The Future of Health Policy

THE FUTURE OF HEALTH POLICY

Victor R. Fuchs

HARVARD UNIVERSITY PRESS
CAMBRIDGE, MASSACHUSETTS
LONDON, ENGLAND   1993

Library of Congress Cataloging-in-Publication Data

Fuchs, Victor R.
The future of health policy / Victor R. Fuchs.
      p.   cm.
Includes bibliographical references and index.
ISBN 0-674-33825-1 (acid-free paper)
1. Medical economics—United States.
2. Medical policy—United States.
I. Title.
RA410.53.F8   1993
362.1′0973—dc20   93-14894
CIP

To Rena, Beatrice, Madeline, and Jed

Contents

Contents

Acknowledgments

Most of the work that forms the basis for this book was supported by The Robert Wood Johnson Foundation; its confidence in my long-term research agenda is greatly appreciated. I would also like to acknowledge grants from the Pew Charitable Trusts and the Andrew W. Mellon Foundation for specific projects: Pew for Canadian health care and Mellon for the well-being of children.

Thanks also to the publishers of previous versions of these chapters; specific credits are given on pages 245–246.

Claire Gilchrist, with her customary skill, attended to the myriad details involved in transforming rough drafts into publications; she also provided many helpful comments for the introduction. Diane Reklis and Joanne Spetz took responsibility for checking and updating references, tables, and figures. I would also like to thank Michael Aronson and Donna Bouvier of Harvard University Press for their editorial contributions. Finally, I offer a special word of appreciation to my wife, Beverly, who critiqued every chapter, and who has been a boundless source of inspiration, assistance, and encouragement for all my endeavors.

The Future of Health Policy

Introduction

When I began research on health economics in the mid-1960s, health policy was just one of many issues competing for priority on the nation's domestic agenda. Indeed, my mentor at the National Bureau of Economic Research, Arthur Burns, concerned for my professional advancement, suggested that I concentrate on a more established subject. Today, health policy looms as the proverbial five-hundred-pound gorilla of American politics, frightening in size, baffling in complexity, and compelling in urgency. Candidates for public office loudly proclaim their intention to cover the uninsured while curbing runaway costs, but their enthusiasm evaporates when they are confronted by the difficult choices necessary to achieve these objectives. This book explains why. It provides the reader with the concepts, facts, and analyses needed to understand the complex issues of health policy. It also shows why there can be no gain for society without pain for some individuals.

I was not the first economist to study health and medical care; Chapter 2 provides a brief history of the field. Nevertheless, my appointments to the President's Committee on Mental Retardation and the U.S. Health Services Research Study Section in the mid-1960s were greeted with some surprise and suspicion by the physicians, sociologists, psychologists, and other traditional guardians of those domains. Today the situation is completely reversed. Economists dominate health services research and health policy discussions because their training makes them appear ideally suited to grapple with the difficult choices that policymakers face. Policymaking usually involves the allocation of scarce resources; the analysis of such allocations, from both positive and normative perspectives, is the bread and butter of economics.

The fact that the editors of prestigious medical journals, deans of medical schools, and secretaries of Health and Human Services now welcome contributions and advice from economists is a source of satisfaction to me, but I must confess to some misgivings as well. There are limits to the contributions that economics can make to health policy, and I suspect that these limits are not always understood either by some of the economists who have recently entered the field or by some of the policymakers who use their research. This book highlights both the contributions and the limitations.

The limitations are of three types. The first was spelled out with his customary clarity by John Maynard Keynes (1923) when he wrote, "The Theory of Economics does not furnish a body of settled conclusions immediately applicable to policy. It is a method rather than a doctrine, an apparatus of the mind, a technique of thinking which helps its possessor to draw correct conclusions" (p. v). Any economist who wishes to contribute to health policy must supplement theory with a firm knowledge of medical institutions and health care technology; recommendations based only on *a priori* theoretical considerations can be irrelevant or harmful. Supply and demand, along with other economic concepts such as the margin and elasticity provide a powerful framework for analysis, but this framework must be filled out with empirical information regarding the special characteristics of medical care markets in order to arrive at sound policy judgments.

Two examples underscore the unusual nature of health care markets. First, in most industries where there is excess capacity, prices tend to fall sharply and some firms are forced out of business. By contrast, in many health care markets there are excess supplies of hospital beds, high-tech equipment, and certain surgical and medical specialists, but charges and fees remain high and the excess capacity persists for decades. Second, in the markets for most goods and services, economic theory correctly assumes that demand is independent of supply. In the market for physicians' services, however, several studies have found that physicians can, to some extent, boost patient demand for their services. This helps explain why an increase in the number of physicians in the 1970s and 1980s (subsidized by public policy) contributed to an escalation in health care costs.

A second limitation in the application of economics to health policy is apparent in the political and social domains. This is particularly evident when policymakers seek to redesign U.S. health care according to some other national model (for example, Canadian or German). Economics can help us understand why health care costs are so much higher in the United States than in these other countries, and it can help us evaluate what we receive for those extra costs. Economics alone, however, cannot explain Canada's superior political capacity to enact and administer universal health insurance or the greater willingness of Germans to obey centrally established rules for health expenditures. But these differences from the United States help explain the success of the Canadian and German cost containment programs. Contemporary experience confirms the wisdom of an observation made by Walton Hamilton more than sixty years ago: "The organization of medicine is not a thing apart which can be subjected to study in isolation. It is an aspect of a culture whose arrangements are inseparable from the general organization of society" (1932, p. 190).

My comparison of Canadian and U.S. health care (Chapters 6 and 7) has convinced me that the Canadian system works better for Canadians than the U.S. system works for U.S. citizens. This is certainly not true in all respects, and is certainly not true for all patients, but when access, cost, and quality are taken into account it is true on average. Does this mean that the United States should adopt the Canadian system? Not necessarily. The powerful grip of lobbyists in Washington and state capitols, the savings and loan debacle, and the scandals at HUD suggest that our political system could not enact a health care plan with the coherence and the rationality of the Canadian system. Furthermore, even if we had such a plan, most of our state governments could not administer it with the efficiency and honesty evidenced by the Canadian provincial governments.

The third and perhaps most important limitation applies not only to economics but to all forms of analysis. It arises from the fact that policy implies choice, and choices depend on values as well as analysis. Imagine a perfectly executed project in health services research using the full power of economics integrated with insights from other disciplines. What can it tell us? At best we will know that if we do x the result will be a; if we do y the result will be b. The research cannot tell us whether we as a society should do x or y; that depends on the values we place on a and b.

Conflicts over values are particularly stark in the health policy arena. By what criteria should a health care system be judged? Some would emphasize the development and diffusion of the most advanced medical technologies. In this respect, U.S. health care is preeminent. But others might put more weight on public health as evidenced by longer life expectancy or the absence of morbidity and disability. From this perspective the United States ranks below average among economically developed countries.

Still another criterion is service, which can be evaluated independently of technology or public health. Is it easy to get to see a physician, or to reach one by telephone? How long does a bedridden hospital patient lie in urine before someone responds to a call? Do health aides regularly visit the homebound elderly? Are dying patients treated with compassion? Canada and Germany provide more physician visits and more hospital days than the United States, but there are many dimensions of service for which no international comparisons are available.

Efficiency in the use of scarce resources to maximize output is another public goal that must be considered. At any given time, labor and capital used for health care are not available for education, housing, automobiles, and the thousands of other goods and services that people want. Much of the criticism of the U.S. health care system arises because Americans spend 40 percent more than Canadians for health care, and the excess over European countries is even greater. England's parsimonious use of resources is particularly noteworthy. High-tech medicine is severely rationed in England, but the level of public health is about the same as in America, and England manages to provide a considerable amount of health service while spending only $1 per capita for every $3 spent in the United States.

Finally, there is the matter of distributional equity. With all else held constant, many people believe that a more equal system is a better system. Indeed, they might even be willing to sacrifice a little from one of the other perspectives in order to achieve more equality. Consider, for instance, a country that has an average life expectancy of 76 years, but also has great inequality. Some of its citizens die in childhood or as young adults, while others live past 90 years of age. Presumably, most people would prefer to be born in a country in which everyone lives to age 75.

Thus, even if there were perfect agreement regarding the consequences of alternative approaches to health care—national health insurance, managed competition, tax credits, or some other program—the policy debate would continue because of differences in preferences regarding the consequences. The nature of the debate would change, however, and its content would be clarified. Health economics can contribute to this clarification by identifying and measuring the costs and benefits of alternative policies, and by showing how behavior is influenced by incentives and constraints.

This is the spirit that motivates this book, which is a sequel to *The Health Economy* (1986), a collection of some of my earlier contributions to health economics and policy. My goal is not to argue for any particular health policy, but to help readers obtain a clearer view of the issues, facts, and likely consequences of alternative courses of action. No easy solutions are proposed because, in my judgment, none exist. With one exception (Chapter 1), the studies were all undertaken in the 1980s and 1990s. Each chapter is based on a previously published paper, slightly adapted, and in a few instances the statistics are updated.

Conceptual Issues

In order to develop sound policies for health we need a clear understanding of what health means. Chapter 1 addresses that question and makes three principal points. First, there is no single concept of health that is ideal for all purposes. Health is multidimensional, and we must choose the concept that seems most useful for the particular question at hand. Age-adjusted death rates (there are several versions), the incidence of illness (acute or chronic), disability, and impaired function are more or less useful, depending on the specific context. Second, we should abandon the notion of a sharp distinction between physical and mental health. "The head is connected to the body" is more than an anatomical fact. New scientific discoveries show that physical problems can have important psychological consequences, and vice versa. Third, it is useful to distinguish between research that focuses on identifying the determinants of health (such as medical care or education) and research that uses health measures to explain other phenomena (such as labor force participation or wage rates). The concepts and methods of economics are applicable to both kinds of analysis.

Chapter 2 describes these concepts and methods and illustrates their application with reference to some of the leading research in health economics. This field draws heavily on four older, more firmly established fields of economics: finance and insurance, industrial organization, labor, and public finance. From finance and insurance come concepts such as risk aversion (the foundation for health insurance) and moral hazard (the effect of insurance on utilization). The need to reconcile the desire for insurance with the fact that insured patients want more care than is socially optimal creates the most fundamental problem of health policy. No nation has solved this problem, or ever will, but some deal with it better than others.

The field of industrial organization provides concepts such as competition and monopoly, productivity, and technologic change—concepts that help illuminate two other major questions of health policy: how to produce health services in the most efficient way, and how to eliminate monopoly profits to providers of health goods and services. Labor economics has developed the enormously valuable concept of human capital, and health is one of the principal fields for its application. Finally, from public finance come such important concepts as public goods and distributional equity, concepts that are crucial to an understanding of many facets of the health policy debates.

Should society put a price on health? Can it be done? These questions are addressed in Chapter 3 and, for the most part, are answered in the affirmative. Any society that consistently acts as if health were a priceless commodity will find itself in deep trouble. But this chapter also discusses why the pricing of health can be problematic, and why society may sometimes wish to keep such pricing implicit rather than explicit.

When I joined the faculty of the Mount Sinai School of Medicine in 1968, I warned my colleagues not to expect economics to provide answers to the problems of health. Its greatest contribution, I suggested, was likely to be in the formulation of new and more relevant questions. My continued belief in this proposition finds expression in Chapter 4, where I propose a series of questions about poverty and health. Many of the questions concern the relationship between these variables: its extent, pattern, and explanations. Others revolve around possible confounding variables, such as education, which is highly correlated with poverty and health. Still other questions focus on medical care: its efficacy in improving health, its value to the poor, and the best way to provide care to the poor.

Empirical Studies

The most difficult problem in health policy (both in the United States and worldwide) is the containment of expenditures. In

Chapter 5 we see that U.S. health expenditures have consistently outpaced the growth of spending for other goods and services: the average differential between 1950 and 1990 was 3 percent per annum. If this differential should continue for another forty years, health care would consume almost one-third of the gross national product. The chapter discusses the many factors that contribute to the growth of health spending and explains why no simple solution is available.

One persistent question in recent years is why per-capita health expenditures are so much higher in the United States than in Canada. Our northern neighbors enjoy almost the same level of income as we do, the standard of medical training is the same in Canada as in the United States, and there are many other similarities between the two countries. But we spend much more for medical care; Chapters 6 and 7 help us understand why. The former focuses on expenditures for physicians' services and shows that the differential is explained entirely by the fact that fees in the United States are more than double those in Canada. The quantity of physicians' services per capita is actually greater in Canada than in the United States. Yet despite the large difference in fees, physicians' net incomes in the United States are only about one-third higher than those in Canada. One reason is that overhead expenses are much greater in the United States. Also, because there are so many more procedure-oriented specialists in the United States, their average work load is much below that of their Canadian counterparts. Chapter 7 focuses on per-capita expenditures for acute hospital care, which are higher in the United States than in Canada even though Canada has more beds, more admissions, more outpatient visits, and double the number of inpatient days per capita. The most probable explanations for the expenditure differential are higher administrative costs in U.S. hospitals and better capacity utilization of equipment and personnel in Canadian hospitals.

The next two chapters in Part II focus on infants and children—that portion of society that seems to me to have been slighted by U.S. policymakers in recent years. Chapter 8 shows that reproduction-related health care claims only a minor share of total health expenditures. Despite huge neonatal intensive-care bills for individual low-birth-weight babies, and despite large hospital charges for the many deliveries by cesarean section, total expenditures for obstetrical care, infant care, contraception, abortion, and infertility services amounted to only 5.5 percent of the total health budget in 1982. The proportion is probably even smaller now because the population over age 65 (the largest consumers of health care) has been growing faster than the birth rate (the principal factor determining expenditures for reproduction-related health care).

Chapter 9 looks at the problems of America's children from a broad perspective, including not only health problems such as suicide and obesity, but also other indicators of well-being. Most of the trends are disturbing: America's children are worse off than those in the previous generation in several important dimensions of mental, physical, and emotional well-being. During the 1960s cultural changes such as divorce and unwed motherhood adversely affected children, while their material condition improved substantially. By contrast, material conditions deteriorated in the 1980s, especially among children at the lower end of the income distribution. This chapter explains why public policies to improve the material condition of children will require a transfer of resources from households that do not have children to those that do. Health programs for children are no exception to this rule.

Policy Analysis

There is a widespread feeling in the United States that expenditures for health care are too high and growing too rapidly. This feeling has stimulated numerous policy proposals for cost containment, including more competition (see Chapter 11), more government involvement (see Chapter 12), and national health insurance (see Chapter 14). In Chapter 10 I address two basic issues. First, why should public policy pay any special attention to health expenditures? I consider and reject two popular explanations—share of GNP and effect on global competitiveness—and then discuss three valid explanations. Second, I show why every approach to cost containment requires pain if there is to be any gain.

The 1980s were said to be marked by a competition revolution in health care, but was there truly an increase in competition among health care providers? What effects did changes in organization and finance have on expenditures, productivity, prices, and the distribution of services? Chapter 11 analyzes this so-called revolution in detail. I then examine the potential contributions of market, government, and professional norms to creating a more efficient and more equitable health care system.

The forces that are likely to produce a reaction to the changes of the 1980s are discussed in Chapter 12. They include the growth of the uninsured and the increasing resistance of the insured to bearing the costs of "free riders." More government involvement seems likely, and the chapter concludes with a brief discussion of some possible dangers of such involvement.

In the long run, there may be no aspect of health policy more important than technologic change. Improvements in diagnostic and therapeutic technologies increase the effectiveness of physicians and other health professionals, but they are also the principal driving force behind the growth of health expenditures. Traditionally, the assessment of new health technologies focused only on safety and efficacy. Chapter 13 explains the need for a broader approach to technology assessment—one that also encompasses consideration of quality of life and the evaluation of costs and benefits. The differences between technology assessment in medicine and in other fields are discussed, and the characteristics of an efficient assessment are explored. The chapter concludes with an appraisal of both the potential and the limitations of technology assessment for improving health policy.

The final chapter of the book draws together almost all of the major issues of health policy through an examination of national health insurance. First, I identify the reasons why some Americans do not have health insurance and show why subsidization and compulsion are necessary and sufficient to attain universal coverage. Next, the "casualty insurance" and "social insurance" approaches to health insurance are compared with respect to efficiency and equity. The chapter reviews the evidence concerning the effects of national health insurance on the cost of care and the health of the population. It concludes with my assessment of the prospects for national health insurance in the United States.

The Future of Health Policy

In the 1970s many observers contended that the American health care system was in "crisis." I questioned this diagnosis, pointing out that "in medicine the crisis is that point in the course of the disease at which the patient is on the verge of either recovering or dying. No such decisive resolution is evident with respect to the problems of health and medical care. Our 'sick medical system,' to use the headline of numerous magazine and newspaper editorials, is neither about to recover nor to pass away" (Fuchs 1974b, p. 9).

Today, I believe the situation is fundamentally different. It *is* a time of crisis. The main problems bear the same names—cost and access—but the level of acuity has risen dramatically. Unless there is radical change within the next ten years, there is a good chance that our health care system will collapse of its own weight.

What is the solution? That's the wrong question; indeed, it's the wrong vocabulary. Nations don't "solve" the problem of health care any more than physicians "solve" the problem of death. Currently, most countries are in turmoil about health policy; most are exploring changes in organization and changes in incentives. It is possible, however, for countries to do better or worse. Even these terms must be used with care, however, because what is deemed better or worse will depend to a considerable extent on a nation's values (Fuchs 1992).

Those who wish to understand the core of future U.S. health policy debates, or to contribute to better policy through research, should pay special attention to three central questions: How can we disengage health insurance from employment? How can we tame but not destroy technologic change in health care? How can we cope with an aging society?

HOW CAN WE DISENGAGE HEALTH INSURANCE FROM EMPLOYMENT?

Except for Medicare and Medicaid, health insurance in the United States is based essentially on employment. This tie originated during World War II, when wages were frozen but employer contributions to health insurance were exempt from such control. Thus, employers used insurance as a legal way to bid for workers at a time of labor shortage. The tie was nourished in the post–World War II era by the tax-exempt status of employer contributions to health insurance, an exemption that became more valuable to workers as wages and taxes rose.

Sooner or later, the inequities and inefficiencies associated with employment-based health insurance will become so apparent as to dictate disengagement. The current system has moved far from the concept of social insurance—that is, the equitable sharing of the cost of medical care across the population. Instead, premiums vary across firms, depending upon the age and health status of their employees. When health insurance was a small percentage of total compensation, and when most insurance premiums were community rated (not firm specific as at present), the distortions were small. Now they are becoming large. Today, workers' choices of job, decisions about job change, and timing of retirement are frequently influenced by health insurance considerations. As a result, labor market efficiency suffers. It also suffers when, as is becoming more common, employer decisions about hiring, training, promotion, and firing are influenced by the impact of such decisions on health-care costs. Concern about labor market efficiency could become a major stimulus for health insurance reform.

HOW CAN WE TAME BUT NOT DESTROY TECHNOLOGIC CHANGE IN HEALTH CARE?

If health care technology is allowed to proceed in the same unconstrained manner as in the past, it will create enormous economic, political, and ethical dilemmas. On the other hand, we must not inhibit technologic change to the point of preventing advancements in medicine that can increase both the quantity and the quality of life at reasonable cost.

From a social point of view, technologic change in health suffers from two serious problems. First, there is too much of it; and second, a great deal of it is misdirected. Third-party payment for health care induces too much technologic change because it insures a market for any change that meets standards of efficacy and safety, regardless of costs relative to benefits. In the rest of the economy (except possibly in defense), technologic change must exceed a satisfactory benefit–cost threshold; otherwise it will not be undertaken. Consider, for instance, the development of a more fuel-efficient automobile engine. Potential buyers can readily compare the savings in fuel against the higher cost of the engine or other possible disadvantages. Knowing that buyers will make this comparison, automobile manufacturers make the calculation first, and do not develop innovations that do not promise to be cost-effective.

The problem of third-party payment aside, the misdirection of innovation in health often arises because of the differential valuation of an identified as opposed to a statistical life. When a patient is facing certain death, the individual, his or her family, and society as a whole are willing to pay heavily for any innovation that offers even a small promise of saving that life. By contrast, the healthy population is not as willing to pay for preventive innovations that would save many more lives for each dollar of expenditure. The executives who make decisions about research and development projects in health care know that this bias exists and therefore understandably fund new projects that offer the greatest profit potential. Legislators and administrators in government also determine the direction of research and development, and they are influenced by the greater political pressure generated by the possibility of saving an identified life.

The point here is not to blame the drug companies or government officials for acting in a rational manner, but rather to call attention to a systemic bias in the signals sent to those who fund and develop new medical technology. The challenge is to develop institutional and scientific resources capable of undertaking comprehensive assessments of medical technologies, combined with incentives and constraints that will ensure that these assessments influence research and development decisions in socially desirable directions.

HOW CAN WE COPE WITH AN AGING SOCIETY?

At the beginning of this century there were ten children (under age 18) in the United States for every person 65 or over. By 1960 the ratio had fallen to four to one; by 1990 it was two to one; and the ratio continues to fall. This demographic revolution has major implications for politics, economics, and social dynamics. The implications for health care are particularly striking because the elderly now consume almost 40 percent of all health care in the United States, and the proportion grows every year. In principle, the amount of health care that the elderly can consume is limited only by the imagination and ingenuity of scientists, physicians, drug companies, and other producers of health care goods and services. Beyond some age, which varies from individual to individual, almost every part of the body can benefit from repair or replacement. Rehabilitation therapy and assistance with daily living for the frail or disabled elderly create two other potentially huge sources of demand. What kind of health policy will keep insured elderly from demanding and receiving all the care that might do them some good without regard to cost?

Currently there is considerable discussion and debate over the right to death with dignity. The goal is to give terminally ill patients or their families the right to refuse certain kinds of treatment that will prolong their dying. Some states are moving further; they propose to give terminally ill patients the right to request physician assistance in ending their lives. As financial and ethical pressures mount, we will probably see the right to death with dignity transformed into an expectation and eventually into an obligation. This development will create enormous stresses for patients and their families, health professionals, and government.

Major improvements in our governmental institutions will be a key to dealing with the three central questions I have just presented. Convinced as I am of the advantages of a free-market approach to most economic issues, my research in health care leads me to conclude that a laissez-faire policy cannot create an equitable, universal system of insurance, cannot harness technologic change, and cannot cope with the potentially unlimited demand for health care by the elderly. In my judgment, major political reform in general, and in the health area in particular, is a necessary precondition for significant improvements in our health care system.

Is such reform possible? Machiavelli, one of the shrewdest political analysts of all time, observed, "There is nothing more difficult to manage, more dubious to accomplish, nor more doubtful of success . . . than to initiate a new order of things. The reformer has enemies in all those who profit from the old order and only lukewarm defenders in all those who would profit from the new order." With these words, Machiavelli provided a prescient commentary on current obstacles to meaningful change in health policy. The problems are formidable, but progress in dealing with them could provide tremendous economic and social benefits to the nation. Moreover, to the extent that we can build a more efficient and equitable health care system, we will strengthen our institutional capacity and resolve to deal with education, childcare, and other major domestic problems.

Some compromise is essential. Neither in health care nor in any other area can we achieve all the efficiency, justice, freedom, and security that we would like to have. Economics can help us understand the trade-offs that we face, but only a commitment to resolving our political and social dilemmas can release us from our present impasse. What is desperately needed is for philosophically opposed groups to recognize that there is some merit in each other's point of view, and to affirm the importance of both individual and collective responsibility in the creation of the good society.

I

CONCEPTUAL ISSUES

1

What Is Health?

"What is health?" More particularly, "What is health from an economist's perspective?" Until recently, this question was seldom asked—and even more rarely answered. This chapter does not propose a definitive reply but, rather, tries to clarify some of the underlying problems. After a brief introduction, I examine several different concepts of health and the relationships among them. Next, I consider health as an object of choice; finally, I discuss some applications of health concepts in economic research.

As far as I can determine, there are no *economic* concepts of health. The concepts and measures of health that a few economists have attempted to incorporate into their theoretical models and empirical analyses (see, for example, Auster, Leveson, and Sarachek 1969; Grossman 1972) have come from other disciplines such as medicine, epidemiology, and demography. Economics is the study of the allocation of scarce resources among competing wants. Simply stated, economics is an intellectual middleman between nature and technology on the *supply* side and the preferences and desires of individuals and society on the *demand* side. Health, in various forms, enters on both sides of the equation. If people want to preserve and enhance their health and are willing to incur costs (monetary, time, psychic) to do so, economics can play a role in broadening our understanding of the process by enabling us to study the effect of such factors as relative prices and income. If the health of the popula-

tion affects the size or productivity of the work force or the demand for medical care, economics can play a role by helping us
trace those relationships.

But which of the many concepts of health should the economist use? Should he or she adopt the World Health Organization
definition that health is "a state of complete physical and mental
and social well-being"? Or should the economist heed the wisdom of René Dubos (1959, p. 1), who wrote, "Complete freedom
fron disease and from struggle is almost incompatible with the
process of living"? Shall the economist measure health by mortality, or morbidity, or disability, or the absence of pain? What
is the economist to do with the statement of epidemiologist J.
N. Morris (1964, p. 40) that "morbidity means what it is defined
to mean: whether a subjective malaise, measurable evidence of
disorder, pathology diagnosed by a doctor, or certified incapac-
ity to work"?

Out of this welter of conflicting views and divergent measures, is there any reasonable rule or strategy to follow in
applying economics to health? One approach that may be useful
is that of *instrumentalism,* a version of pragmatism discussed by
philosopher Abraham Kaplan. According to Kaplan, instrumentalism identifies the procedures of analyzing concepts by an attempt to get at the use that is made of them. "What is insisted
on is that language is an instrument, and that to use language
is to perform an action. The analysis of meanings must therefore
focus on the particular contexts in which the action is performed
and on the purposes which the action as a whole is meant to
achieve" (1964, p. 46). Thus, rather than look for some ideal concept of health, an economist should choose that concept which
seems most useful for the particular problem under consideration.

A Variety of Concepts

Death rates are frequently used as indexes of health, because
they are relatively objective, comparable, and available. There

are, however, many different kinds of rates and many possible uses. For instance, the crude death rate can be a useful measure of health for short-run population projections or for prediction of the demand for funerary services, but age-specific rates become important if one wants to make long-run population projections or to predict the demand for schooling. The aggregation of age-specific rates into an age-adjusted mortality rate is useful for comparing populations with different age distributions (but this may yield ambiguous results because different methods give different weights to the death rates at various ages). Death rates by cause of death can also provide useful information about the health of a population. For example, a finding that most deaths are attributable to infectious disease will point to different conclusions from one that shows heart disease and cancer as the major killers, even though the overall death rates are the same. The crucial point is for the investigator to have a clear idea as to what inference and action depend upon the measure being used.

While different kinds of mortality measures can provide useful indications about the state of health of a population, and particularly about the effectiveness of various programs to improve health, they may be less satisfactory if one is interested in anticipating the demand for health care—that is, utilization of hospitals, physicians' services, and the like. In that case, morbidity would be a more useful measure of health, because it gives more weight to acute illnesses and chronic conditions that may consume large amounts of health services even when not life threatening.

The relationship between morbidity and the demand for medical care is itself very complex. As Kerr White has graphically shown (1973), the morbidity that induces demand for ambulatory care (for example, the common cold, bronchitis, arthritis) tends to be very different from the morbidity that leads to hospitalization (for example, heart disease, fractures and dislocations, mental disorders).

An interest in morbidity may, however, derive from an interest in studying labor force participation rather than in projecting demands for medical care. If so, different concepts of health become more important. Physiological impairment must be viewed in relation to available remedies and to expected functions. Ffrangcon Roberts reminds us that our standards of health vary according to the demands made on individuals by society. "A man who may be quite unfit to be an air-pilot may live a prosperous and healthy life as a hairdresser, while another may become an eminent political economist though a lifelong sufferer from asthma" (1952, p. 23). Or, to mention another well-known example, severe myopia is a serious health problem in the absence of corrective lenses but is much less so when they are available.

Moreover, the decision to seek work, just like the decision to seek medical care, is frequently influenced by much more than the health status of the individual as determined by objective measurements. There is a large subjective element in health, and the economic perspective alerts us to the possible influence of wage rates, prices, income, insurance, and similar variables on an individual's perception of his or her health status, or at least the outward expression of that perception.

Relations among Concepts

While there is not perfect correlation among the different concepts and measures of health, it seems to me an error to assume that there is *no* relationship among them. I found a significant correlation across regions of the United States between age-adjusted mortality and various measures of morbidity (Fuchs 1965a). Michael Grossman (1975) found a significant correlation across individuals between self-evaluation of health status ("Is your general health excellent, good, fair, or poor?") and weeks lost from work because of illness and an even stronger correlation between self-evaluation and number of symptoms reported.

Recent studies showing that the marginal contribution of

medical care to life expectancy in developed countries is very small are sometimes met with the assertion that, while care may not reduce mortality, it certainly is contributing to better health (measured in other ways). This may be correct, but the specification and measurement of these other ways and the significance of the marginal contribution of medical care to health (so measured) remains to be established.

It seems to me that death can be viewed as one end of a distribution of health conditions (see Figure 1.1). I suspect that most factors that reduce mortality also move the entire distribution (adjusted for age) to the left. Thus a finding of no significant relation between mortality and variable X would seem to put the burden of proof on those who claim that X is related to "health."

What about the distinction between mental health and physical health? In my view, too much is made of this distinction. From the economist's perspective, both are aspects of health: both can affect labor force participation and productivity, and both can be affected by genetics, the socioeconomic environ-

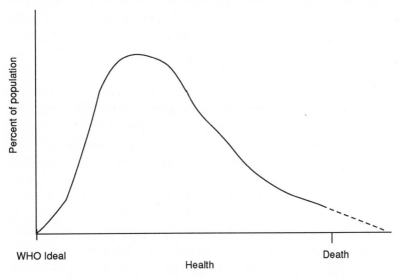

Figure 1.1 Hypothetical distribution of population by level of health

ment, and personal behavior. Indeed, I will speculate that as we learn more about illness we will discover that even from a purely medical-clinical perspective the distinction has been exaggerated. "The head is connected to the body" is more than an anatomical description. Probably the most important difference is the extent to which it is currently possible to make diagnoses and prognoses; this affects insurability as well as social attitudes toward the two types of ill health.

Health as an Object of Choice

The economic perspective tends to emphasize that the health of an individual is, in part, under his or her control; it is not merely a "given." Most economists treat health as an object of choice. To be sure, this choice is subject to constraints—genetic endowment, income, information, and the like—but within those constraints the economic perspective focuses on the choices individuals make. In this respect, health does not differ from any other object of choice—all are subject to constraints. The important point is that, in both the getting and spending of income, individuals make choices that affect their health. The economist is particularly interested in how these choices are influenced by relative prices.

But can one put a price on health? (See Chapter 3.) Here the economist's reply is much the same as that of the old-timer who was asked if he believed in baptism: "Believe in it?" he said. "I not only believe in it, I've seen it." Not only is it theoretically possible to put a price on health, but, if we observe people's behavior, we can see that they frequently do. Some economists have even attempted to estimate that price. (See Chapter 2.)

It is important to distinguish between the price one might place on *certain* death and the price one might place on the probability of death varying by a small amount. For instance, an individual might be unwilling to accept certain death tomorrow, even if offered $10 million, but he or she might be willing to undertake a task with a one in one thousand chance of death in return for a payment of $10,000 (Bergstrom 1974). This is *not* because individuals underestimate the probability of an adverse event when the probability is small. It is, rather, analogous to the case of an individual being willing to give up one unit of commodity X (which he or she normally consumes in quantity q) for price p, while being unwilling to give up consuming X entirely for pq.

It is readily apparent that individuals do consider trade-offs between health and other goals. (Shall I give up $50 to find out if this is a pimple, a wart, or a tumor? Shall I give up eating steak in order to reduce the probability of having a heart attack?) This suggests another distinctive aspect of the economist's perspective—namely, the determination of the optimal level of health. For the economist, the optimal level is usually much lower than is technically attainable. It is the level at which the marginal value of an additional increment of health (however measured) is equal to the value of what is forgone in order to obtain that increment.

This is not to say, however, that free individual choice always results in a socially optimal level of health. If there are significant *external benefits* from good health—that is, an improvement in your health benefits others, and there is no feasible way of arranging compensation for that benefit—a free-market approach may result in suboptimal levels of health, and collective intervention (through subsidies or other means) may be justified to achieve a more efficient allocation of resources. The benefit to others may arise because their health depends, in part, on your health—as in the case of communicable disease—or your ill health may simply be a source of disutility to them.

Use of Health in Economic Research

This chapter has considered some of the conceptual problems that confront economists and other policy analysts in attempting to study health. Health is multidimensional, is partly subjective, and varies depending on the context. As discussed in the next chapter, some economic research focuses on health as a *dependent* variable; economists try to explain variations in health by variables such as medical care, education, and income. The relationship between poverty and health is of considerable interest and is given special attention in Chapter 4.

Some economic research, also discussed in Chapter 2, uses health as an independent variable in order to explain differences in wage rates, labor force participation, and other economic phenomena. Research on health by economists is growing at an exponential rate. The economist's perspective frequently throws new light on health and can contribute to better policies, but it is important to be aware of the limits of economics (Fuchs 1974b) and of the political, social, and ethical aspects of health.

2

What Is Health Economics?

Health economics is an applied field in which empirical research predominates. It draws its theoretical inspiration principally from four traditional areas of economics: finance and insurance, industrial organization, labor, and public finance. Some of the most useful work employs only elementary economic concepts but requires detailed knowledge of health technology and institutions. Policy-oriented research plays a major role, and many important policy-relevant articles are published in journals read by physicians and others with direct involvement in health (for example, Enthoven 1978).

The systematic application of economic concepts and methods to the health field is relatively recent. In a comprehensive bibliography of health economics based on English-language sources through 1974 (Culyer, Wiseman, and Walker 1977), fewer than 10 percent of the entries are dated prior to 1963. In that year a seminal article by Arrow (1963) discussed many of the central theoretical problems, and a few years later a major monograph based on modern econometric methods appeared (M. S. Feldstein 1967).

The literature prior to 1963, thoroughly reviewed by Klarman (1965), was primarily institutional and descriptive. Significant contributions include discussions of U.S. medical care institutions (Davis and Rorem 1932; Ginzberg 1954; Somers and Somers 1961), mental illness (Fein 1958), public health (Weisbrod 1961), and the British National Health Service (Lees 1961). The first U.S.

conference on health economics was held in 1962 (Mushkin 1964) and the first international conference in 1973 (Perlman 1974); the first widely adopted textbook did not appear until 1979 (P. Feldstein 1983).

The field divides naturally into two distinct, albeit related, subjects: the economics of health *per se*, and the economics of medical care. The latter has received much more attention from economists than the former, but it is useful to consider health first because the demand for medical care is, in part, derived from the demand for health, and because many of the theoretical and empirical problems in the economics of medical care arise because of difficulties in measuring, valuing, and analyzing health.

Health

CONCEPTS, MEASURES, AND VALUATION

Health is multidimensional. With the exception of the dichotomy between life and death, there is no completely objective, invariant ordering across individuals or populations with respect to health. Health can be defined according to criteria such as life expectancy, capacity for work, need for medical care, or ability to perform a variety of personal and social functions. Economists' attempts to measure and analyze differences in health across individuals and populations have typically focused on mortality (especially age-specific and age-adjusted death rates), morbidity (as evidenced by symptoms or diagnosed illnesses), or self-evaluations of health status. There have also been several attempts to take account simultaneously of mortality, morbidity, and health-related limitations by weighting years of life according to illness and disability.

Despite claims that health is more important than any other goal and that human life is priceless, economists note that individuals make trade-offs between health and other goals and that the valuation of health (including life itself) is necessary for the rational allocation of scarce resources. The two leading approaches to the valuation of human life are discounted future earnings and willingness to pay. Rice (1966) estimated the costs of various illnesses as the sum of direct expenditures for medical care, the forgone earnings attributable to morbidity, plus the cost of premature death, which is assumed to be equal to the present value of future earnings. Willingness to pay is usually defined as the amount of money an individual would require (pay) in exchange for an increase (decrease) in the risk of death. This approach is preferred on theoretical grounds (Schelling 1968; Mishan 1971; Jones-Lee 1974), but difficult to estimate empirically. Two oft-quoted studies that infer the value of life from risk-related wage differentials differ fivefold in their estimates (Thaler and Rosen 1975; Viscusi 1978).

THE DETERMINANTS AND CONSEQUENCES OF VARIATIONS IN HEALTH

Health is sometimes modeled as a dependent and sometimes as an independent variable, although frequently causality runs in both directions. Health has been studied as a function of medical care, income, education, age, sex, race, marital status, environmental pollution, and personal behavior such as cigarette smoking, diet, and exercise. Grossman (1972) developed a model of the *demand* for health, both as a consumption commodity that enters directly into utility and as an investment commodity that contributes to the production of other goods and services. In his model, variables such as age and schooling affect the optimal level of health by changing its shadow price. Most studies that make health the dependent variable take a *production function* approach, with health depending on income, medical care, education, and other inputs (Auster, Leveson, and Sarachek 1969).

There is a strong positive correlation between income and health among less developed countries, but, *ceteris paribus*, the relationship tends to disappear at higher levels of income. This may reflect a high income elasticity of demand for other goods and services that adversely affect health, or may result from stress or other harmful side effects of earning more money. Also, as the average level of income rises, those diseases that stem from poverty tend to disappear and those that are not related to income form an increasing share of the burden of illness.

Advances in medical care such as the introduction of antibiotics have had significant effects on mortality and morbidity, but holding constant the state of medical science, the marginal effect of an increase in the quantity of medical care on health appears to be small in developed countries. Elimination of financial barriers to care, as in the British National Health Service, has not been accompanied by a reduction in the traditional mortality differentials across social classes. In all countries health is strongly correlated with years of schooling, but the explanation is not firmly established. Education may increase the efficiency with which individuals produce health. Alternatively, some third variable, such as time preference, may simultaneously affect schooling and health (Farrell and Fuchs 1982). Marital status and health are strongly correlated (more so for men than for women), but the causality probably runs both ways. Other interesting correlations include those between wife's education and husband's health, and between parents' education and children's health.

Health has frequently been used as an independent variable to explain labor force participation, particularly at older ages. Not only do retired persons frequently cite poor health as the reason for retirement, but current workers who report a health limitation are more likely to withdraw from work in subsequent years. Health status has also been used to explain wages, productivity, school performance, fertility, and the demand for medical care. The results are often sensitive to the particular measure of health that is used, but the direction of effect generally confirms *a priori* predictions.

HEALTH AS A COMMODITY

Health is both an intermediate commodity that affects production and a final commodity that affects utility directly. When health is included in the utility function several questions arise. Do standard theories regarding risk aversion and time discounting with respect to income apply equally to health? (See Chapter 3.) How is the marginal utility of income affected by changes in health levels? Both income and health are, in part, exogenously determined by initial endowments, and these endowments are likely to be positively correlated. The endogenous aspects of income and health are subject to many forces, some that may produce positive correlation and some the reverse. Although utility is a function of health, there can be a considerable difference between maximizing health (as measured, say, by life expectancy) and maximizing utility. The value of a given reduction in the probability of death (as evidenced by willingness to pay) is higher when the probability is high than when it is low. Thus programs to treat the seriously ill at high cost per death averted are often preferred to preventive programs that avert deaths at lower costs.

Many health problems have a significant genetic component, while others are attributable to unfavorable experiences during the fetal period, at delivery, or in childhood. The resulting heterogeneity among individuals poses a variety of problems for analysis and policy. Unobserved heterogeneity can bias inferences about the effects of health interventions, especially in studies based on nonexperimental data (Rosenzweig and Schultz 1982). For instance, if people born with weak hearts are less inclined to exercise vigorously, the true effect of exercise on heart disease may be less than that inferred from observational studies. When heterogeneity is observable, the problem becomes primarily one of incorporating both efficiency and distributional considerations into policy analysis. Whose health should be considered in setting standards for air pollution or occupational safety? Under what circumstances should persons in poor health be required to pay actuarily fair health-insurance premiums?

The externalities associated with health have attracted considerable discussion. Analysis of the benefits of vaccination or the costs of pollution is fairly straightforward, but other externalities are less conventional. Individuals may derive utility from knowing that the poor sick among them are receiving medical care.

They could attempt to achieve this through voluntary philanthropy, but the amount purchased is likely to be less than socially optimal because each individual's contribution would maximize private utility, ignoring the effects on others (Pauly 1971). These health-centered philanthropic externalities are sometimes invoked to explain the widespread subsidization of medical care for the poor through national health insurance or other institutional arrangements in preference to general income redistribution.

Medical Care

Medical care accounts for more than 13 percent of gross national product in the United States and close to 10 percent in several other developed countries. By contrast, restraints on input prices and quantities result in about a 7 percent share in the United Kingdom. The effect on health of such wide variation in medical care expenditures is not clear. Governments in all countries play a large role as regulators, subsidizers, direct buyers, or producers of medical care. Economists have paid considerable attention to the reasons for and consequences of these governmental interventions. One useful way of categorizing economic research on medical care is to relate it to the older, better established areas of specialization that furnish most of the concepts used in health economics. Some studies, to be sure, draw their inspiration from and enrich more than one area.

FINANCE AND INSURANCE

Risk aversion and uncertainty about future health create a demand for health insurance (Arrow 1963; Phelps 1973). Once insurance is in place, moral hazard leads to overutilization of medical care (Pauly 1968). These two observations have generated a huge amount of research on the role of health insurance in health services (Rosett 1976). The effect of insurance on the demand for care is better understood than is the demand for insurance itself. The usual risk aversion story, for example, cannot explain why many people purchase policies that cover the first dollar of expenditure but have a ceiling beyond which expenditures are not covered.

Asymmetry in information about potential demand for medical care creates another analytical and policy problem for insurance markets. When the consumer knows a great deal more about his or her health status and preferences than does the insurance company, adverse selection can lead to a breakdown in the free market in insurance. Group insurance is a typical solution, with participation achieved by compulsion, direct subsidies, or indirect subsidies via the tax system. Compulsory health insurance is also advocated to deal with the free rider problem. The possibility of free riders implies that even countries without explicit national insurance have public or private programs that provide some kind of implicit universal coverage.

Many research methods, including a large-scale prospective controlled experiment (Newhouse et al. 1981), have been used to study the effect of insurance on the demand for care. As a result, few empirical propositions in economics have been as well established as the downward slope of the demand curve for medical care. Nevertheless, precise estimates of price elasticity (net of insurance) are difficult to obtain, in part because the features of some insurance policies—deductibles, varying co-insurance rates, and limits on indemnity payments—imply that the consumer faces a variable price under uncertainty (Keeler et al. 1977).

One solution to the risk aversion/moral hazard dilemma is for insurance to be provided in the form of contingent claims. For each identifiable condition, the insured would be covered for care up to the point where the marginal benefit equals the marginal cost. Consumers, when well, may prefer that type of contract, but once sick they will want any care that has positive marginal benefit. Furthermore, the physician may want to provide care up to the point where marginal benefit is zero. The insurer's task is to enforce the tighter standard on the patient and the physician. This will often require some deception or nonprice rationing which patients can try to offset by strategic behavior. The resulting loss of trust and less than candid exchange of information between patient and physician can adversely affect the production of care.

INDUSTRIAL ORGANIZATION

Probably the largest range of problems and the largest volume of research in health economics fall in the area of industrial organization. There are many different, though related, industries to study: for example, physicians' services, hospitals, drugs, nursing homes, dental care. The topics covered range from licensure and regulation (Peltzman 1973) to price discrimination (Kessel 1958) and nonprice rationing (Friedman 1978) to technological innovation and diffusion (Russell 1979). Organization in the narrow sense of the term is of considerable interest because of the admixture of public, private nonprofit, and for-profit hospitals, and because the modes of physician practice range from solo fee-for-service to huge groups of salaried physicians. Behavior inside the organization is particularly important in analyzing nonprofit hospitals (the dominant form of organization in the United States) because the trustees, the administrator, the attending physicians, and the house staff all have considerable power and frequently have different objectives.

Medical care is, in many respects, the quintessential service industry. First, it is extremely difficult to measure output. As a result, standard economic accounts show little or no gain in productivity over time despite large expenditures for research and development and rapid technological change. Second, the consumer frequently plays a major role in the production process. This means not only that the value of the patient's time is part of the cost of care, but that the patient's knowledge, skill, and motivation and the level of trust between patient and physician can affect the outcome of the care process. Third, the physician often knows a great deal more than the patient does about the patient's need for various types of care. This asymmetry of information has been used to explain the unwillingness of most societies to rely solely on competitive market forces to insure appropriate behavior by physicians. Fourth, because output cannot be stored and short-run supply is relatively inelastic, productivity is sensitive to changes in demand. The stochastic nature of the demand for hospital care results in excess capacity, and the problem is exacerbated by systematic variation in demand according to day of week and month of year.

Despite the difficulty of measuring output, numerous estimates of hospital short-run and long-run cost functions have been made (Lave and Lave 1970). In the short run, marginal cost is below average cost in most hospitals. Long-run average cost tends to fall with increasing size until about 200 beds and then tends to be constant with a possible rise after a size of about 500 beds. Most researchers have defined output as a day of care or as a hospital admission. Standardization for patient mix can only be done incompletely, and failure to measure the effects of care on health is a serious limitation. To be sure, changes in health are only one aspect of output. A considerable fraction of resources in hospitals and nursing homes is devoted to *caring* for people who are in pain or who are disabled, regardless of whether their health status is (or even can be) improved. Also, a significant fraction of physicians' time is devoted to providing information and validation independently of any intended or actual effect on health status.

The problem of measuring output also increases the difficulty of analyzing the demand for care. Additional complications result from the possibility that physicians may shift the patient's demand (Sloan and Feldman 1978; Evans 1974). Some economists concede that physicians have the power to shift demand but believe that it is sufficiently and uniformly exploited so that further shifting can be ignored. Others argue that the amount of shifting varies with exogenous changes in the physician/population ratio. This follows from a model in which physicians maximize utility as a function of income, leisure, and "correct practice." The empirical evidence is consistent with this model (Fuchs 1978), but it is consistent with other explanations as well.

Perhaps less controversial is the proposition that physicians can and do change their patients' demand for hospital care. One example of this in the United States is the lower hospital utilization by patients enrolled in prepaid group practice plans such as Kaiser Permanente (Luft 1981). Patients pay a single annual premium for total care regardless of the quantity of services used; physicians typically receive a salary or a share of the net income after the hospital and other costs have been paid. An even more spectacular change in hospital utilization emerged when Medicare changed from retrospective cost reimbursement to prospective payment per admission in a particular diagnosis-related group. In just two years the average length of stay of patients 65 years of age and older in short-term general hospitals fell 12 percent without any change in conventional demand variables (see Chapter 11).

The demand for care usually increases as health worsens, but not always. For instance, an elderly person who is in good general health may demand a variety of surgical interventions for specific problems such as hip replacement or lens implantation; a person of the same age who is in bad health may not.

Problems in measuring output imply problems in measuring price. An alternative approach to the estimation of price change is to measure change in the total cost of treating a defined illness or medical condition. A price index calculated by this method was found to rise more rapidly than the conventional medical care price index (Scitovsky 1967), possibly as a result of unmeasured changes in output. Technological advances may have increased the cost of care by making it possible for the physician to do more things for the patient.

Economic research on drugs falls into two main categories that reflect differing policy concerns in the United States before and after the 1962 Kefauver-Harris Amendments to the Pure Food and Drug Act. Prior to the amendments, attention was focused on price fixing, price discrimination (manufacturers' prices vary in several ways, depending upon the type of customer), and alleged socially wasteful expenditures for product differentiation.

Since 1962, economic research has shifted to the volume and character of innovation. A decrease in the flow of new drugs has been attributed to the increased cost of satisfying regulatory requirements (Grabowski, Vernon, and Thomas 1978). Despite the questions raised by economists regarding the net benefit of tighter controls, other countries have tended to follow the policy direction set by the United States in 1962.

In recent years in the United States and many other countries, the major health policy questions have revolved around efforts to contain the cost of care. Most economists have argued for greater reliance on market mechanisms and less on regulation (Zeckhauser and Zook 1981), but an intricate web of social, political, and economic considerations seems to preclude a pure laissez-faire approach to health (Fuchs 1974b).

LABOR ECONOMICS

Much of the research on the economics of health comes out of labor economics, especially the human capital branch. Concerning medical care, labor economists have been primarily interested in the demand and supply of various health occupations. Numerous studies of the earnings of physicians have mostly confirmed the results of a pioneering study (Friedman and Kuznets 1945) that physicians, on average, realize an excellent return on their investment in medical education. Research on choice of specialty and location, however, does not support any simple model of physicians as income maximizers. Some specialities appear to have more intrinsic appeal than others, and the wide geographical variation in the physician/population ratio in the United States is not primarily the result of variation in fees or income. Changes in physician distribution by speciality or location, however, do conform closely to predictions based on standard utility maximization (Newhouse et al. 1982).

Research on nurses in the United States has focused heavily on an alleged persistent "shortage." One explanation is that the principal employers of nurses—hospitals—have monopsony power (Yett 1975). Faced with rising supply curves, hospitals equate the marginal cost of nurses with their marginal revenue product and set the wage on the supply curve. The "shortage" simply reflects the fact that the hospital administrator would like to hire more nurses at the going wage, but has no incentive to raise the wage.

PUBLIC FINANCE

Ever since Bismarck introduced compulsory health insurance to Germany in 1883, the financing of health care has been of increasing concern to governments and to economists who specialize in public finance. Even in the United States, the last major holdout against national health insurance, government pays directly for about 42 percent of all health-care expenditures and pays indirectly for an appreciable additional share through tax exemptions and allowances. Numerous reasons have been offered as to why governments pay for health care, but each has its shortcomings.

All explanations that are health related (for example, "health is a right," "the government has an obligation to reduce or eliminate class differentials in mortality") are suspect because in Bismarck's time there was virtually no connection between medical care and health, and even today the connection at the margin is highly circumscribed. The explanation that medical care is a "merit" good seems circular. Governments are said to subsidize "merit" goods, but the only way to identify them is by the presence of government subsidies. The standard externality–public good explanation applies to the prevention and treatment of communicable diseases, but this accounts for only a small fraction of health care. Subsidies in other industries such as agriculture or the merchant marine can frequently be explained by pressure from producers, but government subsidies for health care have usually been opposed by the producers of care.

Subsidies for health care are frequently defended on the grounds that it is unfair to allow the distribution of health care to be determined by the distribution of income. Many economists counter by saying it would be more efficient to redistribute income and then let the poor decide how much of the increase they want to devote to health care and how much to other goods and services. The crux of the problem seems to be that the amount of redistribution that society wants to make to an individual may depend on the individual's need for care. The greater the need, the greater society's willingness to redistribute. It may be more efficient to combine the determination of need with the redistribution via the delivery of care than to separate the functions.

One special problem arises in this field from the proposition that in order to reduce inequality, governments should limit the amount of care that individuals can obtain. This view is virtually inescapable once a government is committed to equality in health care and constrained to keep the health budget within limits set by general budgetary considerations. No country can afford to provide health care for all its citizens up to the point where the marginal benefit is zero.

Economists spend a great deal of time deploring the fact that no country shows much interest in evaluating the outcome of medical care. It might be more fruitful to try to explain why this is so. No doubt part of the answer is that evaluation is very difficult, but part may be related to the symbolic and political role that medical care plays in modern society. When governments, insurance companies, or employers promise to finance all necessary and appropriate care, they typically have to introduce implicit constraints to keep from going bankrupt. A thorough evaluation would make these constraints explicit and could create a great deal of dissatisfaction.

FUTURE RESEARCH

Because health economics is predominantly applied and policy oriented, future research will undoubtedly be influenced by the changing nature of health problems and by developments in medical science. Thus, it is reasonable to expect to see more attention to the health problems of the elderly—chronic illness and the need for long-term care. Among the nonelderly, health problems stemming from substance abuse are large and growing in importance. The new understanding of the role of genetic factors in disease creates dramatic opportunities for screening and intervention, but these opportunities will pose problems of enormous complexity for analysis and policy. The gap between what is technically possible and what is economically feasible will probably widen; thus, the demand for guidance concerning the efficiency and equity implications of alternative health policies is likely to grow. Further development of health economics as an established field of inquiry will help to meet that demand.

3

The Price of Health

Price is a fundamental variable in economics. What role, then, can economics play in the analysis of a commodity, like health, that is said to be priceless? A central concern of health economics research has been whether health is a commodity like any other. Our answer to this question is an unwavering "yes and no." Health *is* a commodity: it enters into utility; its supply is not unlimited but can be increased through the use of scarce resources (broadly defined); the amount that people demand varies inversely with its price. If societal arrangements for protecting, producing, and enhancing health (including the provision of medical care) ignore this aspect of health—if it is assumed to be a truly "priceless" commodity—these arrangements are likely to be inefficient and unsatisfactory.

In many respects, however, health is unlike other commodities. These differences have profoundly shaped our institutional arrangements—regulatory, financial, organizational—in both the positive and the normative sense. Health is difficult to trade interpersonally. Initial endowments are extremely important. Whereas most commodities are produced by specialists and then sold to the general public, an individual's health status is largely self-produced, being strongly affected by his or her consumption of other commodities. Together, these conditions imply that individuals will not all value health equally at the margin.

Written with Richard Zeckhauser.

Significant externalities of the conventional sort (for example, communicable diseases) affect health; significant interdependent utilities affect its valuation. The symbolic aspects of health are important. Many people believe health should not be allocated like other commodities (that is, on the basis of ability to pay). This sentiment may be expressed more often than it is acted on, but even its ability to command lip service is revealing. For example, Joseph Califano, an enthusiastic convert to the competitive market approach in *America's Health Care Revolution* (1986), tries to soften his message by saying no one should be denied "needed" care.

In this chapter we comment on health in relation to such standard economic topics as wealth, time preference, risk aversion, and utility.

Health and Wealth

Except in extreme cases it is difficult to sort out the precise nature of the relationship between health and wealth. If wealth is very low, health suffers, sometimes to the point of death. Likewise, a person in very poor health may have no capacity to create wealth. Random shocks to health and wealth are usually positively correlated. Within the characteristic range of health and wealth in developed countries, however, the direction and strength of causal connections are more difficult to ascertain.

Initial endowments of health and wealth are probably positively correlated. Children inherit genes that affect health and mental ability, and they also inherit wealth. Parental efforts during childhood are probably also positively correlated. For example, children who receive above-average investment in health probably also receive more investment in education.

Health and wealth also depend on the choices individuals make as adolescents and adults. Some factors, such as rate of time preference, will lead to a positive correlation, but others, such as a trade-off between hazardous work and wages, will lead to a negative relationship.

Health seems to be a normal good in the sense that an increase in wealth leads to an increase in the demand for health. However, the wealth elasticity of demand for health may be less than that of some other commodities, some of which (for example, mountain climbing) may have negative effects on health. In poor countries (unlike the United States), cigarette smoking has a fairly high positive wealth elasticity.

Empirical studies, both cross-section and time-series, suggest that the elasticity of mortality with respect to income (a weighted average of the cause-specific elasticities) approaches zero as income rises. This is to be expected because an increase in income tends to reduce the weight of those causes of death that have large elasticities. Consider infant death rates from congenital anomalies (small elasticity) versus deaths from infectious diseases (large elasticity). In poor societies most infant deaths are the result of infectious diseases, and the overall elasticity is large. As societies become wealthier, a much smaller proportion of infant deaths is due to infectious diseases, and the overall elasticity is small.

When health and wealth are distributed unequally, the question of redistribution poses many complex problems. Suppose that health and wealth depend only on initial endowments, so that incentive effects can be ignored. In this hypothetical situation, many economists would argue for redistribution of wealth toward greater equality—but is there a comparable case for redistributing health? If so, how should it be done? In the real world the choice of appropriate redistributive policies is even more complex; inequality in health is partly the result of initial endowments and partly the result of individual behavior and random shocks.

Time Preference

Health valuation discussions should focus on outputs rather than inputs—for example, days without morbidity as opposed to physician visits—and should take consumer preferences as the building block for welfare evaluation. Thus, not just lives lost but some variant of quality-adjusted life years (QALYs) seem appropriate in assessing health outputs. Should QALYs be discounted the way cash flows are discounted in investment analyses? Many ethically concerned observers have said no, lest we mistreat the future, and they have been joined by others who oppose technologies that impose long-lived threats to human survival. Economists have tended to support discounting, prescribing that some account be taken of life cycle income patterns, the changing cost of QALY increments over the lifetime, and the higher expected wealth of future generations.

The appropriate principle is quite simple; individuals and policy planners should discount the *value of life years*. Changes in quality due to income or age are counted, as are changes in life expectancy or the costs of health production. If we fail to discount, or do not take account of changing valuations, we will be taking Pareto-dominated actions. With life years, unlike most commodities, there is virtually no exchange among individuals, which implies that individuals will value life years differently. Policy planners thus cannot merely add up discounted life years for different individuals. Rather they should add up the individuals' valuations. (If distribution is a concern, planners should weight a dollar to a rich and a poor person for life years in the same way as if they were deciding on sponsoring operas or repaving streets. The weighting could be one for one if a tax-transfer system is available. Symbolic effects—discussed below—would be added separately.)

Choices that affect the health of future generations (for example, disposal of nuclear waste, biomedical research) are qualitatively different from redistributing health from our present to our future selves. Should the distinctive nature of health affect our intergenerational bequests? Should we be any more or less generous in leaving an intact ozone layer, thus diminishing the risk of future skin cancers, than in leaving up-to-date factories? If we assume no altruism, then we will always benefit by pushing health risks off to future generations. In a world that is generationally selfish, there will be too little R&D and too much long-lived pollution. Capital, by contrast, will not be "selfishly" consumed, leaving nothing for the future, since as time rolls forward it can always be sold to the younger generation.

Suppose altruism induces us to leave something to those who follow. Surely we should leave them the mix of health and other endowments that they most prefer among those that cost us the same amount. Allocations to the future then will represent a Pareto-efficient mix, though we will almost certainly fail to make bequests that the future would like to pay for if it could. (With good-specific paternalism, the principle still applies; the net dollar cost of providing different goods to the future will differ, however.)

Most policy planning discussions assume full altruism—future citizens are given equal weight with present citizens—and discount solely for the time value of money. Given this ethical premise, the value of life years to future generations should be discounted at the time-value-of-money rate. If our descendants will be much wealthier than we, our incentive to transfer wealth to them is diminished. But their greater wealth will confer additional value on a life saved in their generation, increasing our incentive to allocate resources so as to improve our descendants' probability of survival. Similarly, just as we tend to value a life saved at age 30 more than one saved at age 80, we should transfer more life-saving resources from current to future generations the greater is their life expectancy relative to ours.

Assessing the present value of life years is just one area where our thinking about discounting has been confused by intergenerational considerations. Economists' discussion of the social rate of discount often founders on the same issue. If it turns out that we collectively value the future more than we express in private actions—for example, I care more about your child's welfare than about yours, but you have no way to charge me for the externalities of your intergenerational transfers—we should adjust our valuations of future benefits upward, not our discount rate downward. Self-respecting economists should not adjust discount rates for externalities stretching to the future or use different rates because it is health that is being valued.

Risk and Risk Aversion

Even physicians and epidemiologists have a hard time specifying the production function for health. The commodity is produced probabilistically, substantially through the lifestyle choices of individuals. The relevant probabilities are often small and hard to judge. If A is inefficient in the production of health—say, eating too much meat relative to fish though A has no strong preference between the two—B cannot poach on A's market; this suggests the potential for X-inefficiency. The costs of producing additional life years vary significantly, between old and young as well as between the athletic and the sedentary. Moreover, individuals value life years differently because of differences in income, attitudes, and age. In sum, even if there were no income inequalities, individuals would have dramatically different values for the same health output.

Some health valuations merely revolve around probabilities of health loss. From von Neumann–Morgenstern utility, we learn we should be linear with gains in survival probability at any particularly time (assuming there is no endowment to be spread across our survival states). In a two-period model, a 1 percent increment in survival probability in the first year is worth a 2 percent gain for the second year, leaving aside time preference and age-related changes in the quality of life. Experiments with hypothetical questions about health suggest that individuals are risk averse with respect to gains but risk preferring with respect to losses, much as Amos Tversky and Daniel Kahnemann (1986) have shown for wealth in their work on prospect theory. This suggests how much behavior can depend on mental frame of reference. The point from which an individual perceives gains and losses to occur can influence his or her choices.

Though life may be priceless—in the sense that there is no monetary amount that an individual would accept to give up life and (even if there were) society would prohibit its sale—probabilistic risks to life in exchange for dollars (or other benefits) may be acceptable. Economists have presented this argument in a variety of regulatory arenas, notably those relating to the environment and workplace. In common parlance, an individual who will not take health risks for money is called risk averse. How does this risk aversion relate to the economist's risk aversion, a hesitancy to take gambles on money (that is, along a single dimension)? The more risk averse a person is with respect to wealth, the more that person will pay to boost his or her probability of survival.

Policy Issues

The government's role in health is pervasive. Government tells consumers what goods and services they can and cannot buy; it tells workers what jobs and working conditions they can and cannot accept; it spends hundreds of billions of dollars each year subsidizing the demand for health care and regulates every aspect of its delivery. Some of these interventions can undoubtedly be explained by economies of scale in the provision of information or a desire to reduce transaction costs, but most cannot. The demand for extraordinarily expensive health care is highly unpredictable, not unlike the demand for firefighting services. To achieve efficient risk spreading, we can collectivize health care and provide it for free (as Britain has done) or employ insurance, possibly government subsidized (the approach of the United States).

Quite often we are dealing with a situation where A thinks that B is not choosing an optimal level of health and therefore favors legislation that will raise B's health level, even at some cost to A. Why does A feel this way? One possibility is pure paternalism. A thinks he is a better judge of what maximizes B's utility than B is, and B's utility matters to A. Alternatively, A may feel a responsibility to ensure that B acts rationally, regardless of any effects on A, or to protect B-future, who is being inadequately considered by B-present. Or, sensing that he may find himself in B's shoes someday, A may vote for some intervention, say mandatory health insurance, as a form of self-control. Finally, it may not be B's utility in general that matters to A, but specifically B's health. A is more troubled by B's poor health than by B's empty wallet. This could be an atavistic reaction left over from a time when most health problems were communicable. Or perhaps A wants to cover up the "raw edges" of inequality in wealth. Thus A is unwilling to let poor people work at hazardous jobs, sell their organs, or otherwise barter health for income.

One popular explanation for the attempts to regulate health behaviors is that A does not want to bear the expense of B's health-damaging behavior through collectively financed third-party payments for health care. But A also shares in the costs of providing B's retirement income and thus stands to benefit financially from B's lower life expectancy. On balance, the externalized financial consequences of B's cigarette smoking, including the excise taxes he pays and his lower-than-average expected Social Security benefits received, may more than offset his higher-than-average expected medical costs. If eliminating financial externalities were the key, perhaps society would take more aggressive action in favor of seat belts, which disproportionately confer health benefits on individuals entering prime earning years, and against cigarettes and their mostly older victims. In any case, many ardent "interventionists" seem completely unaware of the financial externalities argument, so we must look elsewhere for an explanation of their preferences.

The symbolic role of health and health care may play a role. Many of the fundamental beliefs of our society are wrapped up in the valuation of lives and health. Although society cannot avoid making choices that trade health for other resources, the implicit or shadow prices are rarely mentioned; the legitimacy and popular acceptance of the choice process is often as important as the outcome it generates. Because of the special nature of health production, economists cannot make their customary

contribution of pointing out how fewer resources would be required to produce the same commodity elsewhere. Better guard-
rails for B in no way compensate for dirtier air or less health
care for A, however great the net gain in health, and A is not
saving any resources.

That life is priceless need not imply that we will spare no expense to save a life or cure a disease. Yet that myth persists and
gives us comfort. When the myth confronts us head-on, as in a
decision to support renal dialysis for all who need it, we are
likely to flinch and provide. Given our need for myths, many
mechanisms of cost containment must work in the shadows. If
hospital beds or new technologies that are unlikely to be cost
effective are put in place, myth maintenance tends to overpower
cost containment. Distributional equity also plays a significant
role. If a poor person lacks a VCR or even a radio, we are not
overcome by guilt. But let that poor person suffer from a lack
of health, and all the injustices of our society come into stark
relief. It is no surprise that government expenditures on health
care for the poor exceed cash transfers to them.

Conclusion

We cannot produce life years directly or buy them on any market. Goods that cannot be produced or sold often become priceless through a natural process that leads to interdependent
utility considerations, great concerns for equity, probing discussions of obligations to the future, and assertions that these goods
shall not be allocated through the market. Many priceless commodities are collectively owned, or at least we act as though we
have a collective interest in them. Thus, for example, governments rarely sell their natural wonders or peddle outlying territories to other countries; they prevent the export of rare antiques
(the national heritage) and strictly regulate the use of unique
parcels of land, say the greensward near the town center.

Even if we never sell these priceless commodities, we may
need to know their value, so as to decide whether to defend the

Falkland Islands, build a school on the greensward, or devote more resources to health care. Economics must grapple with the priceless commodity health with one axis tied behind its back. Nevertheless, core economic concepts such as discounting, efficient transfers, and risk aversion provide useful guides through perilous intellectual minefields. At the same time, economics itself is enriched by its ventures into the treacherous domain of health production and valuation.

4

Poverty and Health

Gertrude Stein, confidante of the leading writers, artists, and intellectuals of her time, lay dying. Her closest friend and lifetime companion, Alice B. Toklas, leaned forward and said, "Gertrude, what's the answer?" Gertrude looked up and with her last breath said, "Alice, what's the question?"

On the subject of poverty and health we might also ask: What is the question? Or, more appropriately, what are the questions? Opinions no doubt differ, and some may wonder why the issue is raised at all. The purpose of this chapter is to raise theoretical questions about poverty and health in order to elicit answers that might improve public policy.

Who Are the Poor?

A logical place to begin is by asking what we mean by poverty; that is, who are the poor? This question has a long history within economics, and even from the perspective of that single discipline gives rise to considerable controversy over definition and measurement. The question becomes even more important, however, when poverty is discussed in relation to health. As an economic concept, there is general agreement that poverty refers to some measure of income (or wealth) that indicates inadequate command over material resources. At health conferences, however, the concept often gets transformed into an amorphous set of socioeconomic conditions, or an ill-defined "culture of poverty."

Let us try to avoid such confusion. This is not to deny that people can be poor in ways other than economic. They can be "spiritually impoverished," "morally bankrupt," in "poor health," and so on. But, to the extent possible, let us strive for clarity. If we mean low income, let's say low income. If we mean education, let's say education. And if we mean alcoholism, cigarette smoking, crime, drug abuse, fragmented families, hazardous occupations, sexual promiscuity, slum housing, social alienation, or unhealthy diets, let's say so explicitly. If we constantly redefine poverty to include anything and everything that contributes to poor health, we will make little progress either in theory or practice.

Even when poverty is defined in terms of income, there are numerous questions such as adjustment for size and composition of household, but we can leave these questions to the specialists (Palmer, Smeeding, and Jencks 1988). There is one conceptual issue, however, that is so important as to require explicit discussion. Should poverty be defined according to some fixed standard (absolute income), or by position in the income distribution (relative income)? In my judgment, we need to combine both approaches. On the one hand, if we cling only to a fixed standard, economic growth gradually raises almost everyone out of poverty so defined, but the problems we usually associate with poverty persist. So-called "subsistence" budgets are adjusted to new social norms. On the other hand, to define poverty in terms of the bottom 10 or 20 percent of the income distribution does not help us get to the heart of the problem either. In a society with little inequality of income, being at the lower end need not have the same negative implications as when the distribution is very unequal.

People usually think of themselves as poor (and are regarded as poor) when their command over material resources is much less than others. Poverty, as an economic concept, is largely a matter of economic distance. Thus in 1965 I proposed a poverty threshold of one-half of median income (Fuchs 1965b). The choice of one-half was somewhat arbitrary, but the basic idea would not change if a level of four-tenths or six-tenths were chosen instead. There is considerable resistance to such a definition because a reduction in poverty so defined requires a change in the distribution of income—always a difficult task for political economy. But I believe it is the only realistic way to think about poverty. In this respect, as in so many others, Adam Smith had a clear view of the matter over two hundred years ago. He wrote, "By necessaries I understand not only the commodities which are indispensably necessary for the support of life but whatever the custom of the country renders it indecent for creditable people, even of the lowest order, to be without."

What Is the Relation between Poverty and Health?

Once we have identified the poor, the next question concerns their health relative to the rest of the population. We know in general the answer to this question—on average, those with low income have worse health. There are, however, several aspects of the question that deserve further exploration. How does the relation vary with different measures of health, such as morbidity, disability, or mortality? Is the relation different for different diseases? Is it different at different stages of the life cycle? Is the relation stronger in some countries than in others? If any of these questions are answered in the affirmative (and they surely will be), the next step is to determine the reasons for the variation. These findings could then be used to make inferences about causality.

Is Low Income the Cause of Poor Health?

Many writers simply assert that poverty is the cause of poor health, without rigorously testing their hypothesis. In England, social class is often used as a proxy for poverty, but this is problematic, as illustrated in Table 4.1. There is a large differential in mortality between the lowest and the highest class and a large differential in income as well, but more detailed inspection reveals a complex pattern. Class II has only 5 percent greater mortality than class I, even though income is 23 percent lower. In contrast, the differential in mortality between classes IV and V is 21 percent, but the income difference is only 2 percent. It may be tempting to explain these data by asserting that the relationship between income and mortality is nonlinear. Thus, at low levels of income (classes IV and V), even a small increase in income has a strong effect on mortality, while at high levels (classes I and II), the effect is very weak. This explanation won't wash, however, once we note that the mortality differentials between classes I and V were no smaller in 1971 than in 1951. During those two decades real earnings rose by more than 50 percent for all classes; thus if nonlinearity is the explanation for the pattern shown in Table 4.1, there should have been an appreciable narrowing in the class mortality differentials between 1951 and 1971. No such decrease occurred. Furthermore, there was no decrease between 1971 and 1981 despite additional increases in real income (Wilkinson 1986).

England is not alone in experiencing persistence of class (occu-

Table 4.1 Indexes of mortality and income in England and Wales by social class, 1971 (class I = 100)

Class	Age-adjusted mortality, men 15–64 years of age	Gross weekly income
I. Professional	100	100
II. Managerial	105	77
III. Skilled	136	58
IV. Semiskilled	148	51
V. Unskilled	179	50

Source: Adapted from Wilkinson 1986, pp. 2, 11.

pational) differentials in mortality in the face of rising real income and universal coverage for medical care. In Scandinavia, the age-standardized mortality ratio for male hotel, restaurant, and food service workers is double that of teachers and technical workers (Andersen 1991). A Swedish study of age-standardized death rates among employed men ages 45–64 found substantial differences across occupations in the period 1966–1970 and slightly greater differentials in the period 1976–1980 (Calltorp 1989). In Sweden, there is growing recognition that these differentials cannot be explained by differential access to health care. Johan Calltorp (1989) writes, "There is no systematic evidence that the health care system is inequitable in the sense that those in greater need get less care or that there are barriers towards the lower socioeconomic groups" (p. 13).

What Explains the Correlation between Poverty and Health?

The fact that variables a and b are correlated does not, of course, prove that a is the cause of b. Two other possibilities must be considered. First, the causality may run in the opposite direction; b may be the cause of a. The possibility that health affects social class has been explored extensively by British writers (Fox 1984; Stern 1983; Wadsworth 1986). Almost all agree that there is some "selective mobility," but no consensus has emerged regarding its importance. R. G. Wilkinson (1986) concludes that the "contribution [of selective mobility] to observed class differences in health is probably always small" (p. 10). But Roy Carr-Hill (1987) writes, "There is an effect which should not be ignored: the size of the effect could be substantial, but it cannot be estimated properly without a lifelong longitudinal study" (p. 527).

We must also consider the other logical possibility, namely that there are one or more "third variables" that are the cause both of low income and poor health. These variables could include genetic endowment as well as numerous socioeconomic factors. Among the latter, most U.S. studies have focused on schooling. A vast literature explores the relation between health and education (Berger and Leigh 1989; Farrell and Fuchs 1982; Grossman 1975; Kenkel 1991). To be sure, income and education are correlated, but the correlation is not so high as to preclude attempting to sort out their separate relationships with health. In the United States, the coefficient of correlation between education and income within age-sex-race groups never reaches as much as .50 and is typically around .40. When health is regressed on both income and schooling, the latter variable always dominates the former. Indeed, in some studies, income is negatively related to health, once years of schooling is controlled for (Auster, Leveson, and Sarachek 1969).

Why Is There Such a Strong Correlation between Schooling and Health?

One possible answer to the question why schooling and health are so strongly correlated is that schooling is the cause of good health. That is, at any given level of income, those with more education know how to use medical care more effectively, choose better diets and other health behaviors, and so on. This line of reasoning has been developed most fully by Michael Grossman (1975). But again, as a matter of logic, we must consider two other possibilities. Good health may lead to more schooling, or there may be "third variables" that affect both schooling and health. Among the "third variables," my favorite candidates are time preference (Fuchs 1982) and self-efficacy (Bandura 1991).

Time preference is an economic concept that refers to the rate at which people discount the future relative to the present. Individuals with high rates of time preference will tend to invest less in the future: on average they will have less education, lower income, and worse health. A perfect capital market would enable those with low rates of time discount to provide funds to those with high rates until their rates were equal at the margin, but the real world bears little resemblance to this theoretical model. For one thing, low-income individuals who want to borrow a great deal cannot provide effective collateral. Also, many choices about health do not involve money; thus there is no effective market in which individuals with different rates of time preference can make trades.

Self-efficacy is a psychological term that describes people's belief in their ability to exercise control over their own behavior and their environment. Differences among individuals in self-efficacy are probably correlated across several domains, such as health and education, thus helping to explain the close relationship between these variables.

How Does Low Income Affect Health?

Let us return to the line of inquiry that has poverty as a cause for poor health. Within that framework the central question concerns the mechanism through which low income translates into bad health. To what extent does the health of the poor suffer because they have inadequate access to medical care? To what extent is their poor health the result of deficiencies in other health-producing goods and services, such as good food, good housing, and a safe environment? If poor health is attributable to inadequate medical care, are the barriers faced by the poor simply a matter of purchasing power, or are there other impediments?

What Are the Most Important Health Problems Facing the Poor?

In order to determine the most important health problems facing the poor it is useful to distinguish between relative risk and absolute risk, a distinction often obscured in the media and even in policy discussions. For example, infant mortality may be twice as high among the poor as the nonpoor (a relative risk of 2 to 1), while the differential in mortality from heart disease may be only 50 percent (relative risk 1.5 to 1). The absolute level of risk of infant mortality, however, may be very low relative to heart disease mortality; thus, the poor might benefit more from efforts devoted to reducing heart disease rather than infant mortality.

To illustrate this point, consider the tremendous attention given by the media (and many health policy experts) to differences in infant mortality between blacks and whites and the relative neglect of other black–white health differentials. It is true that the black infant death rate is double the white rate, while the difference in overall life expectancy is only 9 percent (75.9 years versus 69.7 years in the United States in 1989). But if the black infant mortality rate were reduced to the white level (and all other age-specific rates remained unchanged), black life expectancy would rise by only six-tenths of a year. Over 90 percent of the black–white difference in life expectancy would remain. Isn't there a danger that undue emphasis on the two-to-one ratio for infant mortality because it can command headlines results in a misallocation of health care resources from the perspective of all African-Americans whose health problems are presumably being addressed?

Which Health Problems of the Poor Are Most Amenable to Solution?

In order to make rational allocations of resources to alleviate the health problems of the poor it is necessary—but not sufficient—to know the relative importance of the problems. It is also necessary to know how readily the problems can be alleviated or solved. Unfortunately, the bulk of health policy research dwells on documenting the problems of the poor, while neglecting the more difficult task of assessing the efficacy of alternative interventions. Policymakers and the public need to know both the costs and the benefits of such alternatives. For example, treatment for infectious diseases may be very efficacious, while treatment for cancer may not be. Some prevention programs such as immunizations may provide a great deal of benefit for little cost, but others, such as mass screening of cholesterol levels, may use a vast amount of resources for limited benefits.

Are There Reasons for Providing Medical Care to the Poor Other than Improving Health Outcomes?

Suppose the contribution of medical care to health at the margin is quite small. Is that sufficient reason to ignore the provision of care to the poor? Not necessarily. In his critique of the Oregon plan for rationing medical care to the poor, Bruce Vladeck (1991) writes, "We expect the health system to take care of sick people whether or not they are going to get better" (p. 102).

Medical care may be valued by the poor (as it is by the non-poor) for the caring and validation services that it provides. If this is the case, serious questions arise concerning the *kind* of care provided to the poor. In particular, is "high tech" overemphasized at the expense of simpler, more valuable services? The fact that medical care has value apart from improving health outcomes provides no grounds for rejecting a cost-benefit approach to resource allocation. But it does highlight the need to incorporate the value of all services in such analyses.

What Policy Instruments Are Available to Help the Poor?

A sociologist tried to explain poverty to a colleague in economics. "You know, the poor are different from you and me." "Yes," replied the economist. "They have less money." This apocryphal exchange highlights a continuing controversy over the best way to help the poor with respect to health or anything else. If more resources are to be allocated to the poor, is it better to provide cash and allow the poor to decide how to spend it, or should the transfers be tied to particular goods and services? The arguments for tied transfers usually derive from a paternalistic assumption that the poor, left to their own devices, will not spend the money "wisely"—that is, they will buy cake when those making the transfers think they should buy bread. A more sophisticated version of this argument invokes "externalities." It may be the case that forcing the poor to spend their additional resources on immunizations rather than alcohol helps the nonpoor because the former creates positive externalities, while the latter creates negative ones (Bruce and Waldman 1991). But the same is true of expenditures by the nonpoor.

Paternalism aside, there is the practical question of whether tied transfers can alter consumption patterns. If a family that previously spent $250 per month on food receives $100 worth of food stamps, there is no reason to expect their spending on food to rise to $350. Indeed, food expenditures are not likely to increase by any more than if they were given $100 in cash. The relative price of food, at the margin, is no different after the transfer than before. The only way to assure a disproportionate increase in food consumption would be to provide food stamps greater in amount than what the family would voluntarily spend on food, given its income plus the cash value of the food stamps.

In devising programs for the poor, physicians usually advocate more medical care, educators more schooling, the construction industry more housing, and so on. But what area(s) would the poor give highest priority? This question cries out for attention from policy analysts.

In choosing between in-kind and cash programs, policymakers should also consider the pecuniary effects of alternative transfers to the poor (Coate, Johnson, and Zeckhauser 1992). One result of Medicare and Medicaid, for example, was higher incomes for physicians—surely not a goal of the Great Society. These programs also led to an increase in the price of medical care for the general public, including many low income people who did not qualify for Medicaid. If, instead of Medicare and Medicaid, the government had transferred to the elderly and the poor an equivalent amount of cash, some of it would have been used for medical care, but much of it would have been used for other goods and services, including food, clothing, consumer durables, and the like. The income and price effects would probably have been very different from those of Medicare and Medicaid, and possibly more egalitarian.

Why Are Americans Less Willing than Others to Subsidize Medical Care for the Poor?

Health policy literature abounds with papers that describe and decry the difficulty faced by poor Americans in obtaining health care. But these papers are typically silent as to why the United States is the only major industrialized country that does not have national health insurance. In 1976, I proposed four answers to this question: distrust of government, the heterogeneity of the population, the weakness of noblesse oblige, and a robust voluntary sector (Fuchs 1976). See Chapter 14 for a reappraisal of these explanations in the light of subsequent political, social, and economic developments.

What Is the Most Efficient Way to Provide Medical Care for the Poor?

The debate on the most efficient way to provide medical care for the poor is clear-cut. On the one hand are those who want to provide the poor with health insurance and leave it to them to obtain the care they need. On the other hand are advocates of special programs directly aimed at providing care for the poor. Inasmuch as both approaches have been tried in the United States and abroad, it should be possible to make some judgments about their relative costs and benefits.

Is it acceptable to provide highly cost-effective care for the poor although the care is different from that available to the nonpoor? A good example is prenatal care and delivery of babies. The Maternity Center Association can provide high-quality midwifery service in their childbearing center for less than half of what Medicaid pays for in-hospital care for a normal birth. At present, some poor women get the high-cost care and some get little or no care.

The question of efficient provision of care to the poor is complicated by the fact that there may be gross inefficiencies in care provided to the nonpoor—overtesting, inappropriate surgery, and so on. Should programs for the poor aim at reproducing these misallocations of resources?

What Is "Two-Tier" Medical Care?

Discussions of medical care for the poor frequently invoke the phrase "two-tier medicine." For strict egalitarians this is a deplorable concept. But others have argued that an explicit two-tier system would serve the American poor better than does the present jumble of services that range from no care (for example, prenatal) to the most sophisticated (for example, neonatal intensive). In thinking about this issue it may be useful to notice that two-tier systems can vary greatly, as shown in Figure 4.1. In both

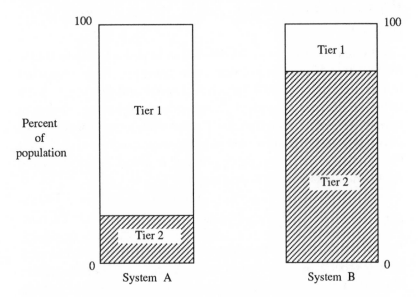

Figure 4.1   Two versions of two-tier medical care

systems, the people in the first tier receive more and better service than those in the second. But in System A most of the population is in the first tier and only the poor are in the second. In System B the proportions are reversed; most of the population is in the second tier and only the affluent and / or well-connected are in the first.

System A provides a safety net; no one is forced to go without any care. System B provides an escape valve; the affluent can get more care then the rest of the population. Most Americans tend to associate two-tier medicine with System A; most other countries have opted for System B. Several interesting questions may be posed about these alternative approaches. Do the two versions have different consequences for cost, access, and quality? For example, consider cost. Suppose expenditures per capita in tier 1 are identical in the two systems and the same is true for tier 2 except that in each country they are 50 percent less than tier 1. Suppose that in System A 80 percent of the population are in tier 1 and 20 percent in tier 2, and that the proportions are reversed in System B. In that case, the average expenditure per person in System A will be 50 percent greater than that in System B.

What are the political, social, and economic factors that lead a country to adopt one version or the other? It would seem that individuals who were certain that they would be in tier 2 under either system would prefer B. Similarly, individuals who were certain that they would be tier 1 under either system might also prefer B. Supporters of A are likely to be individuals who think they would be in tier 1 under A, but in tier 2 under B. Many Americans probably fit that category.

What Is Basic Medical Care?

A frequent conclusion of health policy discussions in the United States is that everyone should have access to basic medical care. Many observers believe that the nonpoor would be more willing to subsidize a basic package than they would complete equality of care. Problems arise, however, in trying to define the contents of that package. Moreover, no matter how it is defined at any point, no one should imagine that the contents can remain fixed over time. In a world of changing technology and rising real income, a fixed approach to basic care will prove no more satisfactory than will a fixed poverty standard based on some notion of subsistence. The basic-care package will constantly have to change in order to include "whatever the custom of the country renders it indecent for creditable people, even of the lowest order, to be without."

In summary, there are numerous questions about poverty and health that need to be addressed. Many of them concern the relation between poverty and health: its extent, pattern, and explanations. Other questions revolve around possible confounding variables such as education, which is correlated with income and health. Still other questions focus on medical care: its efficacy in improving health, its value to the poor, the best way to provide it. In pursuing these questions we need to find a middle road between a mindless optimism that ignores reality and a constricting pessimism that denies the possibility of creating a more efficient and more just society.

II

EMPIRICAL
STUDIES

5

U.S. Health Expenditures and the Gross National Product

The health sector's share[1] of the gross national product (GNP) is a subject of intense interest to government officials, health professionals, business managers, and many others. The story of its rise from well under 5 percent in the late 1940s to 12 percent in 1990 is a familiar one, although there is no consensus concerning the relative importance of technology, health insurance, demography, and other factors in this expansion. The health sector's share in other countries is substantially lower (for example, about 9 percent in Canada and about 7 percent in the United Kingdom) even though they have universal insurance (Schieber and Poullier 1988). Currently, many observers expect the U.S. share to reach 20 percent within two decades. Such growth would increase the possibility of delivering high-tech, state-of-the-art medicine to all Americans, including the one in seven who currently have no health insurance. On the other hand, it would exacerbate the diversion of resources from other pressing needs such as child care, education, the environment, housing, and transportation.

In the course of economic development it is customary for individual sectors to experience spurts of expansion that exceed the national average (automobiles in the 1920s, for example, and computers in the 1970s and 1980s). Such growth industries are usually lauded for their contribution to the overall performance of the economy. The increase in health-care expenditures, however, requires special attention because widespread third-party payment removes the market constraints that discipline spending for most other goods and services (Pauly 1968). The purchaser of an automobile or a computer typically must weigh its cost against its potential benefit, but an insured patient tends to disregard or undervalue cost in making decisions about the use of health care (Newhouse et al. 1981).

There is also widespread concern that the "spurt" of health care has continued for more than forty years and shows little sign of abatement. Moreover, because the health sector is so large in absolute terms (about $800 billion in 1992), its rapid growth has a particularly traumatic effect on other sectors that compete with it for private and public spending. In this chapter I review the factors that influence the health sector's share of GNP and consider possible future trends.

The Gap

What percentage of GNP will the health sector account for ten or twenty years from now? Given the 1990 share (S_0) of 12.1 percent, the share n years in the future (S_n) will be determined entirely by the gap (g) between the rate of growth of health expenditures and the rate of growth of expenditures in the rest of the economy, that is

$$S_n = \frac{e^{gn} S_0}{e^{gn} S_0 + (1 - S_0)}$$

Table 5.1 shows the health sector's share at various points in the future for various values of g. We see that if the gap is 2.0 percent per annum the share will rise to 14.4 percent by 2000, whereas a gap of 3.0 percent will result in almost 16 percent of the GNP being devoted to health care. The further out the projection, the greater the effect of differences in the gap. By 2030 a gap of 2 percent per annum results in a 23.5 percent share, but if the gap is 3.0 percent per annum the health sector will account for 31.4 percent of GNP.

What gap can reasonably be expected? No one can say for certain, but the experience since 1950, summarized in Table 5.2, provides some evidence concerning the range of possibilities. We see that the gap averaged 3.0 percent per annum between 1950 and 1990. In contrast to the United States, 15 European OECD countries during the 1970 to 1987 span showed a median gap of only 1.8 percent per annum (Culyer 1989).

Because expenditures are equal to the product of prices and quantities, the gap can be partitioned into two components (Table 5.2). The first shows the rate of change of health care prices relative to prices of other commodities; the second shows the rate of change of health care quantities relative to the quantities of other commodities. In principle, the quantity of health care services refers to the aggregation of all visits, tests, days in hospital, and other services delivered to patients. Greater intensity is treated as greater quantity—for example, a day in an intensive care unit is more quantity than a day in an ordinary hospital ward, and a visit to a gastroenterologist is more quantity than a visit to a general practitioner. In practice, the quantity series are derived by dividing expenditures by prices. Thus, any error in the measurement of trends in relative prices results in an equal but opposite error in the relative quantities trend.

For the period as a whole the more rapid rise of health-care prices accounted for almost two-thirds of the gap and the change

Table 5.1 The health sector's percentage of GNP in future years for selected values of g (initial share = 12.1% in 1990); g is the difference between the rate of growth of the health sector and the rate for the rest of the economy

g (Size of gap)	Year			
	2000	2010	2020	2030
2%	14.4	17.0	20.1	23.5
3%	15.7	20.1	25.3	31.4
4%	17.0	23.5	31.4	40.5

Table 5.2 Rates of growth of the health sector and the rest of the economy, selected periods, 1950–1990 (percent per annum)

Factor	1950–1990	1950–1970	1970–1990	1950–1960	1960–1970	1970–1980	1980–1990
Expenditures							
1. Health care	10.4	9.3	11.5	7.8	10.8	12.7	10.4
2. Rest of the economy	7.4	6.3	8.5	5.9	6.8	10.2	6.9
Prices							
3. Health care	6.1	4.1	8.2	4.0	4.3	8.2	8.1
4. Rest of the economy	4.3	2.8	5.8	2.5	3.0	7.3	4.2
Quantities[a]							
5. Health care	4.3	5.2	3.4	3.8	6.5	4.5	2.3
6. Rest of the economy	3.2	3.6	2.8	3.4	3.7	2.9	2.7
The gap (g)[a] (1 minus 2)	3.0	3.0	3.0	1.9	4.0	2.5	3.5
Relative prices[a] (3 minus 4)	1.9	1.4	2.4	1.5	1.3	0.9	3.8
Relative quantities[a] (5 minus 6)	1.1	1.6	0.6	0.4	2.8	1.6	-0.4

Sources: Economic Report of the President 1989, pp. 308, 312–373; National Center for Health Statistics 1989a, table 94, p. 144; Waldo et al. 1989, table 1, p. 112; U.S. Bureau of the Census 1975, p. 73.

a. Calculated from unrounded data.

in relative quantities for a bit more than one-third. This is a statistical decomposition, not a behavioral explanation. According to general equilibrium theory, prices and quantities of health care and other commodities are all interrelated, and are determined simultaneously within a demand and supply framework. Also, although there is considerable confidence in the accuracy of the expenditure series, the official price indexes for health care and other commodities are subject to many possible sources of error. For instance, the timing and method of introduction of new goods and services into the indexes, the difficulty of accounting for changes in quality, and the problems of dealing with discounts present formidable obstacles to the accurate assessment of changes in price (Afriat 1977). These limitations apply not only to health care but also to computers, financial services, air transportation, and many other sectors with rapid changes in products or pricing policies.

Relative Prices

Apart from measurement error, the more rapid increase of health care prices can have only two possible explanations: (1) the prices of inputs into health care (that is, labor, capital, intermediate goods, and services) have increased more rapidly than input prices in other sectors, or (2) productivity in health care has increased less rapidly than in other sectors.[2]

INPUT PRICES

Labor is the most important input in health care and many other industries. During the period under study, the price of labor rose faster in the health sector than in the rest of the economy, thus contributing to the increase in relative prices of output. In 1949, rank-and-file health care workers (16 years of schooling or less) earned 15 percent less than their counterparts in the rest of the economy. In 1985 they earned 7 percent more than other workers.[3] This implies that relative wages rose at the rate of 0.6 percent per annum. The rate of change of physicians' incomes over this period cannot be calculated because there are no reliable estimates for the early years. But even if physicians' incomes did not rise as rapidly as those of other health care workers (between 1977 and 1987 they rose more rapidly), the differential trend in the price of labor must have contributed several tenths of a percent per annum to the long-term differential in relative prices.

From 1977 to 1987, wages in most industries failed to keep pace with inflation, but rank-and-file health workers did better, outpacing employees in the rest of the economy by 1.3 percent per annum (see Chapter 11). The net income of physicians (adjusted for changes in specialty mix) grew even faster, rising by 8.1 percent per annum compared with only 5.5 percent per annum for all private nonagricultural workers.[4] This above-average growth of the price of labor in health care was undoubtedly a significant factor in the rapid rise of relative prices in the most recent decade.

The prices of most other inputs, such as goods and services purchased form other industries, tend to rise at about the same rate for health care as for the rest of the economy. If, however, there are inputs that have particularly rapid price increases and loom disproportionately large in the production of health care, the effect will be to increase health care input costs relative to the rest of the economy. An example of this phenomenon is malpractice insurance (Danzon 1985). The rapid growth in the number of tort claims and the size of damage awards has affected liability premiums in all industries, but the impact is greater on health care than other areas because liability insurance represents a larger proportion of total costs. Even in health care, however, malpractice premiums are, on average, under 2 percent of total costs; therefore, the effect on relative prices must be small. The malpractice claim problem has other potential effects, however, on productivity and on the quantity of services.

PRODUCTIVITY

It is important to realize that conventional measures of health care productivity do not take account of the effects of care on health any more than productivity in agriculture depends on whether tobacco or oat bran is better for health. Agricultural productivity is measured by the outputs of tobacco, grain, milk, and the like relative to the labor, land, and other inputs required to produce them. In principle, productivity of the health care sector is similarly measured by an aggregation of physicians' visits, hospital days, tests, and other services relative to inputs, independently of any judgment regarding the effectiveness of those services for health.

Much of the growth of health care prices relative to the rest of the economy between 1950 and 1990 is probably the result of differential changes in productivity, so measured. It is well known that productivity growth in services is slower than in agriculture or industry (Fuchs 1969; Inman 1985), and health care is no exception. In general, industries that depend heavily on individualized personal contact, such as health and education, have not been able to achieve the productivity gains realized in other industries by the routinization of production and the substitution of capital for labor.

Evidence of substantial differentials in labor productivity growth comes from the trends in employment. Between 1950 and 1987 the number of people working in the health sector grew 2.6 percent per annum more rapidly than in the rest of the economy (4.3 percent compared to 1.7 percent per annum).[5] This stands in sharp contrast to the differential trend in relative quantities during that period of approximately 1.0 percent per annum. The rest of the economy achieved some of its gains by substituting capital for labor; thus the differential trend in total factor productivity was smaller than for labor productivity alone. It could, however, still be large enough to account for most of the trend in relative prices.

The malpractice claim problem may have contributed to the productivity shortfall in health care in the following way. As physicians and other health professionals become more aware of the need to be able to defend against malpractice suits, they begin to keep more extensive records. This requires more time input on their part and on the part of other workers, but does not show up as any increase in quantity of output. Another possible development is that physicians may spend more time with each patient on each visit; unless they make an explicit charge for the additional time, it will not be reflected in the quantity index. To the extent that concern about malpractice claims leads physicians to order more visits or more tests, these changes will show up in the quantity index and do not adversely affect productivity as conventionally measured.

The rapid changes in financing and marketing of health care in recent years may also have contributed to poor productivity performance. Physicians and hospitals now face a bewildering array of insurance plans, and they presumably require substantial numbers of clerical personnel to handle the large volume of paperwork. Also, as hospitals and physicians have tried to adapt to the so-called "competition revolution" of the 1980s, there has been a considerable increase in resources going into marketing, advertising, new computer systems, management consulting, and the like (see Chapter 11). It is doubtful that these additional inputs resulted in an equivalent increase in quantity of care. Whether these additional inputs required by hospitals and physicians to adapt to changes in health care finance are one time occurrences or will continue in the years ahead is not known.

Relative Quantities of Output

The possible explanations for the trends in relative quantities of output are more numerous and their interrelationships more complex than for relative prices. The variables that have been mentioned most frequently to explain why use of health care has grown faster than that of other goods and services include defensive medicine, the aging of the population, new technologies, and the rise of third-party payment.

DEFENSIVE MEDICINE

When physicians order tests or other services in order to protect against charges of malpractice, rather than because they believe those services to be of value to their patients, they are practicing defensive medicine. According to some commentators, the rise of defensive medicine is a major factor in the expansion of medical care. The evidence, however, is anecdotal, and there are reasons to question the importance of this explanation. One reason for doubt is that the malpractice claim problem has grown much more rapidly in some areas of the country than in others (for example, California versus Mississippi), but the rate of expansion of health care is more uniform across areas. The timing of change is also problematic. Defensive medicine should have grown most rapidly in the past decade in response to the prior surge in malpractice claims, but as Table 5.2 shows, there was a slower growth of the quantity of health care between 1980 and 1990 than in any of the three previous decades. Indeed, in that decade the quantity of health care (that is, number of hospital days, physician visits, and the like) has not grown as rapidly as quantity (that is, number of automobiles, airplane trips, and the like) in the rest of the economy. If defensive medicine was such a powerful force toward increased use, why has it not resulted in more hospital admissions or longer hospital stays in recent years? Recent changes in the reimbursement policies of Medicare, state governments, and private insurance companies seem to have been more powerful, resulting in fewer admissions and shorter stays.

The regional and time trend evidence, however, is far from conclusive. One could argue that in the absence of the growth of defensive medicine, the cost containment efforts of recent years would have resulted in even more slowing in the growth of quantity of care. One way to think about the problem is to pose the following hypothetical question: "If new national legislation outlawed all future malpractice claims, by how much would physicians and hospitals voluntarily cut their present revenues?" Those who assume that defensive medicine is a big part of the cost problem presumably think that those cuts would be very large. Alternatively, physicians and hospitals might find other reasons for providing something close to the present volume of services as long as facilities, equipment, and personnel are available and there is insurance to pay for them.

AGING OF THE POPULATION

The use of health care varies greatly with age; among adults the pattern is one of sharp increases with increasing age. Under the assumption that the cross-sectional age-spending relation holds constant over time, the effect of the change in the age distribution of the population is estimated by applying the cross-sectional data to the change in the age distribution. One such calculation made with age-specific expenditure patterns in 1977 showed that the change in the age distribution of the population between 1946 and 1986 would have resulted in an increase in use of health care of approximately 0.3 percent per annum (Waldo et al. 1989).

Although this method of estimating the effect of demographic change is widely used, it is problematic. If the change in the age distribution is the result of falling age-specific death rates, the age-expenditure pattern may change over time. One of the main reasons why health care spending rises with age is that the proportion of persons near death increases with age, and expenditures are particularly large in the last year of life. Almost 30 percent of all Medicare expenditures are devoted to the 6 percent of enrollees who are in the last year of life (Lubitz and Prihoda 1984). When age-specific death rates fall over time, there are fewer people in the last year of life at any age; thus their expenditures may be less than those predicted from a previous age-spending pattern. On the other hand, because their life expectancy is greater, they may be deemed suitable candidates for more medical care than previous cohorts at their age.

More certain than the effect of the change in the age distribution is the fact that use of health care by the elderly has grown more rapidly than the rate of use by the population below age 65. For the period from 1965 to 1981, the differential trend on a per capita basis was 1.5 percent per annum, and for the period 1976 to 1981, it was 2.3 percent per annum (Fuchs 1984). Increased spending for physicians' services by the elderly has been particularly rapid in recent years.

What accounts for the differential trends by age? For the years immediately following 1965, Medicare is a sufficient answer; millions of elderly patients suddenly had much better access to care. But the surge in spending after 1976 requires additional explanation. One possibility is that increasing competition among physicians for patients led them to devote more attention to the older men and women in their practices. Also, new medical and surgical interventions may have been particularly applicable to older persons. A third possibility is that improving health of the elderly population made them better candidates for extensive (and expensive) surgical interventions, interventions that would not have been medically justified if the patients were in poor health. These diverse speculations suggest why it is so difficult to find a simple explanation for trends in use.

TECHNOLOGY

Technologic innovation is the primary engine of economic progress. Some innovations are institutional or organizational in character (for example, double-entry bookkeeping, the limited liability corporation, or prepaid group practice of medicine); some are tangible. Innovations in medical care, as in other fields, may appear as new products (such as new operations or new drugs) or as new processes (such as automated blood tests) that enable health professionals to continue doing what they have been doing, but at a lower cost. Most new health care technology involves a change in product rather than process, although the distinction is not always clear-cut (for example, a new diagnostic procedure may be viewed as a change in product or process). Most observers assert that expansion in the character and scope of interventions that physicians can undertake has been a major factor in the growth of health care quantity in recent decades. It must not be assumed, however, that this need always be the case. During the late 1940s and 1950s, the most important technologic advance in medicine, antibiotic drugs, sharply reduced the average length of stay in hospital. Between 1947 and 1957, a period of great advances in medicine, the quantity of health care grew at only about the same rate as the rest of the economy.

This experience should serve as a warning against a blanket

indictment of technology as cost-enhancing. The character of the innovation needs to be considered as well as its magnitude. It is also important to avoid the naïve view that innovations are completely exogenous to the health care system—that is, that they are the inevitable by-products of advances in scientific knowledge. Science plays an important role, to be sure, but the character and magnitude of innovations in any particular sector are partly endogenous, that is, determined by demand emanating from the sector. The third-party cost-based reimbursement system that has evolved in the United States in recent decades has tended to encourage any innovation that promises to improve the quality of care, regardless of cost. Manufacturers of drugs, equipment, and supplies contemplating investment in the development of such innovations have not had to worry about whether the prospective improvement was worth the increase in cost (Grabowski 1986) (see Chapter 13). Moreover, there is an important distinction between potential technology (that is, knowledge of available technology) and technology actually in place. The technology frontier is the same in Great Britain as it is in the United States, but expenditures for health care are much lower in Britain, in part because many technologic innovations are not as readily available to British physicians and patients.

THIRD-PARTY PAYMENT

Fueling the rapid diffusion of new health care technologies, the huge expansion in utilization by the elderly, and the growth of defensive medicine is the pervasive influence of third-party payment. Without the hundreds of billions of dollars available through private and public health insurance, it seems unlikely that the health sector would have grown at anything close to its actual rate. In the early years after World War II the expansion was primarily in private health insurance. Between 1945 and 1960, for instance, the number of persons with hospital insurance jumped from 32 to 122 million, and the number with insurance for physicians' services soared from fewer than 5 million to more than 83 million (Health Insurance Association of America 1985).

The passage of Medicare and Medicaid legislation in 1965 brought health insurance coverage to additional millions of Americans among the elderly and the poor who had not been well served by the private system.

The spread of insurance, however, does not provide a completely satisfactory explanation for all the trends. It doubtlessly contributed to the rapid expansion of health care quantity in the decade or so after 1965, but if insurance alone determined utilization, the relatively flat growth in relative quantities from 1947 to 1957 would be inexplicable. Moreover, during the 1980s insurance continued to be widespread, but both private and public payers introduced new methods of finance and reimbursement in an attempt to stem escalating costs. Medicare's prospective payment system based on diagnosis-related groups (DRGs), the state of California's hospital-specific contracts for Medi-Cal patients, the expansion of deductibles and coinsurance in private insurance plans, and the development of many new health maintenance organizations (HMOs) and preferred provider organizations (PPOs) were all designed to curb use and hold down prices. The results have been spotty: more success with hospitals than with physicians' services; more success with quantities than with prices. Overall, the gap has persisted at nearly 3.5 percent per annum since 1980.

OTHER FACTORS

The decline of the family and traditional religion and the surge of women into paid employment have undoubtedly contributed to an increase in the quantity of health care as recorded in the GNP accounts. The explosion in nursing home care, for instance, which now accounts for almost 1 percent of the GNP, illustrates how social trends can contribute to a switch from home to market production of health services.

More controversial is the question whether the doubling of the ratio of physicians to population since World War II increased the demand for health care. According to standard economic theory it could not; supply and demand are independent except through changes in price. Many economists argue that health care markets conform to this model. Others, however, claim that patient information concerning the need for care is sufficiently imperfect that physicians can induce shifts in demand and are more likely to do so when supply is relatively great.

Future Prospects

This brief review of past trends shows how the expenditures gap can result from the interplay of many factors and that there is little prospect of eliminating or substantially reducing it by trying to identify a single cause. Indeed, in addition to the socioeconomic variables considered here, biological changes can play a role, as evidenced by the AIDS epidemic. Regardless of cause, however, it is clear that political pressures to contain the gap are building. These pressures arise within government because of the large role of health expenditures on the federal budget. They also come from industry and labor, which fear the impact of mounting health insurance premiums on their balance sheets and wage settlements. Sometime during the next decade the government is likely to launch a major assault designed to bring the rate of growth of health care expenditures closer to the rate of growth of the rest of the economy. This will require attention to both price and quantity.

One likely target for restraining input prices is the income of physicians. Such income outpaced the growth of wages in general during the past decade, but may lag behind in the next. Restraining the earnings of other health care workers is likely to prove more difficult, as may be inferred from current discussions about a nursing shortage. As employment opportunities for women expand in other industries, the health sector's disproportionate dependence on women (75 percent compared to 40 percent for the rest of the economy) implies continued pressure for it to increase wages to attract and hold its labor force.

Attempts to lower other input prices (such as for drugs, equipment, and supplies) should also be expected. Federal and state governments, insurance companies, and other large payers are likely to use their massive buying power to attack any monopoly profits that are present in the current pricing policies of firms that supply the health care industry.

Increases in productivity may be sought in several directions. A large one-time gain might be achieved by simplifying our system of finance and reimbursement. This is one area where Canada, for instance, probably has a large advantage over the United States (see Chapters 6 and 7). Canadian physicians bill only one payer (the provincial government), and hospitals do not have to bill at all; they are paid according to a global annual budget. Additional gains could come from holding down the number of physician specialists and subspecialists, thus ensuring fuller work loads for those remaining in practice. The present level of demand leaves many physicians without a full work load in their specialty. The excess supply does not drive down fees, and even low work loads generate sufficient income to attract more new physicians into those specialties. Productivity gains may also be realized if cost containment efforts induce more process innovations and more widespread adoption of cost-reducing technologies by physicians and administrators.

Restraining quantity is likely to prove as difficult as restraining prices. The population will continue to age, and one projection shows an increase in quantity of 0.5 percent per annum simply as a result of the expected change in age distribution between 1990 and 2000 (Sonnefeld et al. 1991). Pressure to provide health insurance for the uninsured will also contribute to expanding quantity. And we can expect increased demand for health professionals to provide services for persons with emotional disorders, marital strife, addictions, and other problems that in an earlier time might have been approached within families or religious communities. One favorable development is the increased attention to technology assessment that may result in discontinuance of ineffective procedures.

Many policy experts look to financial pressures on patients as the principal way of restraining quantity. By introducing more deductibles and coinsurance, and by gearing insurance premiums more closely to expected use, they hope to restrain the demand for care. This approach does reduce demand, but it is likely to encounter substantial difficulties. Most people do not want to risk having to pay very large bills so they seek health insurance, either privately or through government programs. Despite all the efforts to introduce deductibles and coinsurance in the 1980s, the fraction of health care expenditures paid for directly by patients was smaller in 1990 than in 1980 (Levit et al. 1991).

The present enthusiasm for experience rating (that is, the adjustment of insurance premiums for individuals and firms according to their use) is also likely to dissipate. Most Americans feel comfortable about having cigarette smokers pay higher premiums than nonsmokers, but even enthusiastic advocates of experience rating are uneasy about requiring individuals born with genetic defects to pay above-normal premiums. Where should the line be drawn, and who will draw it? Is alcoholism, for instance, to be regarded as similar to cigarette smoking, or is it more analogous to a genetic disease? One probable consequence of genetics research is to make people more aware that there is a genetic component in most diseases. Thus political sentiment is likely to swing back toward an acceptance of collective responsibility for the health care needs of individuals.

More enduring constraints on quantity are likely to emerge from the supply side rather than from demand. The debate over whether or not to ration care is largely irrelevant; the important questions are: Who will ration? Who will be rationed? What will be rationed? There are likely to be attempts to hold down the growth in number of physicians, to limit expansion of medical care facilities and equipment, and to monitor closely the pace and character of technologic innovation. One can only hope that these attempts will be guided by rational analysis, compassion, and an appreciation for the long-run as well as short-run aspects of this complex problem.

6

How Canada Does It: Physicians' Services

American interest in the Canadian health care system is growing rapidly for two principal reasons (Doherty 1989; Moloney and Paul 1989; Iglehart 1990). First, costs have escalated in the United States to such an extent that health care now accounts for approximately 13.5 percent of the gross national product, whereas in Canada the comparable figure is about 9 percent. Second, one in seven Americans have no health insurance, and tens of millions of others have incomplete coverage; in contrast, Canada provides comprehensive, first-dollar health insurance to all its citizens. If U.S. spending could be held to the Canadian percentage, the savings would amount to more than $100 billion a year.

There have been numerous descriptions of the evolution of national health insurance in Canada and of the current federal-provincial system (Andreopoulos 1975; Evans and Stoddart 1986; Iglehart 1986). A detailed statistical analysis of trends in Canada and the United States has identified prospective global budgets for hospitals and negotiated fee schedules for physicians' services as major reasons for lower spending in Canada (Barer and Evans 1986). Other studies have focused on hospital costs (Detsky, Stacey, and Bombardier 1983; Detsky et al. 1986), drug prices (Fulda and Dickens 1979; McRae and Tapon 1985; Scherer 1985), the use of surgical services (McPherson et al. 1981;

Written with James S. Hahn.

Vayda, Mindell, and Rutkow 1982), and administrative costs (Himmelstein and Woolhandler 1986).

This study concentrates on per capita expenditures for physicians' services because in this important sector the ratio between U.S. and Canadian spending is particularly large (1.72 in 1985). In other words, after adjustment for population size and the overall purchasing power of the Canadian dollar, Americans spend 72 percent more than Canadians for physicians' services. The comparable ratio for hospital expenditures is 1.34, and for all other health expenditures combined it is 1.30.

How does Canada do it? Do Canadians receive fewer physicians' services? Are the higher U.S. expenditures attributable entirely to higher fees? Do higher fees result from the use of more resources to produce a given quantity of services (more physicians, nurses, equipment, and the like), or do they reflect higher prices for those resources (higher physicians' net incomes, nurses' salaries, and the like)?

The principal objective of this chapter is to provide quantitative answers to these questions. Our analysis of the ratio between the United States and Canada was supplemented by a parallel comparison of Iowa and Manitoba. The state and the province have small, relatively homogeneous populations, and we had special access to data for the two regions. Our analysis of the ratio between Iowa and Manitoba in per capita expenditures for physicians' services (1.51) served as a check on the comparison between the United States and Canada and helped to sharpen our understanding of the reasons for the differences between countries in spending, fees, and use. The effect of physicians' services on the health of Americans and Canadians is not addressed in this paper.

Methods

Data on health care expenditures, the number of physicians who care for patients, vital statistics, and socioeconomic variables for the United States, Canada, Iowa, and Manitoba for 1985 were gathered from published sources, and the appropriate ratios were calculated.[1] All data in Canadian dollars were converted to U.S. dollars according to the purchasing-power-parity exchange rate of $1 U.S. equals $1.22 Canadian. This rate, calculated each year by the Organization for Economic Cooperation and Development, is based on the relative prices of the same comprehensive basket of goods and services in the two countries. All dollar amounts mentioned in this chapter are in U.S. dollars. Total expenditures for physicians' services were allocated to procedures or to evaluation and management according to a formula based on the distribution of specialists in each country (or region). Details of the allocation are available elsewhere.[2]

FEES

The necessary data on physicians' fees were not available—except from Manitoba—in published form. We therefore relied on data made available to us on a confidential basis by the Health Insurance Association of America, California Blue Shield, Iowa Blue Cross and Blue Shield, and Health and Welfare Canada. Fees in the United States for surgery (thirty-three procedures) and evaluation and management (twenty-two kinds of visits that we combined in five broad categories to achieve comparability with the Canadian data) are based on billed charges reported to the Health Insurance Association of America by its members. The association did not have data for ancillary services; charges for radiology (eight procedures) and anesthesiology (eight procedures) were therefore obtained from California Blue Cross and adjusted to the levels of the association by comparing surgery fees from both sources. Billed charges for Iowa for the same procedures and visits were provided by Iowa Blue Cross and Blue Shield. A list of the procedures and types of visits according to CPT-4 code (Current Procedural Terminology, fourth revision), as well as the precise methods we used to calculate the fee ratios, is available elsewhere (see note 1 above).

All U.S. and Iowa charges were reduced by 20 percent to measure the fees actually received by American physicians more accurately. There are services that are provided but never paid for; there are differences between what is billed and what insurance companies will allow; preferred-provider and health maintenance organizations extract explicit or implicit discounts from billed charges; physicians who accept Medicare assignment may receive less than their usual fee; and Medicaid is frequently the lowest payer of all. A survey of the Medical Group Management Association for 1985 reported that fee-for-service cash collections were 15 percent less than gross fee-for-service billed charges (Medical Group Management Association 1986). It is widely believed that the collection ratio for such groups is higher than the ratio for physicians in solo practice or small partnerships. A sample of Medicare-approved charges for thirty major services and procedures showed a median difference from Health Insurance Association of America billed charges of −23 percent (Health Care Financing Administration 1985). Reducing U.S. billed charges by 20 percent therefore appeared appropriate. No such adjustment was necessary for Canada because bills are paid fully and promptly by the provincial governments according to predetermined, annually negotiated rates.

Fees in Manitoba were taken from the physicians' manual of the Manitoba Health Services Commission and included an adjustment for services provided in rural areas. Because overall Canadian fees were unavailable, Manitoba fees were adjusted to an all-Canada level according to a ratio of benefit rates between Canada and Manitoba that we calculated using provincial data assembled by Health and Welfare Canada. Because there is considerable interest in the United States in reimbursement for procedures as compared with reimbursement for evaluation and management, we calculated separate fee ratios for the two categories of services.

QUANTITY OF SERVICES PER CAPITA

In principle, the quantity of services per capita is the sum of all the visits, tests, operations, and other services provided by physicians. Because comprehensive data to measure these services directly were not available, we estimated the ratios between the United States and Canada and between Iowa and Manitoba by dividing the ratio of expenditures per capita by the appropriate fee ratio. Because expenditures equal the product of fees and the quantity of services, this method provided an indirect measure of the relative quantity of services provided.

PRICE OF RESOURCES

Physicians' services are produced through the use of resources such as physicians, nurses, equipment, and office supplies. We estimated the ratio of the prices of these resources for the United States and Canada (and for Iowa and Manitoba) from physicians' net incomes, nurses' salaries, and other relevant data. The overall ratio was a weighted average (weighted according to expenditures) of the price ratios for four categories of resources: physicians, other personnel, office, and equipment and supplies. This average was then adjusted to take liability-insurance premiums into account.

QUANTITY OF RESOURCES

Of the four categories of resources listed above, we only had data on quantity for the number of physicians. We therefore estimated the ratio of the quantity of resources per capita for the United States and Canada (and for Iowa and Manitoba) by dividing the ratio of expenditure per capita by the ratio of the price of resources. Because expenditures equal the product of the price of resources and the quantity of resources, this method provided an indirect measure of the quantity of resources.

Results

Table 6.1 presents selected background statistics for each country and for Iowa and Manitoba in order to put the data on expenditures in context. Most of the populations of the United States, Canada, and Manitoba are urban, whereas more than half of Iowa's population is rural, which helps to explain the low number

Table 6.1 Selected background statistics, 1985

Variable	United States	Canada	Iowa	Manitoba	Ratio of United States to Canada	Ratio of Iowa to Manitoba
Population (000s)	238,739	25,358	2,905	1,070	—	—
Percent rural	26.3	24.3	52.3	28.8	—	—
Percent in cities of ≥ 100,000	25.4	34.5	10.5	55.5	—	—
Percent over 65 years old	12.0	10.4	14.2	12.5	—	—
Births (per 1,000)	15.8	15.1	14.3	16.0	—	—
GNP (domestic) per capita[a]	16,703	14,801	14,490	13,791	1.13	1.05
Patient-care physicians (per 1,000)[b]	1.81	2.05	1.21	2.02	0.88	0.60
Private-practice general practitioners and family physicians	0.24	0.90	0.29	0.88	0.26	0.33
Other[b]	1.57	1.15	0.92	1.14	1.37	0.81
Short-term general hospitals (per 1,000)[c]						
Beds	4.20	4.43	5.22	4.89	0.95	1.07
Admissions	140	136	142	153	1.03	0.93
Days	994	1,293	1,084	1,317	0.77	0.82
Life expectancy at birth (years)						
Men	71.2	72.9	73.1	72.9	0.98	1.00
Women	78.2	79.7	80.2	79.7	0.98	1.01
Infant mortality (per 1,000)	10.6	8.0	9.5	9.9	1.33	0.96

Sources: American Hospital Association 1986; American Medical Association 1986; Health and Welfare Canada 1988a; Iowa Development Commission 1987; Statistics Canada 1985, 1987b, 1988a, 1988b, 1988c, 1989a; U.S. Bureau of the Census 1986a, 1987, 1988b, 1989a. Calculations in this and the subsequent tables were performed with unrounded numbers.

a. Values are in 1985 U.S. dollars. Canadian figures were adjusted according to the purchasing-power-parity exchange rate. $1.00 U.S. equals $1.22 Canadian.

b. Values include interns and residents.

c. Canadian data include rehabilitation units.

of physicians per capita in that state. Despite its huge territory, 90 percent of Canada's population lives in a narrow band of land just north of the border with the United States. Manitoba, like Canada in general, has a large area, most of which is thinly populated. More than half of Manitoba's population and more than three quarters of its physicians live in one city, Winnipeg. The elderly are relatively more numerous in the United States and in Iowa; were all other things equal, this would lead to a slightly higher use of medical services. The higher per capita gross national product in the United States would tend to increase health care expenditures per capita, mostly through higher incomes for physicians, nurses, and other personnel.

The differences in the number of physicians per capita, both in the aggregate and according to the type of physician, are worthy of special note. On a per capita basis there are more physicians who care for patients in Canada than in the United States, and many more in Manitoba than in Iowa. The disparity with respect to general practitioners and family physicians is very large. In most specialties and subspecialties, however, the ratio between the United States and Canada is much greater than 1. Rates of hospital admission are similar in the two countries; the average length of stay is considerably longer in Canada, partly because some of Canada's short-term general hospitals include rehabilitation units.

Canada does better than the United States with respect to life expectancy and infant mortality, but Iowa does slightly better than Manitoba. There is no reason to believe that access to or the quality of medical care in Iowa is superior to the U.S. average or that care in Manitoba suffers in comparison with care in the rest of Canada. The reversal in ratios therefore suggests that these differences in gross measures of health are determined largely by nonmedical factors, such as personal behavior, the environment, and genetic endowment.

The data on per capita health expenditures (Table 6.2) show that the ratios between the United States and Canada and between Iowa and Manitoba are much greater for physicians' ser-

Table 6.2 Health expenditures per capita, according to type of expenditure, 1985

Expenditure	United States	Canada	Ratio of United States to Canada	Iowa	Manitoba	Ratio of Iowa to Manitoba
Total	$1,780	$1,286	1.38	$1,432	$1,326	1.08
Physicians	347	202	1.72	240	159	1.51
Procedures	193	69	2.78	130	51	2.54
Evaluation and management	154	133	1.16	110	107	1.02
Hospitals	698	520	1.34	541	519	1.04
All other[a]	735	564	1.30	651	648	1.01

Sources: Levit 1985; Waldo, Levit, and Lazenby 1986; Health and Welfare Canada 1987; Organisation for Economic Co-operation and Development 1987; U.S. Department of Commerce 1988; Statistics Canada 1989a.

Note: Values are in 1985 U.S. dollars.

a. Includes expenditures for nursing homes and other institutions, drugs, dentists' services, other professional services, public health, appliances, prepayment administration, construction, research, home care, ambulance services, other personal health care, and miscellaneous expenses.

vices than for hospital services or other expenditures. They also show that within the category of physicians' services, procedures account for nearly all the higher spending in the United States. To understand the difference between the ratios for procedures and for evaluation and management, it is necessary to examine the ratios for fees and for the quantity of services separately.

FEES

Physicians' fees for procedures are approximately 234 percent higher in the United States than in Canada (Table 6.3); the differ-

Table 6.3 Physicians' fees, 1985

Service	Ratio of United States to Canada	Ratio of Iowa to Manitoba
Surgery	3.21	2.76
Anesthesiology	3.73	2.86
Radiology	3.59	4.19
Procedures (weighted average)	3.34	2.99
Moderate office visit[a]	1.56	1.44
Extensive office visit[a]	1.55	1.50
Moderate hospital visit	4.77	3.56
Extensive hospital visit	2.57	2.70
Consultation	1.60	1.64
Evaluation and management (weighted average)	1.82	1.72
All services[b]	2.39	2.18

Note: Values are in 1985 U.S. dollars.

a. "Moderate" visits were limited in scope and duration. "Extensive" visits were longer and broader in scope.

b. Values are weighted averages of the procedures and evaluation-and-management ratios.

ence between Iowa and Manitoba is about 199 percent. By U.S. standards, fees for procedures are exceedingly low in Canada. For example, in Manitoba in 1985 total obstetrical care was reimbursed at $245; the fee for a hernia repair was $186 and for a cholecystectomy $311. Canadian surgical fees are much lower across the board than U.S. fees: for the United States and Canada, 27 of the 33 ratios for surgical procedures are between 2.0 and 4.5; and for Iowa and Manitoba, 29 of the 33 ratios are between 1.75 and 4.25.

Fees for evaluation and management are also higher in the United States than in Canada, but the ratios are much smaller: 1.82 for the United States and Canada, and 1.72 for Iowa and Manitoba. Canadian fees for hospital visits are particularly low; in Manitoba physicians received only $7.20 for a "moderate" hospital visit in 1985 (a visit limited in scope and duration).

The overall fee ratio was moderately sensitive to our allocation of expenditures between procedures and evaluation and management. For instance, if the true share of procedures were five percentage points larger than our estimate, the overall fee ratio between the United States and Canada would increase from 2.39 to 2.47. If the share were five percentage points smaller, the ratio would be 2.32. The exchange rate also affected the fee ratio. If we had used the market rate ($1.00 U.S. equals $1.36 Canadian), which reflects capital movements and speculation as well as the relative purchasing power of the two currencies, the overall fee ratio would be 2.68. Finally, the relation between the fee ratio and our assumption of a 20 percent discount from billed charges for U.S. fees should be noted. If we had assumed a 25 percent discount, the overall ratio would be 2.24; a 15 percent discount would yield a ratio of 2.54.

QUANTITY OF SERVICES PER CAPITA

Table 6.4 provides striking refutation of the hypothesis that lower spending in Canada is achieved by providing fewer services. On the contrary, the ratio between the United States and Canada for all services is 0.72, and between Iowa and Manitoba

Table 6.4 Estimation of the ratios of quantity of physicians' services per capita, 1985

Service	Ratio of United States to Canada	Ratio of Iowa to Manitoba
Procedures		
Expenditures per capita (Table 6.2)	2.78	2.54
Fees (Table 6.3)	3.34	2.99
Quantity of services per capita[a]	0.83	0.85
Evaluation and management		
Expenditures per capita (Table 6.2)	1.16	1.02
Fees (Table 6.3)	1.82	1.72
Quantity of services per capita[a]	0.64	0.60
All services		
Expenditures per capita (Table 6.2)	1.72	1.51
Fees (Table 6.3)	2.39	2.18
Quantity of services per capita[a]	0.72	0.69

a. Values are expenditures per capita divided by fees.

the ratio is 0.69. The disparity in use is much greater for evaluation and management than for procedures. These results are sensitive to possible biases in the fee ratios, but the conclusion that the rate of use is greater in Canada than in the United States appears robust. For instance, if the overall fee ratio between the United States and Canada were 2.0 instead of 2.39, the ratio of the quantity of services per capita would be 0.86, still well under 1.0. These results are not sensitive to assumptions about the exchange rate because using a different rate would change the expenditures and fee ratios in equal proportion; the ratio of the quantity of services per capita would not be affected.

PRICES OF RESOURCES

As a share of total expenditures, the most important resource in both countries is the physician; the physician's net income is 52 percent of gross income in the United States and 66 percent in Canada. In 1985 net income per office-based physician was

$112,199 in the United States and $73,607 in Canada (American Medical Association 1987a; Health and Welfare Canada 1988c). After adjustment for differences in the mix of specialties, U.S. incomes were 35 percent higher than those in Canada, and 61 percent higher in Iowa than in Manitoba (Table 6.5). The price ratio for other personnel was based on the full-time compensation of a registered nurse (U.S. Bureau of the Census 1985; American Hospital Association 1986; Statistics Canada 1987a; Health and Welfare Canada 1988d). The price of occupying and maintaining an office varies greatly depending on geographic location, and direct estimates were unobtainable. We assumed that the price increases as the relative wealth of an area increases; our calculations were therefore based on regional and state per capita income weighted according to the number of physicians in the area. We assumed that the real prices of equipment and supplies used by physicians are roughly the same in both countries; the ratio was therefore assumed to be 1.0.

We calculated the price ratio for all resources as an expenditure-weighted average of the ratios for the four categories, using

Table 6.5 Estimation of the prices of resources, 1985

Resource	Ratio of United States to Canada	Ratio of Iowa to Manitoba
Net income per physician[a]	1.35	1.61
Other resources		
Compensation rate of other personnel	1.09	0.98
Office	1.15	1.05
Medical supplies, equipment, and other	1.00	1.00
All resources[b]	1.24	1.37
All resources, as adjusted for liability insurance	1.30	1.43

a. Adjusted for mix of specialties.
b. Weighted average of all ratios.

the average of U.S. and Canadian weights. Liability insurance is an important item of expenditure for U.S. physicians, but their Canadian counterparts do not incur a similar expense; estimates of liability expenses for Canadian physicians are less than 1 percent of gross receipts. We did not consider expenditures on liability insurance to reflect any real resource used in the practice of medicine; thus, liability insurance was treated as a tax on the prices of all resources. The ratios of resource prices were therefore increased by the share of all expenditures attributable to liability-insurance premiums. We concluded that the prices of resources are moderately higher in the United States than in Canada (Table 6.5), but the ratio is small as compared with the fee ratio of 2.39. Most of the excess of U.S. over Canadian fees must be attributable to the fact that Americans use more resources to produce a given quantity of services.

RATIO OF QUANTITY OF RESOURCES TO QUANTITY OF SERVICES

The results of our estimation of the ratios of resources to services (Table 6.6) were extraordinary. It appears that the United States uses 84 percent more real resources than does Canada to pro-

Table 6.6 Estimation of the quantity of resources relative to the quantity of services, 1985

Variable	Ratio of United States to Canada	Ratio of Iowa to Manitoba
Expenditures per capita (Table 6.2)	1.72	1.51
Price of resources (Table 6.5)	1.30	1.43
Quantity of resources per capita[a]	1.32	1.06
Quantity of services per capita (Table 6.4)	0.72	0.69
Ratio of quantity of resources to quantity of services	1.84	1.53

a. Values are expenditures per capita divided by the prices of resources.

duce a given quantity of physicians' services. The difference between Iowa and Manitoba is somewhat smaller, with a ratio of 1.53.

SUMMARY AND UPDATE

The study's most important results are summarized in Table 6.7. First, higher expenditures on physicians' services per capita in the United States were entirely explained by higher fees; in fact, the quantity of services per capita is actually lower in the United States than in Canada. Second, the higher fees were attributable primarily to the fact that Americans use more resources to produce a given quantity of services. Third, a small portion of the higher U.S. fees was reflected in higher prices of resources, especially physicians' net incomes. Fourth, the results of the comparison between Iowa and Manitoba were similar to those of the comparison between the United States and Canada, except that a larger proportion of the higher fees in Iowa reflected higher physicians' net incomes. Finally, updating the analysis to 1987 with data on changes in each country from 1985 to 1987 yielded results similar to those obtained for the 1985 comparisons between countries.

Table 6.7 Summary and update of estimates

Variable	1985 Ratio of United States to Canada	1985 Ratio of Iowa to Manitoba	1987 Ratio of United States to Canada
Expenditures per capita	1.72	1.51	1.75
Fees	2.39	2.18	2.61
Quantity of services per capita	0.72	0.69	0.67
Prices of resources	1.30	1.43	1.32
Ratio of quantity of resources to quantity of services	1.84	1.53	1.98

Discussion

Two striking conclusions emerged from our statistical analysis of the difference between the United States and Canada in spending for physicians' services. First, the data firmly reject the view that Canadians save money by delivering fewer services. On the contrary, the quantity of services per capita is much higher in Canada than in the United States. Second, as compared with Canada, the United States uses appreciably more real resources to produce a given quantity of services. We will discuss eight possible explanations for these findings: the effects of insurance on demand, the effects of physicians on demand, billing costs, amenities, other administrative costs, overhead accounting, the workloads of procedure-oriented physicians, and the quality or intensity of care.

EFFECTS OF INSURANCE ON DEMAND

Canadians have universal coverage and face no out-of-pocket expenses, whereas U.S. patients pay coinsurance rates ranging from 0 (full insurance) to 100 percent (for the uninsured). Thus, lower rates of use in the United States must reflect in part the price sensitivity of the demand for physicians' services. If, on average, Americans face the equivalent of 25 percent coinsurance, the results of the Rand Health Insurance Experiment predict that there will be 27 percent fewer visits and 33 percent less outpatient expenditure per capita than if they had full coverage (Manning et al. 1987). We found that the use of evaluation and management services in the United States was 36 percent less than in Canada, and the difference between Iowa and Manitoba was 40 percent. Another source has estimated per capita contacts with a physician at 7.1 in Canada in 1985 and at 5.4 in the United States in 1986 (Sandier 1989).

EFFECTS OF PHYSICIANS ON DEMAND

To the extent that higher rates of use in Canada are not fully explained by more complete insurance coverage, they may be explained by demand induced by Canadian physicians (Ginzberg 1969). The number of general practitioners and family physicians is very high in Canada, and their fee per visit is low. They may thus be more inclined to recommend additional evaluation and management services.

BILLING COSTS

In each Canadian province there is only one source of payment for physicians' services. Physicians typically submit one bill, and payment is usually punctual and complete. In contrast, American physicians must bill a myriad of private and public third-party payers, and often must also bill patients directly. Numerous complex forms must be filled out, there are frequently delays in payment as well as disagreements concerning the amount to be paid, and collection efforts impose additional costs. The differences in billing undoubtedly account for some of the additional resources reflected in the U.S. data, but we do not know exactly how much. The order of magnitude can be inferred from the fact that approximately 16 percent of the gross receipts of physicians are devoted to personnel who are not medical doctors. If one-fourth of those personnel are needed for billing tasks that are not required in the Canadian system, then 4 percent of U.S. expenditures can be explained by this factor. There are also additional billing costs for physicians' time, computers, stationery, and postage.

AMENITIES

Fragmentary data from one Canadian province and the American Medical Association suggest that U.S. physicians spend considerably more than their Canadian counterparts for rent and related office expenses, possibly twice as much. It is unlikely that this large difference is primarily the result of higher prices for identical offices. Some portion, probably a considerable portion, reflects a higher level of amenities in the average U.S. office. This may take the form of a more desirable location, more space per patient, newer furnishings, or more elaborate decor. Why would this occur? One reason is that real per capita income in the United States is 10 to 15 percent higher than in Canada; Americans are therefore accustomed to a somewhat higher level of amenities in most aspects of life. But the income difference would probably explain only about a 10 to 15 percent difference in amenities. More important may be the fact that competition for well-insured patients is more intense in the United States, especially among procedure-oriented physicians, many of whom have lower workloads than they desire. Physicians usually do not compete for insured patients by lowering fees, but they can try to attract such patients by offering a higher level of amenities.

OTHER ADMINISTRATIVE COSTS

There are numerous other costs incurred by many U.S. physicians that are lower or nonexistent for their Canadian counterparts. For instance, concern over possible malpractice suits (much rarer in Canada) may cause U.S. physicians to keep additional notes and records, or to undertake other activities that require their time and other resources but that are not reflected in the measures of quantity of services. (If concern over possible malpractice suits leads U.S. physicians to order additional visits and tests, the ratio between resources and services is not affected, because both the additional services and resources required to produce them are accounted for.) Other administrative costs that are more likely to be incurred by U.S. than Canadian physicians involve maintaining contractual relations with preferred-provider organizations, dealing with third-party use reviews, and marketing.

OVERHEAD ACCOUNTING

Overhead makes up 48 percent of expenditures in the United States, but only 34 percent in Canada (American Medical Association 1987a; Health and Welfare Canada 1988c). Some of this difference undoubtedly reflects the greater use of resources in the United States, as discussed above. Some, however, may reflect more stringent scrutiny of overhead accounting by the Canadian government, because the overhead percentage is part of the background for negotiations between the provincial governments and physicians' organizations over fees. This constraint is not present in the United States. If identical accounting practices were applied in both countries, the overhead percentages might be slightly closer to each other and the difference in net income might be slightly larger. Such an adjustment would increase the ratio of the price of resources in the two countries by a few percentage points and decrease the ratio of resources to services by an equivalent amount.

WORKLOADS OF PROCEDURE-ORIENTED PHYSICIANS

There can be little doubt that the average Canadian physician who specializes in procedures does more of them during a year than his or her counterpart in the United States. We estimated that there are about 40 percent more procedure-oriented physicians in the United States than in Canada (relative to the population), but the number of procedures performed appears to be about 20 percent higher in Canada. For some specialties the difference in workloads may be of the order of magnitude of two to one. This explanation is not as relevant for the comparison between Iowa and Manitoba, because the per capita supply of procedure-oriented physicians is about the same in both places. The difference in the supply of physicians may help explain why the ratio of resources to services is much higher between the United States and Canada than between Iowa and Manitoba.

QUALITY OR INTENSITY OF CARE

The most uncertain and potentially controversial explanation concerns possible differences in quality or intensity of care. This question required that evaluation and management and procedures be considered separately. We estimated that approximately two-thirds of the evaluation and management services in Canada are delivered by general practitioners and family physicians, and one-third is delivered by internists, pediatricians, psychiatrists, and other specialists. In the United States the proportions are reversed. Should this be interpreted as a difference in quality of care? Some would argue that care provided by physicians with specialty training should be considered as more care. But there are others who believe that in most cases the quality of care provided by general practitioners or family physicians is as high, and may even be superior because of their greater familiarity with the patient and his or her circumstances. The question of intensity of care arises because of the possibility that some of the additional evaluation and management services provided in Canada are for patients with minor problems such as colds or upset stomachs. Some visits of this type may be deterred in the United States because insurance coverage is not as complete and because patients have been urged by employers and insurance companies not to visit physicians for minor problems. If the category of moderate office visits included fewer patients with minor problems in the United States, an adjustment for intensity would result in a slight increase in the ratio of the quantity of services per capita and a slight decrease in the ratio of resources to services.

With respect to procedures, the question of possible differences in the quality of care arises for other reasons. The technical competence of the specialists performing the procedures in the two countries is probably not an issue. A comparison of surgical mortality in Manitoba and New England concluded that the differences were small (Roos et al. 1990). Timeliness and convenience, however, may differ. Because on a per capita basis there are so many more procedure-oriented specialists in the United States than in Canada, it is likely that Americans with insurance find it easier to have procedures performed when and where they want. From the patient's perspective, this may offer an additional source of satisfaction with the service provided. Whether such differences exist, how large they are, and how they are valued by patients are subjects for further research. These issues are much more muted in the comparison between Iowa and Manitoba than in that between the United States and

Canada, because there are so few physicians per capita in Iowa as compared with Manitoba.

This discussion points up the need for additional studies to determine the magnitude of the many factors affecting fees, use of services, and use of resources to produce those services. Further refinements in the ratios of physicians' fees and the prices of resources would be particularly valuable, given the central role of these ratios in the statistical analysis. Such studies and refinements, however, are not likely to alter the principal lesson of this chapter: U.S. fees are more than double those of Canada, but physicians' net incomes are only about a third higher. The disparity is explained in part by much greater overhead expenses in the United States and in part by the lower workloads of American procedure-oriented physicians as compared with their Canadian counterparts.

7

How Canada Does It:
Acute Hospital Care

Expenditures for acute hospital care were 26 percent higher in the United States than Canada in 1987, after adjustment for population size and the difference in the two currencies. The differential of $129 per person accounted for approximately one-fourth of the total difference in health expenditures of $552 per person. Thus, acute hospital costs, along with physicians' services (see Chapter 6) and administration of health insurance plans (Himmelstein and Woolhandler 1986, 1991), are the principal factors contributing to the high expenditures for health care in the United States relative to Canada. If acute care hospitals in the United States followed the same spending pattern as their Canadian counterparts the savings would have exceeded $40 billion in 1987. By 1989 both the relative and absolute differentials in spending had widened (American Hospital Association 1990; Statistics Canada 1991c).

Why are hospital expenditures greater in the United States? A comparison of patients age 65 and over concluded that admission rates and case mix were similar in the two countries, but cost per case was much lower in Canada (Newhouse, Anderson, and Roos 1988). Other studies have focused on global budgeting and regulation as the principal mechanism for cost control in Canada (Detsky, Stacey, and Bombardier 1983; Detsky et al. 1986; Evans, Lomas, and Barer 1989). Medical practice patterns

---

Written with Donald A. Redelmeier, M.D.

104

may differ because of the higher incidence of malpractice suits in the United States. Also, the health care demands of the two populations may be dissimilar due to the differing cultures and lifestyles (Lipset 1990).

This chapter investigates hospital care for patients of all ages in order to understand why inpatient expenditures are greater in the United States. Do U.S. residents have higher admission rates? Longer lengths of stay? Do U.S. hospitals treat a more complex patient case mix? Do they pay higher wages for the labor resources used to produce hospital care? Do they pay higher prices for drugs and other nonlabor resources? Do they provide more outpatient care? To answer these questions, we compare hospital costs at several levels of aggregation: the United States versus Canada; California (the largest state) versus Ontario (the largest province); and two specific institutions in California versus two in Ontario. The institutional comparisons also include analyses of specific diagnostic services. The ultimate goal is to measure and explain differences in the real resources used to treat comparable patients. The effects of differences in hospital expenditures on patient outcomes are not examined here.

Methods

Details concerning definitions, sources, and statistical adjustments are available elsewhere (see Chapter 6, note 2).

BACKGROUND STATISTICS

General background, health care expenditures, and hospital data on the United States, Canada, California, and Ontario for 1987 were gathered mainly from published sources.[1] This chapter focuses on acute care hospitals; extended care facilities, long-term chronic care units, and nursing stations were excluded. Canadian institutions report on a fiscal year basis (April 1–March 31), whereas U.S. institutions report on the calendar year (January 1–December 31); for comparability we trended back the Canadian data by three months. Canadian currency was converted to U.S. dollars according to the purchasing-power exchange rate of $1 U.S. equals $1.23 Canadian; all dollar amounts mentioned in this chapter refer to 1987 U.S. dollars.

ADJUSTMENT FOR CASE MIX

To adjust for case mix, U.S. patients were classified by diagnosis-related groups (DRGs), Canadian patients by case-mix groups (CMGs). In 1987 these two systems were similar in design and definition (Helyar 1991). We explored possible differences in coding between the two countries by identifying 100 pairs of DRGs with complicated and uncomplicated versions of the same diagnosis and comparing the proportion that were classified as complicated. To quantify overall case mix we analyzed the complete distribution of diagnoses using weights based on California DRG-specific charges. A second summary measure was obtained using weights based on Ontario CMG-specific resource intensities. The results from the two weighting approaches were averaged to obtain the case-mix ratios used in our adjustments.

ADJUSTMENT FOR PRICES OF RESOURCES

Wage comparisons were based on full-time workers' earnings plus fringe benefits. Because the wage comparisons differed depending on the skill level of the occupation, ratios were assessed at three different levels: high (head nurses and general duty staff nurses), medium (laboratory technicians and X-ray technicians), and low (hospital cleaners and food service helpers). To obtain a ratio for wages in general, we calculated a weighted average of the wage ratios for the three occupation categories. Weights of 50, 25, and 25 for the high-, medium-, and low-wage categories were estimated from the distribution of earnings of hospital employees by occupation (U.S. Bureau of the Census 1988a). Alternative averages based on weights of 60, 20, 20 and 40, 30, 30 were also estimated.

The price ratio for pharmacy supplies was derived from an analysis by Schieber, Poullier, and Greenwald (1991). The price ratio for nonmedical resources (such as electricity, water, and telephone) was assumed to be the same as the ratio found by the Organization for Economic Cooperation and Development for all goods and services—that is, the purchasing-power parity exchange rate. To determine the overall relative price of hospital resources, the labor and nonlabor ratios were averaged using expenditure weights of 0.67 for labor and 0.33 for nonlabor to reflect an average of their relative contribution to total hospital costs in the U.S. and Canada (U.S. Bureau of the Census 1990; Statistics Canada 1991a).

ADJUSTMENT FOR OUTPATIENT CARE

To adjust for hospital outpatient services, we developed a model that estimated total admission equivalents as the sum of hospital admissions, emergency department visits, and other outpatient visits (the latter two variables weighted by their relative costs). The quotient of hospital admissions and total admission equivalents indicated the proportion of total expenditures related to inpatient service; for example, a hospital with 8,000 admissions and 2,000 additional admission equivalents (reflecting emergency and outpatient visits) would have 10,000 total admission equivalents and an inpatient share of 80 percent.

We converted emergency and outpatient visits to admission equivalents based on data from the American Hospital Association for individual states in 1987. We used multiple regression to analyze these data for the forty-eight contiguous states and estimated the marginal cost of an average emergency department visit and an average outpatient visit, relative to an average admission. We then applied these estimates to Canadian hospitals, assuming that the difference between the two countries in resource use per outpatient service is similar to the difference for an inpatient admission. The results of the regression model for the state of California and the province of Ontario were compared to estimates provided by the American Hospital Association and the Ontario Ministry of Health; results for the four specific institutions were reviewed by administrators of the respective facilities.

SPECIFIC INSTITUTIONS

Background statistics for the four study hospitals came from published sources, computer files, and confidential reports. The Stanford University Medical Center and the Sunnybrook Health Sciences Center are large tertiary care hospitals located in Northern California and Southern Ontario respectively. Both maintain trauma units, academic teaching programs, and extensive referral networks. The Saint John's Hospital and the Wellesley Hospital are community-oriented hospitals located in southern California and southern Ontario, respectively. Both maintain active obstetrics programs, small intensive care units, and large general medical programs. At all four facilities we evaluated case mix, relative prices, and inpatient share of expenditures by the same methods used in the national and regional comparisons.

SPECIFIC SERVICES

To further examine resource utilization we obtained confidential departmental reports detailing clinical activity at each of the four hospitals. Many services could not be identified across all four hospitals because of differences in accounting and reporting; for this study we selected twelve well-specified diagnostic services. The set of services was chosen to illustrate diverse aspects of care including routine and high-tech procedures.

Results

Table 7.1 presents measures of selected socioeconomic factors that affect hospital expenditures. The United States has a higher percentage of persons age 65 and over and a smaller proportion living in cities of over 100,000. The crude death rate is higher in the United States, but a lower proportion of deaths occurs in hospitals. The birth rate is higher in the United States, and a

Table 7.1 Selected background statistics, 1987

Variable	United States	Canada	California	Ontario	Ratio of United States to Canada	Ratio of California to Ontario
Population (in 000s)	245,807	25,637	28,314	9,270		
Percentage ≥ 65 years	12.3	11.1	10.6	11.3	1.11	0.94
Percentage in cities ≥ 100,000	25.3	34.6	40.4	48.2	0.73	0.84
Deaths per 1,000	8.7	7.3	7.6	7.5	1.19	1.01
Percentage of deaths in hospitals[a]	61.8	72.1	59.4	71.6	0.86	0.83
Births per 1,000	15.7	14.7	18.2	14.7	1.07	1.24
Percentage of births < 2,500 grams[b]	6.9	5.7	6.0	5.4	1.21	1.11
AIDS cases per 100,000[c]	8.3	2.4	16.4	2.8	3.46	5.86
Homicides per 100,000[d]	8.3	2.5	10.8	2.2	3.32	4.91
Patient care physicians per 1,000[e]	1.86	2.14	2.09	2.22	0.87	0.94
GDP per capita[f]	18,338	17,211	21,114	19,619	1.07	1.08
Health expenditures per capita[g]	1,987	1,435	2,365	1,464	1.38	1.62

Sources: Health and Welfare Canada 1988b; Levit 1985; Office of the Registrar General of Ontario 1990; State of California Department of Finance 1990; Treasurer of Ontario and Minister of Economics 1990; U.S. Bureau of the Census 1990; U.S. Department of Health and Human Services 1988; and personal communications from State of California, Department of Health Services, Health Data and Statistics Branch, Feb. 4, 1992; State of New York, Department of Health, Bureau of Biometrics, Feb. 6, 1992; State of Texas, Department of Health Services, Feb. 7, 1992; and Statistics Canada Health Care Section, Aug. 21, 1991.

a. Excludes deaths occurring in private homes, nursing homes, convalescent homes, or dead on arrival.

b. As reported in Office of the Registrar General of Ontario 1990; U.S. Bureau of the Census 1990; and personal communication, Statistics Canada Health Care Section, Aug. 21, 1991.

c. As reported in Health and Welfare Canada 1988b; U.S. Department of Health and Human Services 1988.

d. Refers to murders, manslaughters, and infanticides, as reported in Office of the Registrar General of Ontario 1990; State of California Department of Finance 1990; Statistics Canada 1991a; U.S. Bureau of the Census 1990.

e. Denotes active civilian physicians rendering patient care or services by pathologists.

f. Gross Domestic Product, Gross State Product, or Gross Provincial Product, as appropriate.

g. Canadian dollars converted to U.S. dollars by the purchasing-power-parity exchange rate of $1.00 U.S. = $1.23 Canadian.

larger percentage of U.S. newborns weigh less than 2,500 grams (5.5 lbs.). The homicide rate and the incidence of AIDS are much higher in the United States than in Canada. The differentials between California and Ontario are similar in direction, except there are fewer elderly in California.

Background statistics for acute care hospitals appear in Table 7.2. Expenditures per capita are 26 percent higher in the United States, despite the fact that the number of beds per capita, admissions per capita, and average length of stay are all greater in Canada. In the United States (and California) more beds are in small and medium-size hospitals than is the case in Canada, and a much smaller percentage in hospitals with over 500 beds. The largest difference in age-specific admission rates is for children: a U.S. child is 50 percent less likely to enter a hospital than a Canadian child. Occupancy rates are appreciably lower in American hospitals, but annual admissions per bed (the throughput of patients) is higher. The per capita emergency department visit rate in the United States is less than half that of Canada; the rate of other outpatient visits is approximately equal.

Expenditures per admission are 39 percent higher in the United States than in Canada, and 63 percent higher in California than in Ontario (Table 7.3, line 1); however, to measure the real resource cost of treating comparable inpatients requires taking account of possible differences in patient case mix, wage rates and prices of other resources paid by hospitals, and the allocation of hospital resources between inpatient and outpatient care.

The diagnostic case mix (as measured by DRGs and CMGs) is 14 percent more complex in the United States than in Canada (Table 7.3, line 2). This result is moderately sensitive to the weighting system: an index based only on California DRG-specific charges suggests that the U.S. case mix is 16 percent more complex, and an index based only on Ontario resource intensity weights suggests that the U.S. case mix is 12 percent more complex. Adjustment for case mix reduces the difference in expenditures per admission (Table 7.3, line 3).

Table 7.2 Acute care hospital statistics, 1987

Variable	United States	Canada	California	Ontario	Ratio of United States to Canada	Ratio of California to Ontario
Expenditures per capita	621	492	628	512	1.26	1.23
Hospital beds per 1,000[a]	3.90	5.43	2.92	4.84	0.72	0.60
% in hospitals < 200 beds	34.4	28.5	36.3	23.1	1.21	1.57
% in hospitals 200–500 beds	44.3	38.0	49.6	40.6	1.17	1.22
% in hospitals > 500 beds	21.3	33.5	14.1	36.4	0.64	0.39
Admissions per 1,000 population[b]						
All ages	129	142	106	141	0.91	0.75
Age ≤ 14	49	87	36	85	0.56	0.42
15–24	102	124	102	120	0.82	0.85
25–44	109	118	90	114	0.92	0.79
45–64	147	153	114	151	0.96	0.75
≥ 65 years	327	325	294	351	1.01	0.84
Inpatient days per 1,000 population	929	1,590	678	1,495	0.58	0.45
Mean length of stay	7.2	11.2	6.4	10.6	0.64	0.60
Occupancy rate	65	81	64	85	0.80	0.76
Admissions per bed	33	26	36	30	1.27	1.20
Emergency visits per 1,000 pop.[c]	320	677	280	645	0.47	0.43
Other outpatient visits per 1,000 pop.[d]	683	670	607	736	1.02	0.82
Expenditures per admission	4,814	3,463	5,903	3,629	1.39	1.63

Sources: American Hospital Association 1988; Office of Statewide Health Planning and Development 1990; Statistics Canada 1989b, 1990, 1991b; and unpublished computer data analysis, Ontario Ministry of Health, Information Systems Division, Nov. 9, 1990.
a. Registered units, not necessarily staffed or active, as reported in American Hospital Association 1988 and Statistics Canada 1989b.
b. Excludes normal newborns and includes patients transferred from another facility.
c. Defined as an outpatient visit to a hospital facility having 24-hour staffing and offering immediate care.
d. Each appearance by an outpatient to a unit of the hospital counts as one outpatient visit.

The adjustment for case mix does not take into account possible differences in coding practices between the two countries, nor does it reflect possible differences in severity within each diagnostic group. One test of case mix showed that within each of 100 pairs of DRGs that have complicated and uncomplicated versions of the same diagnosis, the proportions classified as complicated were virtually identical in the two California and two Ontario institutions examined in this project.

Expenditures depend on the quantity of resources and their prices. Prices are, on average, slightly higher in the United States (Table 7.3, line 4). High-wage occupations (such as staff nurse or head nurse) are paid considerably more in the United States,

Table 7.3 Accounting for ratios of expenditures per admission, 1987

	Ratio of United States to Canada	Ratio of California to Ontario
(1) Expenditures per admission[a]	1.39	1.63
(2) Diagnostic case mix[b]	1.14	1.11
(3) Expenditures per adjusted admission[c]	1.22	1.46
(4) Prices of resources[d]	1.04	1.05
(5) Resources per adjusted admission[e]	1.17	1.39
(6) Inpatient share of expenditures[f]	1.06	1.05
(7) Inpatient resources per adjusted admission[g]	1.24	1.46

a. Advanced from Table 7.2.

b. Measure of the relative complexity of case mix calculated from data in Office of Statewide Health Planning and Development 1990; The Hospital Medical Records Institute 1987; National Center for Health Statistics 1987; personal communication, The Hospital Medical Records Institute, April 8, 1991; and unpublished computer data analysis, Ontario Ministry of Health, Information Systems Division, Aug. 21, 1991.

c. (1) ÷ (2).

d. Comparison of prices for labor and nonlabor resources advanced from Table 7.4.

e. (3) ÷ (4).

f. Proportion of expenditures going for inpatient care calculated from data in Table 7.2 and American Hospital Association 1988.

g. (5) × (6).

but for occupations at the other end of the wage scale (such as cleaners and food aides) wages are higher in Canada (Table 7.4). The overall price ratio depends on the weights used to average the ratios for specific resources, but even substantial changes in weights result in a shift in the overall ratio of only about 2 percent in either direction. Adjustment for prices of resources reduces the United-States-to-Canada and California-to-Ontario expenditure ratios (Table 7.3, line 5).

The third adjustment attempts to account for differences in the proportion of total hospital resources devoted to inpatient care. The higher number of emergency department visits in Canada and Ontario suggest that the inpatient share of total expen-

Table 7.4 Estimation of the prices of resources, 1987

	Ratio of United States to Canada	Ratio of California to Ontario
(1) High-wage occupations[a]	1.18	1.23
(2) Medium-wage occupations[b]	0.93	0.93
(3) Low-wage occupations[c]	0.86	0.78
(4) Pharmaceutical products[d]	1.07	1.07
(5) Other goods and services[e]	1.00	1.00
(6) Labor resources[f]	1.04	1.04
(7) Nonlabor resources[g]	1.02	1.02
(8) All resources[h]	1.03	1.03
(9) All resources, adjusted for liability insurance	1.04	1.05

a. Based on head nurses and staff general duty nurses.
b. Based on laboratory technicians and X-ray technicians.
c. Based on housekeeping cleaners and food service aids.
d. Derived from data in Schieber, Poullier, and Greenwald 1991.
e. Assumed equal to 1.00.
f. Weighted average of (1), (2), and (3).
g. Weighted average of (4) and (5).
h. Weighted average of (6) and (7).

ditures is smaller in those hospitals. We estimated that, at the margin, the relative expenditures related to one inpatient admission are equal to 28 emergency department visits (± 14 at 95 percent confidence level) or 77 (± 30) other outpatient visits. These results, when applied to data on admissions, emergency department visits, and other outpatient visits yield inpatient shares of 79.7 percent for the United States and 74.9 percent for Canada. The adjustment for inpatient share is the most problematic of the three adjustments, and readers are cautioned that alternative models and assumptions might yield different ratios for line 6 of Table 7.3.

The net result after adjusting for case mix, prices of resources, and inpatient share shows hospitals in the United States using 24 percent more real resources per adjusted admission than those in Canada; the differential between California and Ontario is 46 percent (Table 7.3, line 7).

Comparisons for the two pairs of California and Ontario hospitals appear in Table 7.5. Length of stay and occupancy rate are much lower at the California hospitals; admissions per bed are considerably higher at Stanford than at Sunnybrook, but Saint John's and Wellesley are approximately equal. The two California hospitals have substantially fewer emergency department visits than their Ontario counterparts, although the proportion admitted is similar at all four facilities. Expenditures per admission before the three adjustments are 23 percent and 22 percent higher in the California hospitals. Part of this differential is explained by a more complex case mix of patients, and part by higher prices of resources. Stanford's prices are particularly high because of higher wages in the Stanford area relative to California as a whole. The outpatient share of expenditures is greater in the two Ontario hospitals. After all adjustments, the two California hospitals use 20 percent (Stanford/Sunnybrook) and 15 percent (Saint John's/Wellesley) more real resources per adjusted admission.

Does the use of more resources per admission by the two Cali-

Table 7.5 Comparisons of individual hospitals in California and Ontario, 1987

	Stanford (U.S.)	Sunnybrook (Canada)	St. John's (U.S.)	Wellesley (Canada)	Ratio of Stanford to Sunnybrook	Ratio of St. John's to Wellesley
Beds	631	620	550	510	1.02	1.08
Admissions (000s)	22.7	16.4	15.6	14.6	1.38	1.07
Emergency visits (000s)	27.2	38.8	22.8	40.8	0.70	0.56
% of emergency visits admitted[a]	17.2	18.6	20.7	16.5	0.92	1.25
Other outpatient visits	161	277	147	137	0.58	1.07
Inpatient days (000s)	143	201	103	173	0.71	0.60
Mean length of stay	6.3	12.3	6.6	11.9	0.51	0.55
Occupancy rate	62	89	51	93	0.70	0.55
Admissions per bed	36	26	28	29	1.36	1.00
Total expenditures ($ millions)	209	123	108	82	1.71	1.31
(1) Expenditures per admission	9,216	7,501	6,898	5,643	1.23	1.22
(2) Diagnostic case mix					1.07	1.04
(3) Expenditures per adjusted admission [(1) ÷ (2)]					1.15	1.17
(4) Prices of resources					1.11	1.05
(5) Resources per adjusted admission [(3) ÷ (4)]					1.04	1.11
(6) Inpatient share of expenditures					1.15	1.04
(7) Inpatient resources per adjusted admission [(5) × (6)]					1.20	1.15

Sources: The St. John's Hospital, Quarterly Financial and Utilization Reports Submitted to Office of Statewide Health Planning and Development (1987) and Annual Disclosure Report Submitted to Office of Statewide Health Planning and Development (Feb. 14, 1988); Stanford University Medical Center, Annual Disclosure Report Submitted to Office of Statewide Health Planning and Development (Dec. 30, 1987) and Auditor's Report on Examinations of Financial Statements (1987); Sunnybrook Health Sciences Center, Annual Return of Health Care Facilities, Part I, Submitted to Health and Welfare Canada (June 16, 1988); The Wellesley Hospital, Annual Return of Health Care Facilities, Part I, Submitted to Health and Welfare Canada (Aug. 31, 1988).

a. 1991 figures.

fornia hospitals result in more services to patients? Comparisons for twelve diagnostic services indicate that U.S. patients receive more of certain services but Canadian patients receive more of other services (Table 7.6). The most common biochemistry test, serum electrolyte assay, is performed particularly less often in the two California hospitals compared to the two Ontario hospitals. The discrepancy in the two most common lung tests is a noteworthy difference in practice patterns: patients in the two California hospitals receive more arterial blood gas tests but fewer chest X-rays than their Ontario counterparts. There are only three procedures—MRI scans of the head, echocardiograms, and arterial blood gases—where both the Stanford/Sunnybrook and Saint John's/Wellesley service ratios exceed the overall case-mix ratios. On balance, the data do not support the hypothesis that the two California hospitals provide more diagnostic services during an admission than do their Ontario counterparts.

Discussion

Canadians spend appreciably less than U.S. residents for acute hospital care, but the savings are not achieved through fewer beds, fewer admissions, or shorter lengths of stay. The differential arises entirely in expenditures per admission, which are 39 percent higher in the United States relative to Canada. Hospitals in the United States have a more complicated mix of patients (as measured by DRGs), and they pay slightly more than Canadian hospitals for the resources used to produce hospital care. On the other hand, the inpatient share of total expenditures is higher in the United States, resulting in a United States/Canada difference of 24 percent for inpatient resources per adjusted admission. The California/Ontario comparisons are similar to the national ratios, but the differential of 46 percent in inpatient resources per adjusted admission is considerably larger. By contrast, comparisons of specific institutions in California and Ontario yielded differentials of 20 percent and 15 percent at the

Table 7.6 Selected diagnostic services per admission at four study hospitals, 1987

	Stanford (U.S.)	Sunnybrook (Canada)	St. John's (U.S.)	Wellesley (Canada)	Ratio of Stanford to Sunnybrook	Ratio of St. John's to Wellesley
MRI scans of the head[a]	0.007	0.000	0.031	0.000	∞	∞
Echocardiograms[b]	0.09	0.06	0.10	0.07	1.49	1.44
Blood cultures[c]	0.65	0.46	0.28	0.37	1.41	0.76
Ventilation/perfusion lung scans[d]	0.018	0.014	0.011	0.017	1.29	0.63
Arterial blood gases[e]	2.99	2.71	0.98	0.39	1.11	2.52
Electrocardiograms[f]	1.05	0.95	1.05	1.03	1.11	1.02
CAT scans[g]	0.22	0.22	0.16	0.15	1.00	1.07
Electroencephalograms[h]	0.032	0.040	0.023	0.060	0.80	0.38
Chest X-rays[i]	0.46	0.66	0.39	0.56	0.69	0.69
Urinalyses[j]	0.96	1.42	0.56	1.20	0.67	0.47
Electrolytes[k]	4.03	6.36	2.20	6.27	0.63	0.35
Prothrombin time assays[l]	1.09	1.79	0.45	0.67	0.61	0.66

Note: Not adjusted for case mix.

a. Denotes Magnetic Resonance Imaging scans of the head.
b. Transcutaneous ultrasound examination of the heart and mediastinal structures.
c. Microbiological assessment of the blood for bacteremia.
d. Represents either a ventilation scan, a perfusion scan, or a combined ventilation/perfusion scan.
e. Denotes an assay of pH, pO2, and pCO2.
f. Excludes measures obtained during electro-physiologic testing.
g. Denotes Computerized Axial Tomography of the body, regardless of region.
h. Multi-channel recording of brain waves obtained from cutaneous electrodes.
i. Radiology of the thoracic cage, regardless of the number of views, and excludes portable X-rays.
j. Standard dipstick examination.
k. Assay of sodium, potassium, chloride, and bicarbonate.
l. May or may not include assessment of partial thromboplastin time.

pair of tertiary care hospitals and the pair of community care hospitals, respectively.

What explains the apparent greater use of inpatient resources per adjusted admission in the United States and California? Can it be simply a problem of inadequate adjustment? We think not. The DRG system is far from a perfect measure of severity, but there is no evidence that within each DRG the U.S. cases are more acute than their Canadian counterparts. Indeed, some analysts have suggested that the prospective payment system of Medicare invites "DRG creep" in the United States, with a bias toward upgrading the severity classification in order to obtain greater reimbursement (Steinwald and Dummit 1989). We also have confidence in the adjustment for the prices of resources. The United States / Canada ratio of hourly compensation in manufacturing has been estimated as 1.04, the same ratio that we found for compensation of hospital employees (Capdevielle 1988). Other investigators, using 1981 and 1985 data, conclude that hospital wages in the United States were actually below those in Canada (Haber et al. 1993). If we have overestimated the wage ratio, then the difference in resources per patient is even greater than that reported here. The greatest uncertainty concerns the adjustment for inpatient share, but it is worth noting that the shares for California, Ontario, and the four institutions were within 5 percent of the values available from other sources.

Further refinements in the measurement of case mix, prices, and inpatient share are desirable, but we do not believe they will overturn our most important conclusion: United States hospitals use more real resources per adjusted admission. There are four possible explanations for this differential.

COST OF ADMINISTRATIVE SERVICES

United States hospitals must keep more extensive records to facilitate billing to state and federal governments, insurance companies, and patients, and in anticipation of malpractice suits. (The greater administrative cost for physicians in the United

States relative to Canada was discussed in Chapter 6.) According to Woolhandler and Himmelstein (1991), administrative costs account for 20 percent of hospital expenditures in California but only 9 percent in Canada. If they are correct, and if California and Canada are representative of the United States and Ontario, we can calculate the differentials in nonadministrative resources per admission as 10 percent for the United States versus Canada, and 28 percent for California versus Ontario. Thus, roughly half of the differences reported in Table 7.3 would be explained by administrative costs. However, administrative costs may be proportionately higher in California than in the rest of the United States; if so, the United States / Canada differential in nonadministrative resources per admission would be greater than 10 percent.

COST OF OTHER NONCLINICAL SERVICES

In addition to administration, hospitals provide other nonclinical services frequently referred to as "hotel services" or "amenities." Most American hospitals are in competition for well-insured patients, raising the possibility that the quantity and quality of such services are greater in the United States than in Canada. Reliable, comparable data to test that possibility are not available, but there are several reasons for doubting that such services contribute significantly to higher costs per admission in the United States. First, U.S. patients have shorter average lengths of stay; therefore, they require fewer meals, less waste disposal, and smaller amounts of laundry service per admission. Second, these services are usually performed by low-wage workers whose salaries tend to be lower in the United States than in Canada. Finally, the nonlabor resources consumed in these activities, such as the food supplies and cleaning products, represent only a small fraction of total hospital expenditures (Donham and Maple 1989).

COST OF PRODUCING A GIVEN CLINICAL SERVICE

In Canada, specialized procedures are performed in a relatively small number of large hospitals, whereas in the United States most community hospitals strive to provide a wide variety of tertiary care services. For example, after adjusting for differences in population size, in 1987 there were three times as many hospitals with open-heart surgery units in California as in Ontario, five times as many with magnetic resonance scanners, and ten times as many with extracorporeal lithotripters. One consequence is much fuller utilization of capacity in Canada. The lithotripter at the Wellesley Hospital has an average utilization of almost 50 cases per week. At Stanford, as at many U.S. hospitals, average utilization is less than one-tenth that level. Among the more than 100 California hospitals that offer open-heart surgery, half do fewer than 200 procedures per year (Office of Statewide Health Planning and Development 1991). Canadian centralization, reliance on referral, and establishment of waiting lists result in less idle capacity of high-cost equipment and associated personnel.

United States hospitals may also use relatively more resources to produce routine clinical services. The tremendous emphasis on early discharge in American hospitals creates a need for additional equipment and personnel ready to provide routine laboratory, radiological, and other services on short notice. By contrast, the relatively long stays in Canadian hospitals are conducive to a queuing approach, which probably results in better capacity utilization. In the United States and California the majority of patients are in small to medium-sized hospitals, which do not enjoy the relative efficiencies associated with performing routine services in large volumes. Also, greater variability in occupancy rates in U.S. hospitals from day to day and week to week makes it more difficult for them to schedule equipment and personnel with maximum efficiency.

QUANTITY OF SERVICES DELIVERED PER ADMISSION

It is widely believed that U.S. hospitals are more service intensive. This is certainly true if the unit of comparison is a patient day; however, the greater intensity per patient day may be offset by the more than 50 percent longer average stay in Canadian hospitals. As is true of physicians' services, U.S. patients get a different mix of services but not necessarily more services. The longer stays in Canadian hospitals imply that Canadian patients get more evaluations of vital signs, more dressing changes, and more of other services that are provided on a daily basis. Direct measures of the quantity of twelve diagnostic services per admission at Stanford compared with Sunnybrook, and Saint John's compared with Wellesley, do not support the hypothesis that U.S. hospitals provide more diagnostic services when treating comparable inpatients.

Canadian patients pay a price for their higher-capacity utilization of equipment and personnel. The more centralized hospital system can cause delay or inconvenience in obtaining access to specialized services (Katz, Mizgala, and Welch 1991; Naylor 1991). In some cases it results in a delay of discharge (Iglehart 1990). On the other hand, the quality of care in U.S. hospitals may suffer when complex procedures are performed relatively infrequently in smaller hospitals (Hughes, Hunt, and Luft 1987).

In summary, the United States spends more than Canada for acute hospital care even though the number of beds, the number of admissions, and the average length of stay are all greater in Canada. U.S. hospitals treat a more complex case mix and pay slightly higher prices for labor and other resources, but Canadian hospitals have a higher ratio of outpatient to inpatient care. After all adjustments, we find that the United States devotes more real resources to acute care hospital inpatients, standardized for case mix, than does Canada. The most likely explanations for the differential include greater costs of administration in U.S. hospitals and more intensive use of centralized equipment and personnel in Canadian hospitals. Our comparisons of a limited number of diagnostic procedures per admission in the four study hospitals do not support the hypothesis that U.S. hospitals deliver more clinical services, but this subject warrants further investigation.

8

Expenditures for Reproduction-Related Health Care

There are 58 million American women of childbearing age (15 to 44 years), of whom about 55 percent use some form of contraception, including sterilization. Approximately 10 percent have the opposite problem—difficulty in conceiving—and annually about 1 million couples seek medical advice or treatment for infertility. Each year approximately 6.5 million women learn that they are pregnant. One-fourth of the pregnancies end with an induced abortion, and another 15 percent of these confirmed conceptions end in miscarriage or stillbirth. About 4 million infants are delivered, of whom almost 40,000 die within a year of birth. Nearly all of the infants receive some medical care; a small percentage receive a great deal.

Currently there is considerable controversy about "high-tech" obstetrical methods, costly neonatal intensive care, and other reproduction-related expenditures, but there is little solid information available about these health services from an economic perspective. What fraction of total health care spending is accounted for by this sector? How is it divided among contraception, infertility treatment, abortion, and obstetrical and infant care? What are the prospects for future spending in this area?

This chapter presents systematic estimates of the direct money costs of reproduction-related health care in 1982. Indirect costs, such as the value of time lost from work by pregnant women

Written with Leslie Perreault.

or psychic costs that may be associated with contraception and abortion, are outside the scope of this article, as are nonhealth costs related to reproduction, such as adoption proceedings. The direct money costs estimated herein are just one element, but a critical one, in health planning or in a full-scale analysis of costs and benefits.

Sources, Methods, and Results

In the absence of overall expenditures data, the estimates are constructed primarily by multiplying estimated quantities by estimated prices. These data are drawn from a variety of sources, ranging from national surveys to small clinical studies. All prices and quantities are for 1982 unless otherwise stated. A few estimates are based on data from earlier years, extrapolated to 1982 with the aid of related price and quantity series. The sources, methods, and results are presented in considerable detail to enable readers to assess their reliability and to facilitate substitution of alternative estimates for particular quantities or prices while utilizing the other results within the same overall framework.

OBSTETRICAL CARE

The largest category of reproduction-related expenditures is obstetrical care, including prenatal, delivery, and postnatal services. We estimate total charges for these services at $8.2 billion, approximately $2,230 per live birth. Hospital charges account for nearly 60 percent of the total. Another 35 percent represents physicians' fees, and the remainder is accounted for by laboratory tests, roentgenograms, and the like (Table 8.1).

Of the 3.7 million babies born in 1982, 99 percent were delivered by physicians in hospitals or other medical facilities. These admissions accounted for 10.5 percent of all hospital admissions in that year, but because maternity stays are relatively short—an average of 3.4 days compared with 7.1 days for all admissions—only 4.6 percent of total hospital days are for women having babies (National Center for Health Statistics 1985a). The average hospital charge for a normal birth with labor and delivery rooms was $1,130. Cesarean births—17.6 percent of all births in 1982—cost $1,930 (Health Insurance Association of America 1982). Total obstetrical hospital charges of $4.7 billion imply an average cost of $374 per day, which is very close to the average expense per patient-day of $380 for all admissions to nonfederal short-stay hospitals in 1982 (American Hospital Association 1984).

According to the Health Insurance Association of America, the average physician fee for complete obstetrical care was $600 for a normal delivery and $785 for a cesarean delivery (Health Insur-

Table 8.1   Direct costs of obstetrical care, 1982

	Number (thousands)	Average cost	Total cost (millions)
Live births			
Hospital charges			
Normal delivery	3,033	$1,130	$3,427
Cesarean section	648	1,930	1,251
Nonhospital charges			
Attending physician			
Normal delivery	3,033	600	1,820
Cesarean section	648	785	509
Anesthetist			
Normal[a] delivery	1,520	150	228
Cesarean section	648	250	162
Tests, laboratory, and other[b]	3,681	150	552
All live births	3,681	2,160	7,949
Miscarriages and stillbirths	966	260	252
All obstetrical care	4,647	1,765	8,201

a. Assumes anesthesia is used in half of normal births.
b. Estimated as 17% of nonhospital charges.

ance Association of America 1982). We use these estimates although they are somewhat lower than those found in a survey of physicians by *Medical Economics,* which reported a median charge for normal obstetrical care of $700 for obstetricians, $500 for family practitioners, and $450 for general practitioners (Kirchner 1982). This results in an average charge of $655 if 80 percent of babies are delivered by obstetricians and the remaining births are spread equally between family and general practitioners (National Center for Health Statistics 1984a).

The average anesthetist's fee for a normal delivery was $150 and approximately $250 for a cesarean delivery (Health Insurance Association of America 1982). Assuming that all cesarean deliveries and half of normal deliveries require the services of an anesthetist, the total bill for their services is $390 million.

In addition to hospital charges and physicians' fees, there are costs associated with new diagnostic procedures. Of women having live births in 1980, 29 percent of those aged 35 years and older and 4 percent of younger mothers underwent amniocentesis. In addition, 30 percent of all mothers underwent at least one ultrasound examination and 13 percent received at least one medical roentgenographic examination (Kleinman et al. 1983; Hamilton et al. 1984). These procedures and other tests not covered by the obstetrician's basic fee accounted for 17 percent of all nonhospital maternity costs at the Palo Alto Medical Clinic in 1981 (Anne Scitovsky, unpublished data, 1984). This ratio applied to our estimates adds another $550 million to the cost of having babies.

In addition to the cost of live births, there were charges incurred for miscarriages and stillbirths. We assume that the cost of stillbirths occurring after 28 weeks of pregnancy is the same as for live births. The proportion of these stillbirths delivered by cesarean section is as high as among live births, and electronic fetal monitoring is used almost as frequently (Placek et al. 1984). For those stillbirths occurring between 20 and 28 weeks, we estimate the average charge at three-fourths of the cost of a live birth, and for miscarriages prior to 20 weeks we estimate a physician's fee equal to one-third of the fee for a normal delivery.

INFANT CARE

Babies in their first year of life used medical care costing approximately $6.5 billion in 1982. Of the total, 60 percent was spent on newborn care. Another 30 percent was paid for medical care for infants requiring subsequent hospitalization during the first year. Only 10 percent was spent on well-baby care, preventive care, and medical care for problems not requiring hospitalization (Table 8.2).

The majority of infants are normal and healthy, leaving the hospital after a routine nursery stay. Pediatric care for a normal newborn is $64, and the average hospital charge is $100 per day, or $350 total (Health Insurance Association of America 1982). Approximately 5 percent of newborns, however, require intensive neonatal care. Many are normal-weight infants born with congenital defects; a substantial portion have low birth weight ($\leq$ 2,500 grams, or 5.5 lbs.). Although only one baby in fourteen

Table 8.2 Direct costs of infant care, 1982

	Number (thousands)	Average cost	Total cost (millions)
Newborn care			
Normal care			
Hospital	3,496	$ 350	$1,223
Physician	3,496	85	299
Intensive care	185	12,000	2,220
Other infant care			
Hospitalization			
Hospital	340	5,140	1,748
Physician	340	675	230
Physicians' office visits	3,681	177	652
Laboratory, immunizations, etc.	3,681	35	129
Total infant care	3,681	$ 1,766	$6,501

is born at low birth weight, they account for over half of all infant deaths and three-fourths of all neonatal deaths (deaths within the first 28 days).

There are no national data on the utilization of neonatal intensive care. Expenditures must be estimated from clinical studies, often based on atypical populations and small samples. In one study of 1,185 infants weighing at least 500 grams (1.1 lbs.) at birth, total physician and hospital costs for the first year of life averaged $8,000 per infant. The infants were treated in the intensive care nursery at the University of California San Francisco Moffitt Hospital during a 30-month period in 1976–1978. Average total cost was $19,000 for babies weighing 501 to 1,000 grams (1.1 to 2.2 lbs.) at birth, but only $5,600 for those weighing at least 2,500 grams (5.5 lbs.) (Phibbs, Williams, and Phibbs 1981). Another study of 75 babies weighing less than 1,000 grams reported average hospital costs (1976 dollars) of $14,000 for the 45 infants who died and $40,000 for the 30 survivors (Pomerance et al. 1978).

Budetti et al. (1981) conducted a study of the costs and effectiveness of neonatal intensive care for the Congressional Office of Technology Assessment. They estimated that average expenditures per patient in 1978 were about $8,000. Adjusting their estimate by the consumer price index for medical care, we set the average cost per admission at $12,000 in 1982.

In addition to lengthy hospital stays at birth, a substantial portion of low-weight infants are rehospitalized during their first year of life. McCormick et al. (1980) estimate that 19 percent of these infants have at least one additional hospital episode, with an average of 12.5 hospital days during the year. Normal-weight infants have a rehospitalization rate of 8.4 percent, with an average stay of 7.8 days. These figures imply that infants used 2.9 million hospital days in 1982.

The National Hospital Discharge Survey conducted by the National Center for Health Statistics (1984d) reports much higher figures—1,702 hospital days per 1,000 infants in 1982, or a total of 6.3 million days. Some possible reasons for the huge disparity are that National Hospital Discharge Survey estimates may include neonates who are transferred to another hospital or to an intensive care unit within the same hospital. Since the study by McCormick et al. excluded all hospitalizations before the infant went home for the first time, their estimate would be lower. In addition, the estimates of McCormick et al. relied on interviews with parents of infants alive at 1 year. Actual utilization would be underestimated if the infants who died required more hospital care or if parents forgot to report some of the hospital days. This chapter uses an average of the two estimates—4.6 million hospital days. At $380 per day (the average expense per day for all admissions), hospital costs are estimated at $1.7 billion. Physician fees for these hospitalizations add another $230 million, assuming an average charge of $50 per day.

According to unpublished data from The Robert Wood Johnson Foundation National Perinatal Regionalization Program, normal-weight infants have an average of 10 physician visits during the first year (McCormick 1985). On the other hand, the National Ambulatory Medical Care Survey reported only 4.4 office visits to pediatricians per infant per year in 1980–1981. If 70 percent of all physician's office visits by babies younger than 2 years were to pediatricians (National Center for Health Statistics 1983), the National Ambulatory Medical Care Survey estimate implies an average of 6.3 visits per infant per year. We split the difference between the sources and assume 8 visits per year. Physician charges are estimated as $30 for an initial office visit and $21 for a follow-up visit (American Medical Association 1983). Thus, physician care during the first year amounted to $650 million. Immunizations and other services not included in the physician's fees added another $130 million, assuming average charges of $35 per infant.

CONTRACEPTION

Approximately 54 percent of American women aged 15 to 44 years use some form of contraception. The cost in 1982 was about $2.4 billion, or $81 per woman using contraception and $44 per woman of childbearing age. Of those who are not using contraception, most are sexually inactive, noncontraceptively sterile, pregnant, postpartum, or seeking pregnancy. About 4 million women aged 15 to 44 years, however, are sexually active and not trying to conceive, but use no method of birth control.

The majority of persons using contraception use one of the most effective methods: male or female sterilization (33 percent), birth control pills (28 percent), or intrauterine devices (IUDs) (7 percent). Expenditures for these methods amount to over $1.9 billion, 80 percent of the total. Another 23 percent of persons using contraception use barrier methods: diaphragms, condoms, or foam. The remaining 9 percent employ the least effective methods, mainly rhythm and withdrawal. Contraceptive sterilization has increased sharply in popularity during the last decade, replacing the pill as the most common method of birth control. Over half of contraceptive users aged 30 to 44 years rely on sterilization, but among younger women the pill is still preferred (National Center for Health Statistics 1984b).

Expenditures for the different contraceptive methods vary in the size and timing of outlays. The one-time payment for surgical sterilization averages $1,180 for tubal ligation and $241 for vasectomy. Physician visits and the purchase of contraceptive devices contribute to high first-year expenditures for prescription methods—an average of $154 for pill, IUD, and diaphragm. In subsequent years, the IUD is costless, while expenditures for pill and diaphragm are substantially reduced, depending mainly on the cost of supplies (Torres and Forrest 1983). Whereas the costs of sterilization, pill, and IUD are fixed for all women who use these methods, the expense associated with barrier methods depends on the frequency of intercourse.

Because of the unevenness in timing of expenditures, estimates of the annual cost of contraception vary depending on the technique of estimation. One technique is to count outlays in the year that they are incurred. Alternatively, the total cost can be regarded as spread smoothly over the entire period of protection. Because one-time contraceptive expenses are paid at the beginning of the investment period rather than in annual installments, an implicit interest charge must be added to the total. (Money available now is worth more than an equal amount available in the future because it can be invested to earn more money. Thus, prepaying a lump sum is more costly than paying an equal amount in installments.) The yearly cost becomes the imputed annual payment for interest and amortization on one-time expenses, plus the costs that are incurred year after year.

In Table 8.3, contraceptive expenditures are calculated using the interest and amortization technique. Conceptually it makes more sense to spread the costs of contraception evenly over the period of protection. In 1979–1980, women obtaining tubal sterilizations were, on average, 30 years old (Centers for Disease Control 1983b). Thus, the cost of sterilization is amortized over the approximately 15 remaining years of reproductive life. One-time costs of the pill, IUD, and diaphragm are spread over a three-year period. This assumes that each year one-third of these contraceptive users are first-time users or are incurring equivalent costs for checkups or replacement devices. (This portion of the cost estimate is particularly sensitive to the number of years a method is assumed to provide protection.) A real (that is, adjusted for inflation) interest rate of 4 percent per annum is applied to unamortized balances of onetime costs. Recurring costs are then added to arrive at a total annual cost.

ABORTION

According to the Alan Guttmacher Institute, nearly 3 percent of all women between the ages of 15 and 44 years had an abortion in 1982. We estimate the cost of these 1.5 million abortions at $484 million. This is approximately $307 per abortion, or about $9 per woman of childbearing age (Table 8.4). The Centers for Disease Control's estimate of the number of abortions is about 20 percent lower. Their figure, however, is based on summary reports from individual states and is probably incomplete (Cen-

Table 8.3 Direct costs of contraception, 1982

Type of contraception	Annualized one-time cost[a]	Recurring cost	Total annual cost	Number (thousands)	Total cost
Female sterilization[b]	$106	—	$106	6,486	$ 688
Male sterilization[b]	22	—	22	3,189	70
Pill[c]	23	$107	130	8,377	1,089
Intrauterine device[c]	47	—	47	2,108	99
Diaphragm[c,d]	27	84	111	2,432	270
Condom[d]	—	30	30	3,621	109
Spermicides[d]	—	50	50	1,135	57
Other	—	—	—	2,108	0
All types	NA[e]	NA	81	29,455	2,382

a. Unamortized cost incurs interest at 4% per annum, assuming the following initial costs: female sterilization, $1,180; male sterilization, $241; pill, $65; intrauterine device, $131; and diaphragm, $76.

b. Amortized over 15 years.

c. Amortized over 3 years.

d. Assumes coital frequency of 100 per year.

e. NA indicates not applicable.

ters for Disease Control 1983a). Publicly funded abortions (210,000 in fiscal year 1982) had an average cost of $322, which is close to our overall estimate of $307 (Nestor and Benson 1982).

Approximately 82 percent of abortions are performed in clinics and physicians' offices; the remaining 18 percent are done in hospitals. About 90 percent are performed in the first trimester and 10 percent in the second trimester (Henshaw, Forrest, and Blaine 1984). Over one-third of second-trimester procedures take place in hospitals, while only 16 percent of earlier abortions are hospital procedures (S. Henshaw, oral communication, April 1985). The estimates of the cost per abortion by site and trimester are based on samples. A 1981 survey of 240 clinics reported charges of $190 and $358 for first- and second-trimester abortions, respectively (Henshaw 1982). We inflated these charges slightly to bring them to 1982 levels because the price of an abortion has been rising slowly in recent years (Henshaw, Forrest, and Blaine 1984). Charges for in-hospital abortions are based on very small samples and are probably less reliable.

INFERTILITY SERVICES

There are no published estimates of average or total expenditures for infertility services; in our judgment they were still quite small in 1982, but probably growing rapidly.

Table 8.4 Direct costs of abortion, 1982

	Number (thousands)	Average cost	Total cost (millions)
Clinic[a]	1,291		
First trimester	1,202	$195	$234
Second trimester	89	370	33
Hospital	283		
First trimester	230	775	178
Second trimester	53	740	39
All abortions	1,574	307	484

a. Includes abortions performed in physicians' offices.

The National Survey of Family Growth (National Center for Health Statistics 1982) reports that 4.4 million women (8.2 percent of women aged 15 to 44 years) have impaired fecundity (they are nonsurgically sterile, it is difficult or dangerous for them to have a baby, or they have had no pregnancy during three or more years of sexual activity without contraception in a stable relationship). In addition, 4.2 million are surgically sterile for noncontraceptive reasons. More than half of these 8.6 million women say they would like to become pregnant. In addition, about one-fourth of women who have been sterilized for contraceptive reasons (or whose partners are contraceptively sterile) indicate a desire for children (Mosher 1984; National Center for Health Statistics 1985b). Thus, the potential demand for infertility treatments, surrogate mothers, and related services is probably very large. In 1982, among ever-married women aged 15 to 44 years, 6.3 million had sought medical attention for infertility at some time in the past and approximately 1 million reported at least one infertility visit during the previous 12 months (National Center for Health Statistics 1984c).

About half of infertility is partly or entirely due to a problem of the male, and an estimated 10,000 couples per year turn to artificial insemination by donor. Usually two or three inseminations are performed each cycle at a cost of approximately $75 per insemination (Menning 1982). About 80 percent of the women receiving artificial insemination conceive within three to six months (Feldschuh and Feldschuh 1982). Diagnostic workups to detect female infertility are usually more extensive than for males. With new drugs and improved surgical techniques, 50 to 60 percent of infertility can be successfully treated; these treatments, however, are often expensive. One cycle of menotropins (Pergonal) to induce egg production in women who do not ovulate naturally can cost between $250 and $750 (Glass and Ericsson 1982).

The birth of the world's first test-tube baby in 1978 gave new hope to infertile women with severely damaged or missing fallopian tubes, but widespread use of this experimental technique is still far in the future. In the United States in 1982, there were probably fewer than 100 births resulting from in vitro fertilization. Each attempt at fertilization cost about $3,000 for medical expenses alone, and only 15 percent of couples using this technique succeeded in having a live birth.

We conclude that most couples spend little or nothing for infertility problems; a few spend an extraordinary amount. As a rough estimate we assume an average expenditure of $200 per couple who seek help, yielding a total of $200 million for 1982. Even if the correct figure is twice as high, the overall estimate for reproduction-related health expenditures would increase by only 1 percent.

SUMMARY

Expenditures for reproduction-related health care amounted to $17.8 billion in 1982; this was 5.5 percent of total health care spending of $322 billion. The reproduction-related sector was dominated by obstetrical care and infant care, which took 46 percent and 37 percent, respectively. Contraception accounted for 13 percent, while abortion and infertility services shares were 3 percent and 1 percent, respectively. Expenditures per woman of childbearing age were $329; this figure varied considerably with age, as shown in Figure 8.1. Although only 39 percent of women of childbearing age were in their twenties in 1982, they accounted for two-thirds of all births and 55 percent of abortions.

Comment

Our estimates show that reproduction-related health care accounts for only a small part of total health care spending. The 5.5 percent figure is not precise, but it is unlikely that the true figure is below 4.5 percent or above 6.5 percent. By contrast, health care spending for persons aged 65 years and older in 1982 amounted to 33 percent of total health expenditures, or an average of $4,000 per person. Just in the last year of life alone, persons aged 65 years and older utilized 10 percent of all U.S. health services. Thus, while newspaper headlines may feature stories about individual babies with health care costs of $100,000 or more, reproduction-related health care at present is not using a large part of health resources. If there were an insurance mechanism to spread the cost of high-tech neonatal intensive care over all babies delivered in a given year, it would add only a small amount (between 5 and 10 percent) to the total cost per live birth.

To be sure, reproduction-related health care spending could grow rapidly in the future. Whether it does so or not will depend on an interdependent set of demographic, technologic, economic, and sociolegal factors. The most immediate determinant, the number of women of childbearing age, points toward lower expenditures in the future. This figure was unusually high in 1982 (23.6 percent of total U.S. population) because of the 1950s baby boom. It is expected to fall to 21.5 percent by the end of

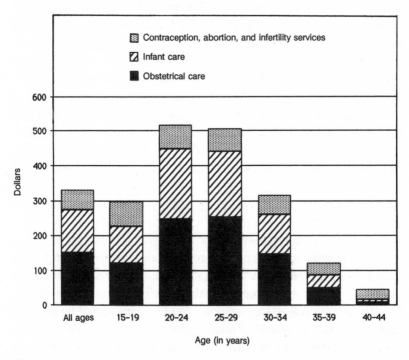

Figure 8.1 Reproduction-related expenses per woman, by age, 1982

this century (U.S. Bureau of the Census 1984). Changes in the age distribution within the 15-to-44-year-old age group will also lead to lower expenditures as the baby boomers move out of their twenties and early thirties and the smaller cohorts that follow enter the peak childbearing ages. The fertility rate is an important determinant, but there is no consensus among experts whether this rate will rise, fall, or stay at slightly below the replacement level (i.e., 70 births per year per 1,000 women). Other important demographic determinants are the age and marital status of the mothers. Unmarried women are twice as likely as married women to deliver a low-birth-weight baby, and teenagers are at higher risk regardless of marital status. Older women are also at greater risk of having a low-birth-weight baby and have the highest cesarean section rates.

Technologic advances, such as electronic fetal monitoring and ultrasound, affect the level of spending, as do new fertility drugs and improved surgical techniques. The pace and character of technologic change depend in part on exogenous advances in science (for example, the discovery of DNA) and on the level of funding provided by the National Institutes of Health and other sources. But the development and diffusion of applied technologies are also influenced by the willingness and ability of society to pay for medical care. New methods of financing health care aimed at cost containment (see Chapters 10 and 11) are likely to dampen the growth of expensive new technologies and shift the emphasis toward innovations that reduce costs.

Trends in insurance coverage and reimbursement methods could have a significant impact on the overall level of expenditures. For instance, per capita or per admission reimbursement tends to reduce expenditures, as does the introduction of copayment into conventional insurance. At present, treatment of infertility is only partially covered by third-party payment. Given the large number of Americans who might benefit from such services, and given the high cost of some interventions (such as in vitro fertilization), expenditures could increase greatly if such services were covered by private or public insurance.

Sociolegal considerations can affect expenditure for reproduction-related services in many ways. Laws governing abortion, contraception, surrogate mothering, and the like can change the total volume of spending and its distribution among various services. Prevailing norms regarding socially acceptable behavior in areas such as premarital and extramarital sex can be important. These attitudes may alter as a result of fundamental shifts in philosophy and religion, reaction to advances in technology (for example, female-controlled contraceptive techniques), fear of sexually transmitted diseases, or changes in the economy (for example, growing opportunities for women in paid employment). Prenatal screening for genetic disorders has large potential for growth. How extensively these services are utilized will depend in part on laws and attitudes concerning selective abortion, and on the provisions made for children born with congenital problems.

Laws governing malpractice suits also affect expenditures, as evidenced by the recent sharp rise in malpractice insurance premiums for obstetrical care. The fear of product liability suits may be a significant factor in preventing the fall in the price of contraceptive drugs, even though many of these products are no longer under patent protection.

Thus, the future of spending for reproduction-related health care is fraught with uncertainty. What is certain is that the present level is relatively low in comparison with the total bill for health care.

9

America's Children

American children are in trouble—not all children, to be sure; but many observers consider today's children to be worse off than their parents' generation in several important dimensions of physical, mental, and emotional well-being. Has the status of children really worsened over the past three decades? If so, why? And what policy options are available that might help children?

Most explanations can be classified as cultural or material. In the cultural realm observers point to the waning influence of religion on the daily lives of most Americans, the fragmentation of the family through divorce and unwed motherhood, and the harmful influence of television on intellectual development and physical activity.[1] In this vein, some observers relate the problems of children to a permissive society in which adults fail to set high standards or provide sufficient attention and discipline. In *Childhood's Future*, Louv (1990) argues that children today experience a freedom that is closer to abandonment.

The other set of explanations emphasizes changes in the material realm. Has government failed to provide the goods and services needed by children? Have changes in the distribution of household income (both earned and transfers from government) adversely affected the ability of parents to provide for their children? What has happened to the production of goods and

---

Written with Diane M. Reklis.

services for children within the household (meals at home, childcare, and help with homework)?

In this chapter we focus primarily on the material side, but we also consider important interactions between the two sets of explanations. Cultural changes, such as the growing incidence of divorce and unwed motherhood, reduce the income available to children. Material changes, such as a decrease in household income—either absolute or relative to expectations—may induce both parents to seek paid jobs, with possible negative implications for families and neighborhoods.

One frequently mentioned explanation that can be dismissed at the outset is that children are increasingly born to women of low education. There is a significant gap between the schooling of women with children and those who are childless, but the relative gap was not appreciably greater in 1988 than in 1960. In absolute terms, today's parents have much more schooling than those of the previous generation. The proportion of children living in households with a woman who had not completed high school was 50 percent in 1960 but only 21 percent in 1988; the proportion where the woman had four years of college or more jumped from 5 to 15 percent.

The Status of Children

Between 1960 and 1990 the number of children in the United States remained roughly constant at about 64 million. During that same period the number of adults aged 18 to 64 increased from 100 million to 152 million, and the number of Americans 65 and older jumped from 17 to 31 million. With many more adults available to provide and care for children, a substantial increase in the well-being of children might have been expected. Instead, the reverse seems to have occurred. A national household survey of parents in 1988 reported that nearly 20 percent of children aged 3 to 17 had one or more developmental, learning, or behavioral disorder (Zill and Schoenborn 1990). By age

12 to 17, one in four adolescents had suffered at least one of these disorders. Comparable data for the previous generation are not available, but several other indicators suggest deteriorating conditions for children, both absolutely and relative to adults (Table 9.1).

Declining performance on standardized tests between 1960 and 1980 has been well documented and is only partially accounted for by the characteristics of those taking the tests. Between 1980 and 1988 test scores rose slightly, but then fell again between 1988 and 1991, with results on the verbal portion reaching an all-time low (*New York Times*, 27 August 1991, p. 16). The tripling of the teenage suicide rate occurred during a period when the age-adjusted suicide rate for adults 25 and older remained approximately constant. Homicide rates have increased at all ages, but more rapidly for teenagers than for adults. The sharp increase in obesity in children is of concern because it raises the risk of hypertension, psychosocial problems, respiratory disease, diabetes, and orthopedic problems (National Institutes of Health 1985). Poverty rates for children and adults dropped sharply between 1960 and 1970, but since then the incidence of poverty among children has increased while remaining roughly constant among adults (Bane and Ellwood 1989).

Not all trends have been adverse. In particular, infant and child mortality has fallen by more than 50 percent since 1960. Life expectancy tables for 1960 show 41 of every 1,000 newborns dying before their twentieth birthday; by 1988 the comparable figure was only 19. On the other hand, reported rates of child abuse tripled between 1976 and 1986 (U.S. Bureau of the Census 1990); whether this reflects only better reporting is not known. A recent assessment of proficiency in mathematics revealed that only one in seven eighth graders could perform at the level that educators expect for that grade (*New York Times*, 7 June 1991, p. 1). Even at age 17, one-half of all high school students cannot "compute with decimals, fractions, and percentages; recognize geometric figures; and solve simple equations" (Applebee,

Table 9.1 The status of children, selected years, 1960–1988 (children are under age 18 unless otherwise specified)

Variable	1960	1970	1980	1988
SAT scores[a]				
Verbal	477	466	424	428
Math	498	488	466	476
Suicide rate, ages 15 to 19[b]	3.6	5.9	8.5	11.3
Homicide rate, ages 15 to 19[b]	4.0	8.1	10.6	11.7
Obese (%)[c]				
Ages 6 to 11	18[d]		27[f]	
Ages 12 to 17		16[e]	22[f]	
Children in poverty (%)[g]	26.9	15.1	18.3	19.5
Children whose parents divorced during the year (%)[h]	0.72	1.25	1.73	1.68[i]
Births to unwed mothers (%)[j]	5.3	10.7	18.4	25.7
Children in households with only one adult (%)[k]	5.5	9.2	12.1	14.2
Married women in the labor force with children under age 6 (%)[l]	18.6	30.3	45.1	57.1

a. Data for 1960 from Educational Testing Service, personal communication; data for 1970, 1980, 1988 from U.S. Bureau of the Census 1990, table 244.

b. Rate per 100,000. From National Center for Health Statistics 1960, pp. 5–202; 1970, pp. 1–24; 1980, p. 33; 1988, p. 36.

c. Data from Gortmaker et al. 1987.

d. About 1964.

d. About 1968.

e. About 1968.

f. About 1978.

g. Data from U.S. Bureau of the Census 1989a, table 20, p. 59.

h. Data from 1960 from London 1989, table 1, p. 14. Data for 1970, 1980, 1988 from U.S. Bureau of the Census 1990, table 131.

i. 1986.

j. Data for 1960 from U.S. Bureau of the Census 1983, table 97. Data for 1970, 1980, 1988 from U.S. Bureau of the Census 1991, table 92.

k. Data from U.S. Bureau of the Census 1960, 1970, 1980b, 1988a.

l. Data from U.S. Bureau of the Census 1990, table 636.

Langer, and Mullis 1989, p. 21). To what extent are these problems of children correlated with trends in government spending and household income and behavior?

Government Purchases of Goods and Services

In 1988 purchases of goods and services by government (federal, state, and local) amounted to $962 billion (Table 9.2). Some of these purchases were clearly intended for children—for example, public spending for elementary and secondary schools. Others were clearly intended for adults—for example, Medicare and higher education. We allocated to children or to adults all clearly identifiable purchases; some items (amounting to 57 percent of the total in 1988), such as national defense or general administration, could not be allocated by age. Similar estimates for 1960, 1970, and 1980 were adjusted to 1988 dollars by a price index of goods and services purchased by government.[2] Government transfers of money to households through programs such as Social Security retirement or Aid to Families with Dependent Children are not part of government purchases; they are included in the estimates of household income to be discussed below.

The data in Table 9.2 show that government purchases of goods and services for children (in real dollars) have risen throughout the period, both in the aggregate and on a per-child basis. Although the allocation of purchases by age is not precise, separate analyses of the most important components of government spending for children reveal the same upward trend. For instance, expenditures per pupil in public elementary and secondary schools adjusted by the input price index for education rose by 2 percent per annum between 1975 and 1987 (U.S. Bureau of the Census 1989b). Government spending for personal health care per child, adjusted by the medical care component of the consumer price index, also rose by 2 percent per annum between 1977 and 1987 (Waldo et al. 1989).

Although Table 9.2 gives no support to the notion that government purchases of goods and services for children have

Table 9.2 Federal, state, and local government purchases of goods and services for children (< 18) and adults (≥ 18), selected years, 1960–1988

Variable	1960	1970	1980	1988	Rate of change, 1960–1988 (% per year)
Aggregate purchases (billions of dollars, 1988)[a]					
Children	83.1	141.6	154.3	188.1	2.92
Adults	34.0	102.8	160.2	228.7	6.81
Not allocated by age[b]	381.0	461.7	450.3	545.7	1.28
Number of persons (millions)[a]					
Children	64.5	69.7	63.8	63.8	−0.04
Adults	116.1	133.5	162.8	182.0	1.60
All ages	180.7	203.2	226.5	245.8	1.10
Purchases per person (1988 dollars)[a]					
Children	1,289	2,032	2,420	2,946	2.95
Adults	292	770	984	1,257	5.21
Not allocated by age[b]	2,109	2,272	1,988	2,220	0.18

Note: Purchases adjusted by the GNP-implicit price deflator for government purchases, Economic Report of the President, 1991, p. 291.

a. Data taken from the following sources:
Total government purchases from Economic Report of the President, 1991, p. 380.
School expenditures from U.S. Bureau of the Census 1983, table 214 (1960); 1990, tables 208 and 209 (1970–1988).
Government health allocations from Waldo et al. 1989.
Government expenditures and Medicare from U.S. Bureau of the Census 1960, table 96 (1960); 1990, table 135 (1970–1987; 1988 extrapolated from prior years).
Federal food programs from U.S. Bureau of the Census 1980d, table 214 (1960); 1990, table 605 (1970–1988).
U.S. population from U.S. Bureau of the Census 1983, table 27 (1960); 1990, table 22 (1970–1988).
b. For example, national defense, general administration, and public safety.

declined, it does show that purchases for adults have increased at a much faster pace, primarily as a result of the introduction of Medicare and Medicaid in 1965 and the subsequent rapid growth of those programs. Moreover, those who argue that children's problems result from insufficient government spending argue that the increase in purchases has not been sufficient to allow the schools and other publicly supported institutions to cope with the greater problems they now face. These problems are attributed to an increase in the percentage of children coming from non-English-speaking homes, from one-parent homes, or from homes where both parents are in paid employment. Also, more resources are needed to "mainstream" children who were previously neglected by public institutions because of physical, mental, or emotional disabilities.

Money Income

Most goods and services consumed by children (and adults) depend on the money income received by households (Table 9.3).[3] Using public use samples of the 1960, 1970, and 1980 censuses of population, and the March 1988 *Current Population Survey*,[4] we calculated the money income of each household, including wages and salaries; self-employment income; dividends, interest, and other nonwage income; transfers from government, such as retirement income or welfare payments; and private transfer income received in the form of alimony or child support payments. Within each household, we allocated the money income equally on a per-person basis to the adults and the children, if any, in the household.[5] The children are then arrayed from the lowest to the highest income, and the income per child at various points in the array, such as the first quartile, the median, and the third quartile, is determined. Similar calculations are performed for adults as a whole and for adults divided into two age groups, those between 18 and 64, and those 65 and older. Income estimates in current prices for 1960, 1970, and 1980 are converted to 1988 dollars by a price index of goods and services purchased by households.[6]

The first row of Table 9.3 shows a substantial increase in the median money income per child, from $4,133 in 1960 to $6,917 in 1988. The rate of increase over the entire period in real dollars was 1.84 percent per annum. Although this was slightly lower

Table 9.3 Household income per child and per adult, selected years, 1960–1988

Variable	Household income (1988 dollars)				Rate of change, 1960–1988 (% per year)
	1960	1970	1980	1988	
Total income					
A. Median					
Child	4,133	5,470	6,220	6,917	1.84
Adult	6,201	8,145	9,342	10,992	2.04
18 to 64	6,375	8,513	9,665	11,281	2.04
≥ 65	4,924	6,232	7,687	9,831	2.47
B. First quartile					
Child	2,390	3,284	3,568	3,555	1.42
Adult	3,598	4,812	5,579	6,310	2.01
18 to 64	3,788	5,107	5,750	6,313	1.82
≥ 65	2,841	3,623	4,978	6,152	2.76
Income minus earnings of women in households with children					
C. Median					
Child	3,726	4,603	4,839	4,866	0.95
Adult	5,568	7,273	8,249	9,539	1.92
18 to 64	5,708	7,383	8,416	9,511	1.82
≥ 65	4,719	6,031	7,554	9,679	2.57
D. First quartile					
Child	2,005	2,501	2,312	2,015	0.02
Adult	3,175	4,154	4,664	5,081	1.68
18 to 64	3,254	4,343	4,611	4,854	1.43
≥ 65	2,782	3,619	4,876	6,017	2.76

Sources: U.S. Bureau of the Census 1960, 1970, 1980b, 1980c, 1988a, adjusted for differences in census and CPS data by using both in 1980.

Note: Household income is adjusted by GNP-implicit deflator for personal consumption expenditures.

than the 2.04 percent per annum increase experienced by adults, these data provide little support for the view that a fall in household income available to children is the cause of their declining well-being. This conclusion, however, needs to be qualified in three important ways.

First, the growth of median income per child was much more rapid between 1960 and 1970 (2.80 percent per annum) than between 1970 and 1988 (1.30 percent per annum).

Second, our calculations reveal that inequality in income among children increased appreciably, especially between 1980 and 1988. Thus, looking at income per child at the lower end of the distribution (first quartile) (B of Table 9.3), we see that the rate of growth was appreciably slower than at the median; between 1980 and 1988 there was no growth at all. By contrast, the rate of growth for children at the third quartile (not shown in the table) was 1.94 percent per annum between 1960 and 1988. Adults do not show any increase in inequality between 1960 and 1988; the rates of growth at the first quartile, median, and third quartile were all between 2.01 percent and 2.06 percent per annum.

The third important qualification concerns the source of income for children. Since 1960 there has been a huge increase in the proportion of mothers in paid jobs (Table 9.1).[7] The importance of their earnings in sustaining income for children can be seen in parts C and D of Table 9.3, where the calculations are identical to those in parts A and B, except that the earnings of women in households with children have been subtracted from total income.[8] That adjustment reduces the rate of growth of the median income per child to only 0.95 percent per annum, while the rate for adults remains at a sizable 1.92 percent per annum. The earnings of women in households with children became most important at the first quartile; without them, the gains of the 1960s were completely offset by losses between 1970 and 1988.[9]

An important trend adversely affecting children's income is the increase in households without an adult male. In 1960 only

7 percent of children lived in such households; by 1988 that proportion had jumped to 19 percent. The median income per child in 1988 was $7,640 with an adult male, but only $2,397 without an adult male. As a rough approximation, if the proportion of children without an adult male had stayed at 7 percent, average income per child in all households would have been about 9 percent higher than it was in 1988.[10]

Figure 9.1 shows that income trends have varied by type of household and type of measure. With an adult male present, median and first quartile income rose in all three decades. These households, however, became increasingly dependent on women's earnings over time as evidenced by the widening gap between the curves that do not include women's earnings (dashed lines) from those that do (solid lines). This effect is particularly strong for children at the lower end of the income distribution: without women's earnings, real income in 1988 was no higher than in 1970. In households without an adult male, median and first quartile income rose in the 1960s and 1970s, but declined between 1980 and 1988. No trend is shown for the first quartile in households without an adult male when women's earnings are subtracted because the value was zero in all four years.[11]

Nonmarket Production

Children's material well-being depends primarily on three sources: the goods and services provided by government, the goods and services purchased for them by their parents with household income, and the goods and services provided by adults to children within the household through so-called nonmarket production. Data on nonmarket production comparable to the government and money income time trends are not available. However, data on the proportion of children in one-adult households and the labor force participation rates of married mothers suggest a downward trend in nonmarket production.

We see in Table 9.1 that the percentage of children living in households with only one adult almost tripled between 1960 and

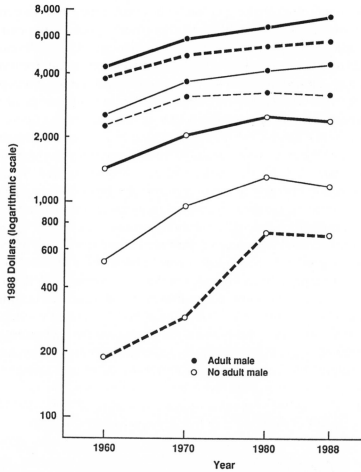

Figure 9.1 Income per child in households with and without an adult male (thick lines represent the median; thin lines, the first quartile; solid lines, all income; and dashed lines, minus women's earnings). *Sources:* U.S. Bureau of the Census, 1/1000 sample, public use tapes (for 1960, 1970, 1980); *Current Population Survey,* March 1988, public use tapes (for 1988), adjusted for differences in census and CPS data using 1980 CPS public use tapes.

1988. Even more striking is the jump in the proportion of married women with one child or more under age six who are in the labor force. Such large changes in the number of adults and in their employment status probably resulted in some decrease in home-cooked meals, help with homework, and other nonmarket goods and services since 1960. By 1986, in white households with children, there were about 10 hours less per week of potential parental time (total time minus time in paid work); the decrease for black households with children was approximately 12 hours per week (Fuchs 1988). The principal reason for the decline was an increase in the proportion of mothers holding paid jobs, but the increase in one-parent households was also important, especially for black children.

Consideration of women's earnings, nonmarket production, and the presence of an adult male shows that the cultural and material explanations are not completely distinct. Divorce or birth to an unwed mother usually has an adverse effect on the material well-being of children quite apart from any psychological or social implications. The slow growth of the real earnings of young fathers since 1970 (especially for those at the first quartile of the income distribution) induced more mothers to take paid employment, with repercussions for the cultural realm. Interactions between the two realms need to be considered in any discussion of policy options to help children.

Policy Options

The menu of policy options to help children tends to divide into two categories similar to the cultural and the material explanations. There are those who argue that only a return to more traditional family structures and values can provide the combination of care and discipline that children need. Some advocate changes in public policy, such as more stringent divorce laws or holding parents responsible for the antisocial acts of their children, in order to reverse the cultural changes of recent decades.

Most advocates for children tend to emphasize the necessity to improve children's material condition through new or expanded programs of education, health, childcare, and the like. Because society's resources are fixed at any given time, such programs must involve a reallocation of resources from adults to children, either within households that have children or from households that do not have children to those that do. The mechanisms for reallocation may involve business firms or the government, but ultimately all resources flow from and to households.

One possibility is for adults in households that have children to devote more money and time to the children and less to themselves. In practice it is difficult for public policy to compel such redistributions; except for extreme abuse, parents are free to treat their children as they wish. However, to the extent that parents care about their children's well-being, a well-chosen combination of taxes on adult consumption and subsidies of children's goods and services might induce some reallocation of household income toward children.

The most likely source of additional revenues for children is from households that do not have children. Such households have grown in relative importance, from 49 percent of the total in 1960 to 62 percent in 1988. In households headed by someone between 25 and 44 (the prime ages for having children) the proportion without children has almost doubled—from 20 percent in 1960 to 37 percent in 1988. Given the present distribution of income in the United States, revenue transfers to households with children would be "progressive," from higher- to lower-income persons. Among all households without children, median income per person is 67 percent higher than among households with two children (1988). Holding the age of the householder constant, the differential is substantially larger.

Comparisons of income per person tend to exaggerate household differences in living standards for two reasons: first, a child may not require as much income as an adult; second, large households may not require as much income per person as small households in order to achieve the same level of material well-being. The official poverty rate calculations adjust for these factors; for example, a household with two adults and two children is assumed to require only twice as much income as a one-adult household in order to exceed the poverty level of living. Nevertheless, poverty is more likely in households with children, and the incidence rises sharply for households with three or more children. Regardless of the method of comparison, it is indisputable that a redistribution of income from households without children to those with children would result in greater equality. A corollary is that a general redistribution from higher to lower income (without regard to the presence of children) would tend to benefit children.

One way of achieving redistribution to children is to require employers to offer benefits such as paid parental leave or subsidized child care, with the costs of such benefits spread among all workers (in the form of lower wages or foregone other benefits) or among consumers (in the form of higher prices). The employer-mandate mechanism appeals to many in government because it avoids difficult budgetary choices, but it will usually be less efficient and less equitable than direct government programs supported by general taxation.

Mandated child-benefit programs reduce economic efficiency because the costs fall disproportionately on the consumers of particular products and on workers in particular industries and firms—those that employ relatively more women of childbearing age. These distortions in relative prices and wages cause consumers and workers to change their behavior and reduce the overall efficiency of the economy much as if the government put a special tax on commodities that were produced by women with small children. Moreover, firms would be less likely to hire women of child-bearing age or to promote them to higher-level positions. Even if the mandate legislation is gender-neutral, the Swedish experience indicates that many more women than men will use the benefits (*Sweden Now* 1986).

The distributional consequences of employment-based child benefit programs are particularly regressive, as may be seen in Table 9.4. Most poor children do not live in households that would be the chief beneficiaries of employer-mandated programs. Indeed, the households that would receive the bulk of the benefits (where both the woman and the man are employed) have the highest income and the lowest poverty rate. Paid parental leave would provide the greatest dollar benefits for children with the best-paid parents; many of the poorest children would receive no benefit at all because their mothers are not employed and have poor job prospects. Those women who are raising children alone and are not currently employed have, on average, only eleven years of schooling.

An alternative way to help children is for government to provide tax credits, subsidies, or child allowances with the costs met by raising taxes or cutting spending for other programs. These benefits could be means tested (available only to children below a certain income level), or they could be available to all children. Even the latter approach, if financed by general revenue, would

Table 9.4 Characteristics of households with one or more children under 6 years of age, by presence and employment status of adults, 1988 (employment is defined as paid employment for at least 1,000 hours in year)

Adults in household	Children < 6 (%)	Poor children < 6 (%)	Median income per person	Schooling of women (years)
One woman and one man				
Both employed	27.1	3.2	$9,956	13.5
Man employed	37.7	21.0	7,028	12.8
Woman employed	2.5	2.1	5,361	12.9
Neither employed	6.1	16.2	2,535	11.9
One woman				
Employed	3.9	5.1	5,233	12.7
Not employed	8.0	33.8	1,388	11.0
Other[a]	14.7	18.7	5,702	11.1

Source: U.S. Bureau of the Census 1988a.
Note: Totals may not equal 100 because of rounding.
a. Includes two or more women, three or more adults (with at least one man), and one or more men (with no women).

have a progressive distributional impact because so many children are in households with low income. A major challenge for government is to devise tax credits or allowances for children without exacerbating cultural changes (such as more divorce or more births to unwed mothers) that would increase the number of children in poverty.

Conclusion

Both cultural and material changes have probably contributed to the problems of America's children; the relative importance of the different explanations, however, varies over time. Between 1960 and 1970 the fall in test scores, the doubling of teenage suicide and homicide rates, and the doubling share of births to unwed mothers cannot be attributed to economic adversity. During that decade purchases of goods and services for children by government rose very rapidly, as did real household income per child, and the poverty rate of children plummeted. Thus, we must seek explanations for the rising problems of that period in the cultural realm.

By contrast, material conditions did deteriorate in the 1980s, especially among children in households at the lower end of the income distribution. Between 1980 and 1988 real income per child at the first quartile declined slightly, and even the gain of 1.0 percent per annum at the median was almost entirely accounted for by mothers taking on paid employment. At the first quartile, income per child fell at the rate of 1.4 percent per annum if women's earnings are excluded. Moreover, the sharp increase in the proportion of children living in households in which all adults are employed implies a decrease in time available for nonmarket production of goods and services.

What of the future? Expressions of concern about the well-being of children span the political spectrum (National Commission on Children 1991), but no consensus has been reached regarding the causes of children's problems or the policies that would alleviate them. Some analysts seek to reverse the cultural changes of the past several decades by making divorce more difficult or holding parents responsible for their children's antisocial acts. Even those who emphasize cultural changes, however, experience difficulty devising public policies that would bring them about. How can government change the public's values and lifestyles without intruding on what many claim are fundamental individual rights?

Most policy discussions focus on improving the material well-being of children through government mandates on employers or direct government programs, such as tax credits or child allowances. Implicit in many of the proposals is the hope that higher income for households with children will lead to more parental inputs at home and less time spent in paid employment. Alternatively, credits and allowances could facilitate the purchase of more services for children.

In order to formulate an efficient and equitable set of policies about children, society must reach some agreement concerning the objectives of such policies, the means to reach those objectives, and the distribution of the costs. There seems to be some truth to both conservative critiques of the cultural changes that were launched in the 1960s as well as liberal complaints about the uneven prosperity of the 1980s. But mutual recrimination does little to help children. All adults need to recognize that the nation's future depends critically on our willingness and ability to help America's children today.

III

POLICY
ANALYSIS

10

Cost Containment: No Pain, No Gain

There is a widespread belief in the United States that expenditures for health care are too high and growing too rapidly. This belief has stimulated numerous policy proposals for "cost containment," including such diverse approaches as managed care, managed competition, insurance company regulation, DRG reimbursement, global budgets, and expenditure caps. The pros and cons of competing approaches to cost containment have been debated extensively; I do not intend to add to that debate. Instead, I propose to address two basic issues. First, why should public policy pay any special attention to health expenditures? I will consider and reject two popular explanations—share of GNP and effect on global competitiveness—and then discuss three valid explanations. Second, I will show why every approach to cost containment requires pain if there is to be any gain.

The basic facts are clear. In 1992 Americans spent approximately $3,150 per person for health care, for a total bill of about $800 billion. By comparison, expenditures for education—public and private, kindergarten through graduate school—amounted to only $375 billion. Defense expenditures were even less, about $300 billion. Even more important than the level of spending is the rate of change. As discussed in Chapter 5, between 1950 and 1990 health expenditures grew 3 percent per annum faster than expenditures for all other goods and services. If health spending continues to outpace the rest of the economy at the same rate, by 2030 the health sector will consume almost one-third of the gross national product.

These are clearly large numbers. But, are they *too* large, in the sense that public policy ought to try to make them smaller? And if so, why? Many of the reasons that are frequently offered in support of cost containment are misleading; they do not get to the heart of the problem.

Consider, for instance, the claim that the United States spends a larger share of the GNP on health than does any other country. The claim is correct. Most industrialized nations spend around 7 to 9 percent of GNP on health, while the United States now spends over 13 percent. But why should that be a cause for concern? Every country must spend 100 percent of its GNP on something. If the United States spends a larger share on health care, Japan may spend a larger share on food, Canada on housing, and so on. Is there any reason why it is better to spend on videotapes than on X-rays, or on computers rather than on coronary care? We shall return to this question shortly.

In addition to the GNP share argument, critics often assert that high health expenditures make U.S. companies less competitive in the global economy. That's nonsense. Health expenditures have no more relationship to competitiveness than do expenditures for hotels or haircuts. Employer contributions to health insurance are part of a total compensation package that includes basic wage rates, overtime premiums, and a wide variety of fringe benefits. If total compensation is high relative to productivity, the firm will not be competitive; that should be obvious. But the form of compensation—wages, health insurance, or whatever—is irrelevant. The rise in the price of health care lowers the worker's standard of living, just as a rise in the price of food or any other commodity would. But as long as total compensation is consistent with productivity, the firm's competitiveness is unaffected. Food is much more expensive in Japan than in the United States, but no one claims that the high price of food has made Japan uncompetitive in the global economy. One reason for confusion and controversy over this point is that many employers were fond of telling their employees that they were "giving" them health insurance. In fact, the insurance was no more of a gift than were wages. But now, when employers need to cut back on insurance benefits or require employee contributions to premiums, they meet fierce resistance because it seems they are taking away something that they formerly "gave" to the workers.

There are, however, three good reasons why public policy should attempt to contain costs. First, there is a presumption, well supported by economic theory and empirical research, that many of the health services currently utilized do not provide benefits to patients that are commensurate with their costs. Much has been written about defensive medicine—that is, services that provide zero benefits to patients, but are recommended by physicians as protection against possible malpractice claims. There is also a great deal of discussion regarding unnecessary care, that is, care that on balance does patients more harm than good, but is nevertheless provided either as a result of ignorance or greed on the part of the physician, or because of pressure from the patient.

Examples of defensive medicine and unnecessary care are not hard to find, but they are only part of the problem; there is another category of care that has an even greater impact on expenditures. These are the services that *do* provide some patient benefit, but the value to the patient is less than the cost to society of providing them. Low-yield medicine is not no-yield medicine. The extra test, the extra visit, the extra day in the hospital frequently have some value to patients. If they are insured, the patients will probably want them, and the conscientious physician who is trying to act in the patient's best interest will recommend them. It is this kind of medical care that is the most difficult to constrain.

The much greater utilization of X-rays in the United States than in England helps to illustrate this point. Why do Americans get four times as many X-ray films as the English? Some of the differential probably reflects defensive medicine. But it is doubtful that most American physicians needlessly expose their patients to harmful X-rays when there is no possibility of obtaining any information of value. Similarly, some of the differential may be attributable to physicians who make a handsome profit from their X-ray equipment. But again, it is unlikely that most of the differential can be explained by American physicians callously jeopardizing their patients' health for financial gain. In my judgment, most X-rays are taken because the physician (or the patient) believes that they *may* provide some information that will be of value. Uncertainty is the common enemy of the physician and the patient, and a great deal of medical care is undertaken to reduce uncertainty. The fact that the expected benefit of an X-ray or an MRI scan is small relative to its cost does not make it unnecessary. From a social point of view, however, it does make it undesirable.

A second reason for concern about costs involves inefficiency in the use of resources to produce health care services. There is a growing body of evidence that suggests that the U.S. health care system uses more resources than necessary to produce the services that it currently provides. The waste of resources occurs principally in two areas: administration (including marketing, billing, and collecting) and excess capacity of facilities, equipment, and specialized personnel.

Public policy is needed to reduce inefficiency because, unlike many industries, the markets for health insurance and health care are not self-correcting. For instance, in a typical industry, excess capacity has two dramatic effects. First, prices fall, and second, some firms go out of business. Even the airlines, with only a half-dozen major competitors, and only two or three on many routes, offer tremendous discounts and have periodic price wars; several carriers have been forced to discontinue operations altogether. In health care this adjustment process is much slower and weaker, and is often nonexistent. In many U.S. cities hospital beds, high-tech equipment, and certain procedure-oriented specialists are all in excess supply, but charges and fees remain high and the excess capacity persists for decades.

Consider, for example, the proliferation of high-tech high-cost services in California community hospitals. In 1990, there were 113 such hospitals that offered open heart surgery, despite the fact that only 76 hospitals in the state had 300 beds or more. One-half of the open heart surgery units perform fewer than 200 procedures per year. Open heart surgery is not an esoteric exception. Magnetic resonance imaging was offered in 90 hospitals, X-ray radiation therapy in 107, angioplasty in 124, and so on. The failure to concentrate high-tech services in a relatively few regional centers raises the cost of providing them. It may also contribute to worse outcomes in hospitals with low volume.

The least important, but still valid, reason for cost containment is to eliminate abnormally high returns to some producers of health care goods and services. The drug industry, for example, consistently earns a rate of return that is far above the average for other manufacturing industries. Some of the difference is attributable to differences in accounting practices, but not all of the excess profit can be explained that way. The drug companies frequently succeed in establishing excessive product differentiation that allows them to charge monopoly prices. Other countries have countered by developing strategies for dealing with drug companies that result in substantially lower prices than in the United States.

American physicians also enjoy higher earnings (relative to the average employed person) than do physicians in most other industrialized countries. As shown in Chapter 6, U.S. physicians earn about 35 percent more than Canadian physicians after adjustment for specialty mix. The average wage differential between the United States and Canada for all workers is only about 5 percent. Part of the higher income of U.S. physicians is economically justified as compensation for higher tuition in the United States, but this cannot account for all of the differential. The Canadian example shows that hard bargaining by the buyers of care can hold down physicians' incomes without significant effects on the supply of physician services.

Compared to reductions in services or improvements in efficiency, however, the potential savings from elimination of excess returns to the suppliers of care are small. If drug company profits were slashed in half, health care expenditures would fall by less than 1 percent. A cut of 20 percent in the net income of physicians would reduce the total health care bill by only 2 percent.

This brief review of the reasons why society would benefit from cost containment also reveals why this goal has been so elusive. There are only three possible routes to lower costs: reduce services, produce the services with fewer resources, or cut the prices paid to the resources. Each route involves pain.

Consider, for instance, a cutback in services. If the costs of the eliminated services are greater than their benefits, there is a gain to society as a whole. But services are not provided to society as a whole; they are received by particular individuals and groups. For example, almost 40 percent of care is provided to Americans aged 65 or over, and this group's share of services that have a low benefit-to-cost ratio is probably even higher because life expectancy is much lower at older ages. Any serious attempt to reduce the total quantity of medical services will require some cutbacks to the elderly, but such an attempt will probably be resisted by the American Association of Retired Persons (AARP). The Children's Defense Fund would protest cutbacks in services to children, perhaps with more justification than the AARP, since the United States spends proportionately less on children than do many other countries. Veterans' organizations want more, not fewer, services for veterans; and so on. Advocacy groups concerned with specific diseases will also make their voices heard. Proposals to reduce services to AIDS victims, or to sufferers from asthma or arthritis, would surely be opposed by those who represent such patients.

Patients are not the only ones who will resist reductions in services. They will be joined by those who provide the services. Are radiologists likely to recommend fewer radiological services? Both their desire to use their hard-won technical skills and their desire to preserve their income suggest otherwise. Will transplant surgeons welcome measures to reduce the number of transplants? Not likely. Thus, in most situations the interests of individual patients and of individual providers will override the public interest. This problem does not arise with videotapes or computers or most other goods and services because the purchaser must balance the cost against the prospective benefit. But when it comes to medical care, neither the insured patient nor the insured patient's physician must make a similar type of reckoning.

Improvements in efficiency, like reductions in services, will also impose burdens on particular individuals and groups. Every dollar spent on administration is a dollar of income to someone, and it should come as no surprise that where one stands on the issue of "administrative waste" depends on where one sits. Elimination of excess capacity sounds like a tempting strategy, but in practice it requires reducing the number of hospitals that offer high-tech services and curbing the proliferation of surgical and medical specialists. Some patients would undoubtedly be inconvenienced by the elimination of excess capacity, either because they may have to wait for procedures or because they may have to travel to a different hospital or even a different city in order to obtain them.

The pain experienced by physicians and drug companies when their income and profits are reduced is so obvious as to require no elaboration. Such reductions may also have negative effects on some patients through changes in the behavior of physicians or in the research activities of the drug companies.

In summary, there are three good reasons why American society would be better off if less were spent on health care and more on other kinds of consumption and investment. But society as a whole does not consume health care; the services are delivered to particular individuals and groups by particular individuals and organizations. A careful assessment of the only three possible ways to contain spending shows that if there is no pain there will be no gain.

11

The "Competition Revolution" of the 1980s

Any attempt to assess the effects of a revolution that is only a decade old and still in progress is fraught with danger. The relevant data appear only with a lag and are subject to revision. Some of the most important effects necessarily occur slowly, and at this point any evaluation of recent changes in health care must contain large elements of forecast as well as measurement after the fact. An additional problem arises because the health care revolution has been widely advertised as one of "increasing competition." Is this characterization correct? To what extent have recent changes in organization and finance increased competition among health care providers? To answer these questions we first must consider what economists mean by competition and appraise the factors that limit competition in health care. The major portion of this chapter deals with the effects of the "revolution" regardless of whether related to competition or not. We will see that the cost-containment efforts of the 1980s did not result in a slowing of expenditures for health care. The reasons for this apparent failure and the implications for the future are discussed.

Health Care Competition in Context

Health care is, in many respects, similar to other goods and services. It is produced with resources that are scarce relative to human wants. Thus every society must have control mechanisms for determining how much health care to produce, how to produce it, and how to distribute it among the population. In principle, only three types of mechanisms are available: the market, central direction, and traditional norms. Kenneth Boulding (1968) has characterized these alternatives as the exchange system, the threat system, and the integrative system.[1] All modern societies use a combination of the three, but the proportions vary greatly from country to country and from time to time within the same country.

For the market approach to succeed, competition must be present. Without competition, sellers with monopoly power or buyers with monopsony power can take advantage of their customers or their suppliers with results that are neither efficient nor equitable. Most health care markets depart substantially from competitive conditions, sometimes inevitably and sometimes as a result of deliberate public or private policy (Fuchs 1972). One question of interest is the extent to which the changes in finance and reimbursement of recent years have moved health care markets toward a more competitive structure. Another, to be discussed at the end of this chapter, is whether the competitive market approach is the goal toward which health policy should strive.

The term *competition* has a long and complex history in economics. To Adam Smith it was a powerful, beneficent instrument of change that would liberate the economy from the deadening influence of mercantilist restrictions. With extraordinary vision, he saw that if the anticompetitive influence of government were eliminated, the market system literally could create the "wealth of nations." He also warned against private attempts to limit competition, especially the propensity of people of the same trade to meet together "even for merriment and diversion, but the conversation ends in a conspiracy against the public."

Following the prescriptions of Smith, Ricardo, and other classical economists, nineteenth-century England developed the competitive market approach in full force, and the British economy prospered. Many noneconomists, however, railed against the evils of competition, and the term began to acquire an odious connotation (Marshall [1890] 1936).

In modern times, economic theorists have defined competition (and its many variants) with greater precision. *Perfect competition* means that the individual seller or buyer is so small relative to the total market that the actions of that seller or buyer have no effect on the market price.[2] Each producer's output is indistinguishable from competitors', and there is perfect information on both sides of the market. Given certain assumptions about preferences, income distribution, and economies of scale, perfect competition constitutes an ideal in the sense that if it prevailed in every market, resources would be allocated in a socially optimal way.

A more practical approach to the question of competition emphasizes the following conditions: (1) a large number of buyers and sellers, no one of whom is so big as to have a significant influence on the market price; (2) no collusion among the buyers or sellers to fix prices or quantities; (3) relatively free and easy entry into the market by new buyers or sellers; (4) no governmentally imposed restraints on prices or quantities; and (5) reasonably good information about price and quality known to buyers and sellers.

In short, the structure of the market (number of firms and their size distribution), barriers to entry, and privately initiated or government-sanctioned collusion generally determine the extent of competition. In health care markets there is another consideration: Are the buyers of health care sensitive to costs? If they are not, the question of competition among suppliers is less relevant. One consequence of competition, in health care as well as other markets, is a reduction in profits.

Let us look at each sector of the health care industry and ask whether recent changes have moved the sector in a more competitive direction. Health insurance has always been competitive, with hundreds of firms seeking business in most large markets. Nationally, over 1,200 firms sell health insurance, and the number has not changed materially in the 1980s. In some markets, Blue Cross and Blue Shield (the "Blues") have a dominant share, and they have been accused of competing "unfairly" by getting discounts from hospitals. Health insurance company profits are not known precisely and fluctuate markedly from year to year. The conventional wisdom is that they were low in the early 1980s, rose sharply in 1984 and 1985, and fell in the latter half of the decade. Much of the recent pressure on profits comes from insurance company ventures in health maintenance organizations (HMOs) and preferred provider organizations (PPOs).

The number of hospitals certainly has not increased in the 1980s; indeed, it has decreased slightly, and this decrease has been widely applauded. Many hospitals have no close competitors because they are located in areas with small populations. Hospitals located close to one another have always competed, but in the past the target was usually physicians, and the bait was better equipment, bigger support staff, and the like. Now the target is more likely to be patients, who are wooed with amenities and services on the one hand, or with price discounts (to large buyers) on the other. If the total amount of competition among hospitals increased in the 1980s, profits should have fallen; however, there is no evidence of that through 1985. In that year, profits from the prospective payment system (PPS) were estimated at $5.1 billion, or a profit/revenue rate of 15.3 percent (Simmons 1987). After 1985, however, profits probably did fall as the large buyers of care, both public and private, began to press harder on price and utilization.

The number of physicians has increased in the 1980s, but the rate of increase has been no more rapid than in the 1970s, when competition was rarely mentioned. Moreover, during the 1980s, there has been an effort to get medical schools to reduce enrollment or to close altogether, and the number of independent physicians has declined as a result of a trend toward larger groups and organized practices.

There has been a large increase in the number of organized

health plans and a big increase in competition in that sector. Thus, an organization such as Kaiser Permanente, which frequently was the only plan in an area, undoubtedly has perceived a big increase in competition. At one time Kaiser was the only organization offering managed care in many markets, and their low costs relative to conventional insurance plans insulated them from competitive pressures. All that has changed. Furthermore, the increased emphasis on self-insurance by large firms and on experience rating by health insurers threatens the survival of Kaiser's community-rating approach.

With respect to collusion, there probably has been some reduction through the elimination of laws that prohibited selective contracting. Price discounting is more widespread now than in the past, although until we have information on utilization and quality of care we will not know whether discounts truly lower the cost of care. It is ironic that selective price discounting by hospitals and physicians now is hailed as evidence of competition, when one of the most frequently cited articles in health economics, "Price Discrimination in Medicine" (Kessel 1958), concluded that the existence of sliding fees proved that physicians had monopoly power.

Most of the barriers to entry into health care markets—licensure, accreditation, and certification—are about the same today as in 1980. The growth of for-profit firms, however, with their access to equity capital, may have encouraged entry in some areas. There certainly has not been any reduction in governmentally imposed prices; at the state level, especially, the trend has been toward more government intervention.

Finally, with respect to information available to buyers, there has been a small increase in the form of health plan evaluations and some primitive quality-of-care measures for hospitals. Yet the fundamental problem remains: patients frequently have great difficulty determining how much and what kind of medical care they need, and they probably always will.

In short, except for the growth of organized health plans, I would not characterize the 1980s as a period of substantial increases in health care competition. I say this even though most physicians, hospital administrators, and other health professionals feel that they are under increased pressure, which they attribute to competition. Most of this pressure, however, really comes from another source, namely, more activist policies by the buyers of health care. The large buyers have decided to exert "countervailing power" against the sellers (Galbraith 1956). This may be socially desirable, but it is not the same as competition. However, a shift away from open-ended, cost-unconscious third-party reimbursement is resulting in more emphasis on price as opposed to nonprice competition. Also, a shift from inpatient to ambulatory care has forced many hospitals to seek new sources of revenue.

What Really Happened?

In the three decades preceding 1980, demand for health care increased enormously, beginning with the rapid diffusion of private health insurance. The number of persons with hospital insurance jumped from 32 million at the end of World War II to 122 million by 1960, and coverage for physicians' services soared from fewer than 5 million to over 83 million. Then, when the spread of private insurance ran out of steam, tens of millions of additional Americans obtained health insurance coverage through the Medicare and Medicaid legislation of 1965.

Changes on the demand side were accompanied by substantial shifts in supply. Between 1950 and 1980, the number of short-term hospital beds per 1,000 population rose from 3.3 to 4.4, hospital personnel per patient soared from 1.8 to 3.8, and physicians per 1,000 population jumped from 1.5 to 2.1. Generous funding from the National Institutes of Health (NIH), as well as heavy investment by drug companies and other private firms, contributed to a scientific and technologic transformation of medical practice.

For three decades, "highest-quality care for all" dominated the health policy agenda. Not surprisingly, spending for health care jumped from 4.6 percent to 9.1 percent of the GNP. As 1980 approached, however, concern shifted from increasing access and raising quality to curbing the skyrocketing cost of health care.

In assessing the possible mechanisms to achieve cost containment, policymakers ruled out self-regulation by physicians and hospitals as ineffective. A so-called voluntary approach had been tried in the 1970s and been found wanting. Direct regulation by the federal government, as implied in the Carter-Califano proposals, also was rejected as inconsistent with the political-economic temper of the times. With air transportation, trucking, banking, and other industries being thrown open to the rigors of the unregulated marketplace, there was little support in Washington for close regulation of health care. A few states, however, did adopt a regulatory approach through hospital commissions charged with setting rates and controlling utilization.

PROSPECTIVE PAYMENT

Probably the most important change in the 1980s was the introduction by the federal government of a prospective payment system (PPS) for Medicare beneficiaries, based on diagnosis-related groups (DRGs). Although this change has helped to slow the rate of growth of hospital expenditures, it has little to do with competition. To see this, imagine that all hospitals were owned by one giant corporation, HMA (Hospital Monopoly of America). The switch from a system of cost reimbursement to a prospectively set fixed fee could result in a slowing of expenditures and put great pressure on HMA even though its monopoly position was unchanged.

The impact of PPS on hospital length of stay has been substantial (Feder, Hadley, and Zuckerman 1987). Hospitals reimbursed under PPS had much smaller increases in costs per case than those still covered by the previous Tax Equity and Fiscal Responsibility Act (TEFRA) system (+7.6 percent versus +18.1 percent between 1982 and 1984). The most important factor was a more rapid decline in average length of stay in the hospitals paid by PPS (−14.6 percent versus −7.9 percent).

The role of competition in this decline is unclear. A study of California hospitals by Melnick and Zwanziger (1987) concluded that those located in highly competitive markets were more responsive to cost containment in 1983–1985 than were hospitals in areas with very little competition. In 1983, however, the hospitals in the highly competitive markets had almost 50 percent higher expenses per admission, so it is not surprising that they would be affected more by PPS and similar cost-containment efforts. In a national study, Robinson and Luft (1987) reported that costs actually are higher in hospitals located in competitive markets than in hospitals that have no close competitors (controlling for wage rates, patient case mix, state regulatory programs, and teaching status of hospitals). In the past, competition between hospitals typically took cost-increasing, nonprice forms such as meeting physicians' requests for new technologies. Currently, there probably is more emphasis on price competition, but extensive expenditures for advertising, community relations, and outreach programs show that nonprice competition is still significant. The new nonprice competition is focused more on patients and less on physicians.

Another aspect of cost containment in the 1980s is a reversal of the egalitarian ethos of the 1960s and 1970s. In recent years, we have seen reductions in health care programs for the poor, elimination of cross-subsidies by tying premiums more closely to experience, and attempts to reduce utilization via deductibles and copayment. Regardless of whether these changes are good or bad, they should not be mistaken for changes in competition among suppliers.

Consider the RAND health insurance experiment, which conclusively demonstrated that the "general law of demand" applies to medical care as well as to wheat and widgets (Manning et al. 1987). In a prospective, carefully controlled study, families with full insurance coverage used more care than those with cost sharing. Although this result often is cited in support of the competition argument, no such inference is warranted. Both the free-care families and the cost-sharing families received their care in the same markets, and the cost-sharing effect on utilization was as large in a site that had fewer than two dozen physicians as in a site that had several thousand.

From a theoretical perspective, it is not clear that more competition would enhance the cost-saving effects of deductibles and coinsurance. Given the inevitability of imperfect information, rival health plans faced with decreasing demand might increase marketing expenditures more than a monopoly would. At least some of these expenditures would be a dead-weight loss from the point of view of consumer welfare.

HOW EFFECTIVE WAS COST CONTAINMENT?

The question of competition aside, did cost containment reduce the rate of growth of health care expenditures? The answer is that it did not. As shown in Table 11.1, the overall growth of real expenditures per capita was more rapid after 1980 than in the previous decade. Disaggregation reveals that expenditures for hospital care did slow appreciably between 1983 and 1986, but then resumed rapid growth. Expenditures for physicians' services accelerated throughout the 1980s. The growth of nursing home expenditures slowed somewhat after 1980, and government public health expenditures also grew less rapidly. These changes bear no relation to market structure.

Failure to Decrease Spending

To gain insights regarding the failure of the health care revolution to slow spending in the 1980s, it is useful to begin with a cost-containment identity:

$$\text{Expenditures} \equiv \left(\begin{array}{l}\text{quantity of inputs per}\\\text{unit of service}\end{array}\right)\left(\begin{array}{l}\text{price of}\\\text{inputs}\end{array}\right)\left(\begin{array}{l}\text{quantity of}\\\text{services}\end{array}\right)$$

Table 11.1 Rates of change of national health expenditures and components, adjusted for population growth and inflation, selected periods, 1960–1990, percent per year

	1960–1970	1970–1980	1980–1983	1983–1986	1986–1990
National health expenditures	5.8	3.9	4.4	3.6	4.8
Health services and supplies	5.7	4.2	4.6	3.8	4.8
Personal health care	5.7	4.0	4.5	3.7	4.7
Hospital care	6.7	4.8	4.8	2.1	4.1
Physicians' services	5.2	3.1	5.2	5.3	5.9
Dentists' services	4.3	3.0	1.7	4.4	3.2
Other professional services	4.9	9.4	5.8	7.7	8.5
Drugs and medical sundries	3.1	0.8	3.3	5.1	3.2
Eyeglasses and appliances	4.9	0.1	-0.5	7.5	5.3
Nursing home care	11.6	5.9	4.7	3.6	4.5
Other personal health care	3.4	5.5	4.7	4.5	7.6
Program administration and net cost of private health insurance	4.2	6.5	7.0	4.4	6.6
Government public health activities	8.3	8.2	2.5	6.5	4.2
Research and construction of medical facilities	7.1	-0.6	1.9	-2.2	4.1
Noncommercial research	6.2	1.7	-2.6	5.8	4.7
Construction	8.0	-2.8	6.0	-9.7	3.7

Sources: Levit et al. 1991, p. 47; Letsch, Levit, and Waldo 1988, p. 113; Economic Report of the President 1992, pp. 302, 305.
Note: Figures are deflated by the implicit gross domestic product (GDP) deflator.

By definition, expenditures depend upon the reciprocal of productivity (the first term) multiplied by the price of the factors of production (including profits) multiplied by the quantity of services (including quality as one dimension of quantity). For cost containment to have had an effect, it would have had to have worked through one or more of these three terms.

PRODUCTIVITY

The first term, the reciprocal of productivity, is extremely difficult to measure, but in my judgment there was not much improvement in the 1980s. This term measures *production efficiency* in the narrow sense of the quantity of services delivered to patients, regardless of the value of those services. It does not purport to measure efficiency in the broad sense of changes in health outcomes or other aspects of patient satisfaction. Unfortunately, a good deal of the discussion of cost containment has blurred the distinction between these two concepts of efficiency. The elimination of "unnecessary care," or care with low value relative to costs (efficiency-enhancing in the broad sense), is possible and desirable but has little to do with making hospitals and physicians' offices run more efficiently in the narrow sense.

The limited measures of productivity that are readily available, such as the number of hospital personnel per patient or number of physicians per 1,000 patient visits, show no improvement since 1980, and perhaps a deterioration. To be sure, the quantity of services per patient day and per visit probably increased, but we do not know by how much. We do know that after 1980 there was a considerable increase in resources going into marketing, advertising, new computer systems, management consulting, and the like. Whether these additional inputs resulted in an equivalent increase in services to patients is unclear. Also unclear is whether the additional inputs required by hospitals and physicians to adapt to the changes in health care finance are onetime or whether they will continue. For the period 1980–1986, I would not be surprised if subsequent research shows that productivity made a negative contribution to cost containment.

INPUT PRICES

The second term on the right-hand side of the cost-containment identity refers to the price of inputs (of given quality), including inputs of capital and entrepreneurial skill. Thus this term includes profit as a price. The most important input to health care is labor, and fortunately we have good data on wages in health and other industries. These data show that hourly earnings of health care workers grew faster than the earnings of other American workers between 1979 and 1985 (Table 11.2).[3]

The gap of over one percentage point per year cannot be explained by differences in employment growth. It is true that employment grew much more rapidly in health than in the goods sector (mining, manufacturing, and the like), but employment in other services (banking, finance, retail trade, personal services, education, and so on) grew almost as rapidly as in health.

A more promising explanation is that health workers are

Table 11.2 Rate of change of hourly earnings in health relative to other sectors, 1979–1985, percent per year

	Health relative to service sector (excluding health)		Health relative to goods sector	
	Unadjusted	Adjusted[a]	Unadjusted	Adjusted[a]
All	1.4	1.3	1.1	1.3
White women	1.4	1.2	0.4	0.4
Black women	0.5	0.7	−1.6	−0.6
White men	0.3	0.5	−0.1	0.4
Black men	3.4	3.0	2.1	1.9

Source: Current Population Survey Tapes, March 1980 and March 1986; calculations by author.
a. Multiple regression analysis is used to control for changes between 1979 and 1985 in the sex, race, age, and education distributions of workers in each sector.

disproportionately female, and women's earnings rose more rapidly than men's in the 1980s (Fuchs 1986b). Women constitute 75 percent of employment in health, but only 49 percent in the rest of the service sector and 26 percent in the goods sector. Given the differential change between women's and men's earnings of about 1 percent per year, the differences in gender proportions could produce a differential between health and the rest of the service sector of about 0.25 percent per year and between health and the goods sector of about 0.50 percent. But even if one looks only at women's wages, those of health workers grew more rapidly. In the most thoroughly controlled comparisons, looking only at white women age 25 to 34 and 35 to 44 at three specific levels of education, the rate of growth of earnings in health was slightly greater than the rate in the rest of the service sector (Table 11.3). Whatever else cost containment did, it did not noticeably depress the price of labor—the most important input. This is not surprising. The health industry must offer competitive wages if it is to be able to attract the quantity and quality of labor it needs.

QUANTITY OF SERVICES

If changes in productivity and input prices did not contribute much to a slowing of health care expenditures, that leaves the third term, quantity of services, as the only significant mechanism through which costs can be contained. Sooner or later the way to cut health care spending significantly is to reduce the quantity of services delivered to patients.

Table 11.4 suggests that recent cost-containment efforts did have a major impact on the quantity of hospital care delivered to Medicare beneficiaries. The number of bills (a good index of number of admissions) declined in the 1980s instead of rising rapidly as in the late 1970s; average length of stay decreased more dramatically than before; and the number of days of care stopped rising and then fell rapidly. However, the number of persons covered by hospital insurance increased by almost 2 percent per year. Total charges (deflated) continued to rise, but

Table 11.3 Hourly earnings of white women in health sector and service sector (excluding health)

	Average hourly earnings, 1985 (dollars)		Average rate of growth of real hourly earnings, 1979–1985 (percent per year)[a]	
	Health	Service sector (excl. health)	Health	Service sector (excl. health)
Ages 25–34				
Years of education				
12	6.66	6.33	0.1	-0.2
13–15	8.55	7.55	-0.1	0.5
16	10.36	8.90	1.2	0.4
Ages 35–44				
Years of education				
12	7.03	6.59	0.0	-0.1
13–15	8.97	8.27	1.4	1.0
16	11.28	9.66	1.3	1.0
Simple averages				
Two age groups				
Years of education				
12	6.84	6.46	0.0	-0.1
13–15	8.76	7.91	0.7	0.8
16	10.82	9.28	1.1	0.7
Three education groups				
Ages 25–34	8.52	7.59	0.3	0.3
Ages 35–44	9.10	8.17	1.0	0.7
Six age-education groups	8.81	7.88	0.7	0.5

Source: Current Population Survey Tapes, March 1980 and March 1986; calculations by author.
a. Deflated by the Consumer Price Index.

at a much lower rate than before 1980. The rate of increase in charges per bill was relatively unchanged, but reimbursement per bill rose 1 percent per year faster after 1980, contributing to better profit rates for hospitals under PPS.

With respect to the population under age 65, the growth of participation in HMOs from 5 percent to 12 percent of the population (1980–1986) also must have had an appreciable effect on hospital use. HMO members typically use only about two-thirds as much hospital care as the rest of the population; thus the shift in proportions would explain a decrease in hospitalization of 0.4 percent per year even if everything else remained constant.

It seems clear that cost-containment efforts did have an impact on hospital services, not only for the Medicare population but for patients under 65 as well. For the total U.S. population, the 1985 discharge rate (short-term general hospitals) of 148 per 1,000 was the lowest since 1971 and represented a decline of over 10 percent since 1980. Virtually all of the decline occurred after 1983. Average length of stay was dropping prior to 1980, but the rate of decline accelerated after that date. Hospital expenditures did respond to the shift to HMOs, the changes in reimbursement methods, the closer scrutiny of hospital admissions and lengths of stay by third-party payers, and a slight increase in the propor-

Table 11.4 Rates of change of Medicare short-stay hospital bills approved for payment, percent per year

	1974–1980	1980–1985
Number of bills	5.1	−1.9
Average length of stay	−1.6	−3.5
Total days of care	3.4	−5.5
Total charges (deflated)	10.7	3.4
Charges per bill (deflated)	5.6	5.3
Reimbursement per bill (deflated)	4.3	5.3

Source: Social Security Bulletin 1987, table Q-13, p. 78.

tion of hospital bills paid directly by patients, from 7.4 percent to 9.4 percent.

Cost containment has yet to make an impact on physicians' services. The number of bills for Medicare beneficiaries grew somewhat more slowly after 1980 than in the 1970s, but the growth rate for allowed charges continued at almost 8 percent per year, deflated (Table 11.5). Reimbursement in relation to allowed charges was less favorable in 1980–1986 than in 1974–1980, especially for physicians providing medical as distinct from surgical care. This undoubtedly contributed to physicians' sense of unease.

For the population as a whole, there is uncertainty about the trend in number of visits to physicians. The National Health Interview Survey shows an increase from 4.8 to 5.1 per person between 1980 and 1983, but the access surveys sponsored by The Robert Wood Johnson Foundation (1987) show a decline from 4.8 to 4.3 ambulatory visits per person between 1982 and 1986. At this point, the most reasonable conclusion is that number of visits probably did not change much one way or the other, but the intensity (i.e., services) of each visit probably increased. Some observers expected an increase in deductibles and coinsurance to slow spending for physicians' services, but no slowing

Table 11.5 Rates of change of Medicare physician bills paid, percent per year

	Total		Medical		Surgical	
	1974–80	1980–86	1974–80	1980–86	1974–80	1980–86
Number of bills	12.9	9.7	13.5	9.8	9.2	8.3
Allowed charges (deflated)	8.7	7.6	9.2	7.0	8.1	8.6
Allowed charges per bill (deflated)	−4.2	−2.0	−4.3	−2.9	−1.1	0.3
Reimbursement per bill (deflated)	−3.3	−1.8	−3.2	−2.9	−0.6	0.8

Source: Social Security Bulletin 1987, table Q-15, p. 80.

is evident. One likely explanation is that the proportion of physicians' spending paid directly by patients did not increase between 1980 and 1986; it actually fell from 30 to 28 percent.

Other Explanations

The failure of cost-containment efforts in the 1980s to have much effect on expenditures does not come as much of a surprise to those who emphasize supply factors—hospitals, physicians, and technology—as major influences on costs. In 1980, a huge hospital capacity was already in place, and fewer patient days do not translate into equivalent reductions in costs until hospitals actually close. The data from Feder and colleagues indicate that costs per patient day (in current dollars) jumped 28.1 percent between 1982 and 1984 in the hospitals covered by TEFRA and almost as rapidly, 26.4 percent, in the hospitals reimbursed by PPS (Feder, Hadley, and Zuckerman 1987). Hospital closure comes slowly, but the pace is increasing: 83 in 1986 compared with 61 in 1985 and an average of 54 per year in 1980–1984 (Mullner, Kralovec, and McNeil 1987).

PHYSICIAN SUPPLY

A large physician supply also was in place in 1980 and continued to increase after that date. It takes at least a decade for changes in demand to affect the flow of new physicians into the market, and even longer for changes in the flow to have a significant effect on the size of the total stock and its distribution among specialties.

Fees for specialty care and the number of specialists have, as yet, been relatively untouched. Consider ophthalmological surgery, for example. My discussions with physicians in San Diego County led to the conclusion that there are at least four times as many ophthalmologists practicing there as are needed to meet the surgical needs of the community at current rates of utilization. Nevertheless, fees remain high (and new medical school graduates continue to flood into ophthalmology). An ophthalmologist with a reasonably full workload—say, ten cataract operations (or their equivalent) per week for forty weeks per year —would gross almost \$1 million per year. Most of them, of course, do not make that much, but there is large excess capacity for surgery, for which the community pays a high cost. The failure of fees to fall to a level that would eliminate the excess capacity while still providing a fair return to physicians with reasonably full workloads indicates that this market is far from the one envisaged by economists when they talk about competition.

TECHNOLOGIC CHANGE

In addition to numbers of physicians, a major factor affecting costs is the pace and character of technologic change. In our pluralistic, heavily insured, malpractice-sensitive system, once a new technology is in place it tends to be used. Over the long run, technology, more than anything else, drives the cost of care. The technologic innovations that were introduced during the first half of the 1980s were mostly developed prior to the cost-containment efforts. It takes a long time to slow the pace of innovation. Unless this happens, however, other cost-containment efforts tend to have only a onetime effect. In the long run, changes in the rate, or at least the character, of technologic innovation must play a critical role in slowing the rate of growth of health care expenditures.

Technologic change depends in part on new scientific knowledge, but it also is affected by demand. The old cost-based reimbursement system tended to encourage any innovation that promised to improve the quality of care, regardless of cost. Manufacturers of drugs, equipment, and supplies contemplating investment in the development of such innovations did not have to worry about whether the prospective improvement was worth the increase in cost (Grabowski 1986). Under the prospective closed-ended reimbursement that has been growing since 1980, developers of new technology are concerned much more with prospective benefit / cost ratios. This pressure probably will slow the overall rate of innovation and will shift the emphasis away from improving quality regardless of cost to innovations that are valued primarily for their cost-saving potential.

Moreover, there is an important distinction between potential technology (that is, knowledge of available technology) and technology actually in place. Potential technology is presumably the same in Great Britain as it is in the United States, but British physicians practice medicine at lower cost than American physicians, in large part because many technologic innovations are not available to them.

Thus, it was unreasonable to expect the cost-containment efforts of the 1980s to have any marked effect on health care spending within just a few years. To slow spending, it is necessary to slow the rate of growth of services. The demand for services by patients can be affected by deductibles and coinsurance, but it seems likely that third-party payment will always predominate. Thus the major constraints on services must come from the supply side: the number of physicians, their specialty distribution, their training, the incentives they face, and, most important, the facilities and technology at their disposal. Changes in these factors can come only with a long lag, but they probably will come if the large buyers of health care maintain and extend their cost-conscious behavior.

Distributional Effects

The cost-containment efforts of the 1980s did not slow the overall rate of growth of spending for health care but did affect the distribution of care. Between 1981 and 1986, the days of hospital care per 1,000 population declined more rapidly for the poor than for the nonpoor in both absolute and percentage terms. Similar disparities occurred in trends for blacks compared to whites and females compared to males (Moss and Moien 1987). The Robert Wood Johnson Foundation's national access surveys in 1982 and 1986 showed that access and utilization measures for the poor and minorities deteriorated relative to the nonpoor and whites (1987). This reversed the trend of the 1960s and 1970s, when differentials were narrowing. National Health Interview Survey data show that the percentage of persons without any health insurance coverage rose from 11 percent in 1978 to 13.3 percent in 1986 (Ries 1987). The trend in the late 1960s and early 1970s was toward increased coverage.

These distributional shifts should not be regarded as unintended effects of cost containment. They are inevitable if one seeks to eliminate cross-subsidization and to make patients more cost-conscious in their use of care. In the absence of third-party payment, each patient would make his or her own calculations of marginal benefit (versus marginal cost). The result would be different standards of care for different people because, other things equal, the trade-offs would depend on income. In the absence of cross-subsidies for insurance, the poor and the sick will decrease their purchases of insurance and use of medical care.

Critics of a single standard of care are correct in asserting that some people get more care than they want (in the sense that they would rather use the resources for something else) while some get less than they would want. However, the egalitarian approach can be justified for its symbolic value, or because it contributes to political stability, or because the wealthy do not want to redistribute money to the poor for them to use as they choose but are willing if the money is used for health care.

The Future of the Health Care Market

Dissatisfaction with the cost-containment effort is mounting. Critics say that it is not stemming the growth of expenditures, it is leaving more individuals with little or no insurance, and it is making life difficult and uncertain for the manufacturers of drugs, equipment, and other health care supplies. Some critics allege a decline in the quality of care, but the evidence offered is largely anecdotal.

Physicians blame cost containment for forcing them into new modes of practice and for their loss of power to managers and administrators. Some reorganization and loss of power were inevitable, but where physicians have taken the leadership in efforts to control costs (as in prepaid group practices) there is greater potential to retain professional satisfaction than when controls on utilization are imposed from the outside.

A counterrevolution in health care finance is brewing, based on dissatisfaction and fear among many different elements (see Chapter 12). At some point, a coalition of business interests, consumer advocates, and providers is likely to unite in a call for more federal involvement in health insurance and health care, although they will disagree on the form of that involvement.

Efforts to improve the current situation should be encouraged, but they should be based on realistic assessments of what has happened and what is possible. The failure of health spending to slow in the 1980s probably reflects the recency of the cost-containment efforts more than inherent ineffectiveness. Indeed, there has been a demonstrable impact on hospital utilization, which was the primary target.

Most important, any attempt to build a better system for providing health insurance and controlling health care must recognize certain fundamental problems. On the demand side, most people do not want to risk having to pay very large bills, so they seek health insurance, either privately or through government programs. Once individuals have insurance, however, they want to consume more medical care than they would consume without it—and more than is socially optimal.

Another difficult policy problem is deciding when the premiums people pay for health insurance should be based on their expected utilization and when they should not (see Chapter 14). Most Americans seem to feel comfortable about having cigarette smokers pay higher premiums than nonsmokers, but even enthusiastic advocates of experience rating are uneasy about requiring individuals born with genetic defects to pay above-normal premiums. Where do we draw the line? Is alcoholism, for instance, to be regarded as similar to cigarette smoking, or is it more analogous to a genetic disease?

There also are fundamental problems on the supply side of health care. Competition often is impossible or undesirable because of economies of scale. For instance, how many hospitals are needed to serve a population of 100,000 efficiently? Probably only one; at most two. Similar constraints apply to competition in physicians' specialty care, especially if the physicians work full-time at their specialties. It is doubtful that a population of one million is large enough to justify enough independent maternity services or open-heart surgery teams to approximate competitive conditions. Thus, it is wrong to think that competition can serve as the only control mechanism for health care.

Even in markets large enough to sustain large numbers of hospitals and physicians, it is not clear that the public interest is best served by insisting that health professionals maintain rigorous arm's-length competition with one another. Patients can benefit from cooperation among physicians and hospitals, in both reduced costs and better service.

This chapter began by noting the similarity between health care and other goods and services. The differences also are important. The patient/physician relationship often is highly personal and intimate, similar in many ways to relationships within families or between teachers and pupils or ministers and congregants. It is, in part, what Boulding calls an integrative relationship, one that depends on mutual recognition and acceptance of rights and responsibilities enforced by traditional norms as well as market pressures and government regulations.

The production function for health is a peculiar one; it usually requires patients and health professionals to work cooperatively rather than as adversarial buyers and sellers. Mutual trust and confidence contribute greatly to the efficiency of production. Thus the model of atomistic competition usually set as the ideal in economics textbooks often is not the right goal for health.

The necessity for dealing with dying and death also reveals the problematic nature of standard solutions based on fully informed consumers and competitive suppliers. There are, of course, many advantages to providing more information to the consumers of health care, but there also are potential disadvantages. If there is cost sharing, fully informed consumers will be forced to make painful decisions concerning limitations on care for loved ones, decisions that can leave a lifelong residue of guilt and regret. Not infrequently, families and society as a whole would prefer to have physicians take responsibility for these difficult decisions, keeping implicit rather than explicit the inevitable trade-offs between life and goods and services. If there is no cost sharing, patients and their families usually will want any care that could possibly help, regardless of cost. The rationing will have to come from the supply side, and full disclosure is unworkable.

The market is a subtle and powerful instrument of control, and competition is an important component in making markets work well. But Alain Enthoven (1986, 1988) has concluded that competition in health care must be managed, and that government must be one of the principal managers. Moreover, I believe we err in thinking that the only options are markets or government regulation. There is room for, indeed need for, a revitalization of professional norms as a third instrument of control in health care. As long as physicians continue to perform priestly functions, as long as they are our ambassadors to death, as long as they control the introduction of new technology, they must be endowed with certain privileges and held to certain standards of behavior different from those assumed by the market or regulation models.

In my view, we will never be able to introduce enough direct patient payment into the system to make that a significant instrument of cost containment. Thus, we inevitably will have to rely on physicians and other health professionals to do much of the rationing. How equitably and how efficiently they do that, along with constraints on supply and on the quantity and character of technologic change, will determine the success of cost containment in the long run.

12

The Counterrevolution in Health Care Financing

The revolution in health care financing is transforming American medicine. Medicare's prospective payment system based on diagnosis-related groups, the spread of health maintenance and preferred-provider organizations, the increased use of deductibles and copayments, and a wide variety of statewide cost-containment programs have dramatically altered the incentives and constraints facing physicians and other health care providers.

The roots of the revolution, which had been growing for years, included overuse of services resulting from open-ended third-party reimbursement, inadequate evaluation of new technologies, inefficient and inequitable cross-subsidization, and excess supplies of hospital beds and specialists. Radical changes in health care financing and organization were bound to come, but the timing of the revolution was determined primarily by the slow growth of the economy after 1973. Slow growth in economic productivity, combined with a continuing escalation of health care expenditures, jolted decision makers in both the public and private sectors into action. The particular forms that the changes took—emphasizing segmentation of insured populations, competition, and utilization review by payers—can be attributed partly to the antiegalitarian mood of the 1980s and partly to a loss of faith in federal regulation or professional norms as instruments of control.

Some physicians have welcomed the revolution; most have

not. Even as its merits are being debated, however, new pressures are building. No revolution lasts forever, and the outlines of a counterrevolution can already be discerned. Its exact form remains to be determined, but the essential element will be greater federal involvement in health care. This involvement will arise for at least six reasons.

Growth in the Uninsured Population

Approximately 15 percent of the U.S. population has no health care insurance, and many additional millions of persons have only limited coverage. These numbers are likely to grow as insurance markets become increasingly segmented and groups at high risk face ever higher premiums. Current efforts to cover the uninsured through surcharges, local taxes, and similar devices will probably fail. The more coverage provided and the better the quality of care delivered under such programs, the greater the incentive to workers and employers to forgo carrying their own insurance. Even today, most of the uninsured are employed persons and their dependents.

Resistance to Double Payment

As the number of uninsured persons grows and the need for surcharges, local taxes, and the like increases, workers and employers who are paying for their own insurance will increasingly resent paying for the uninsured as well. They will begin to view more sympathetically a system that mandates coverage for everyone and forces everyone to pay a share.

Concern about Quality

Cost containment inevitably means fewer services than would otherwise be delivered. Although curtailment of some services may not jeopardize the quality of care (or may even enhance it), some reductions will undoubtedly be perceived as lowering quality, and some of these perceptions will be correct. The media will dramatize stories of patients who died after an "early" discharge and will associate other mishaps with the changes in health care financing. As competitive pressures on hospitals and physicians increase, the number of such stories is also likely to increase, and fears about deterioration in quality are likely to increase exponentially.

Concern about the Physician/Patient Relationship

Closely related to the concern about quality is the likely deterioration in the physician/patient relationship. Physicians have traditionally idealized the ethic of duty to their patients, and patients have derived considerable comfort from believing that physicians hold to this ethic. As physicians increasingly practice in organized groups, and as these groups are subjected to more competition, the conflict between commitment to the patient and commitment to the organization may grow. Patients' perceptions of a conflict of interest can lead to an erosion of the trust, confidence, and candor that are essential elements in the physician/patient relationship and in the delivery of high-quality care.

Financial Difficulties of Large Health Care Corporations

One of the most striking developments in the past decade has been the emergence of the very large, publicly owned health care corporation. Some observers have predicted that a relatively small number of these multibillion-dollar companies will dominate health care by the year 2000. If dominance depends on the ability to deliver high-quality care efficiently and effectively, such predictions are probably wide of the mark. Most health care is locally produced and locally delivered; it does not allow the large economies of scale that characterize industries such as automobile manufacturing. On the contrary, the layers of bureaucracy that are inevitable in any large organization are usually antithetical to the efficient delivery of care. Many of these large health care organizations will begin to experience financial difficulties; indeed, some are already operating at a loss. They will try to postpone the day of reckoning by mergers and restructuring, but competition will drive some to the wall, much as it has in the airline industry. Firms that face bankruptcy are likely to go to Washington for help.

Fears of Employees in Health Care

Many millions of Americans earn their living in hospitals and other health care settings. Even before actual bankruptcies occur, competition within the health care system will adversely affect these workers in several ways: loss of jobs, a stepped-up intensity of work, and slow wage growth or even wage cuts. As the pressures build, health care employees are likely to add their voices to those calling on the federal government to act.

When will the counterrevolution come? Possibly within five years; probably within ten. What form will it take? That depends primarily on the level and rate of growth of the economy as a whole. If long-term rapid growth in real income is under way, the new federal involvement will be more expansive than if the crisis occurs during a period of stagnation or depression. The form will also be influenced by the strength or weakness of the egalitarian ethos at the time. If the political mood of the country resembles that of the 1960s or earlier periods that emphasized greater equality, the counterrevolution will look different from the way it will look if the political mood is otherwise.

Those who are now suffering the trauma of the revolution may be tempted to celebrate the prospect of a reversal, but this enthusiasm should be tempered. Far from giving three cheers, those carefully considering the scenario outlined above may find one or two cheers more than sufficient. If the primary thrust of the counterrevolution is to prop up inefficient health care corporations, or if detailed federal regulations are substituted for market mechanisms, there may be little reason to cheer at all. The problems that triggered the current revolution are real, not imagined. A successful counterrevolution must continue to concern itself with costs, even as it pays renewed attention to problems of access and quality.

13

Technology Assessment and Health Policy

Stimulated by concerns about the quality, effectiveness, and escalating cost of health care, interest in medical technology assessment (TA) is growing (Institute of Medicine 1985; Roper et al. 1988). Technology assessment—the application of scientific methods to the evaluation of health practices—has a long history (Major 1954). Traditionally, TA focused merely on safety and efficacy. Today it has expanded to encompass consideration of quality of life and patient preferences (McNeil, Weichselbaum and Pauker 1978; Fowler et al. 1988), and evaluation of costs and benefits as well as safety and efficacy (Office of Technology Assessment 1980).

Some view this newly powerful tool with hope, others with trepidation. Insurers and patients hope that TA will reduce expenditures while maintaining or even improving the effectiveness of health care. Many practicing physicians fear that this new wave of TA will further erode their ability to practice as they deem best. Further, medical researchers, pharmaceutical manufacturers, and producers of medical devices fear that these assessments will inhibit the development and diffusion of new technologies. Although TA is not universally welcomed, its broad application is inevitable and promises to significantly influence the diffusion of medical technologies.

The following discussion addresses the ways in which the new

Written with Alan M. Garber, M.D.

TA differs from traditional TA, the characteristics that distinguish TA in medicine from TA in other fields, the features that make an assessment credible, the timing for first performing and revising an assessment, and the goals and limitations of TA.

The Evolution of Technology Assessment in Health Care

The distinguishing features of the new TA can be discerned in the manner in which it approaches specific technologies. Recent progress in detecting genetic defects reveals a need for newer approaches to TA to address contemporary concerns about health interventions. For example, a new test for the prenatal diagnosis of cystic fibrosis might be used to detect most cases of this fatal disease (Kerem et al. 1989; Lemna et al. 1990). Traditional TA would evaluate the technical performance and safety of the test, but these are only two of its important characteristics. While the new TA also attempts to verify that the test detects the abnormality, it also seeks to answer such additional questions as: Will the test lead to an unacceptable number of false positives? What actions will families take after learning that a fetus has a positive test for cystic fibrosis? How do the costs of screening for cystic fibrosis compare with the benefits? What are the ethical implications of using the new tests to screen the general population, when even small false-positive rates will lead to the abortion of many normal fetuses? Like traditional TA, the new TA explores the biomedical characteristics of the technology, but it also addresses broad social and economic issues.

As TA has moved beyond the purely biomedical characteristics of health interventions, the expertise required to perform it has changed. Initially TA was carried out by scientists and physicians who developed the technology or used it in caring for their patients. As formal interventional trials became more common, biostatisticians and other specialists in the design and performance of clinical trials assumed important responsibilities. With an increased emphasis on cost, quality of life, and patient satisfaction, the new TA continues to draw upon the traditional areas of expertise. However, it also requires evaluations by specialists with training in additional disciplines, especially economics, epidemiology, operations research, and psychometrics. These researchers use a wide variety of sources and methods to carry out their evaluations.

As the scope of TA has broadened, its audience has become more diverse. Formerly, reports of assessments were communicated through professional journals and scientific meetings aimed primarily at physicians or regulators. These groups remain targets of the new TA, but reports are also directed toward health insurance companies, employers, government agencies, policymakers, and the general public, who often learn of assessment results through television and other mass media.

How TA in Medicine Differs from TA in Other Fields

Technical complexities, the ubiquity of health insurance, and the highly fragmented nature of the industry distinguish technology assessment in health care from similar efforts in other industries.

Though complexity is not unique to health care, it is particularly difficult for medical consumers to become fully informed. The complexities of TA in the health care industry are apparent when health technologies are contrasted with an innovation such as a more fuel-efficient automobile engine. While the engineering that produced the new engine may be comprehensible only to experts, the average driver can readily determine and understand how this innovation translates into more miles per gallon. By contrast, even expertly designed clinical trials carried out by experienced investigators may not yield clear, quantitative answers concerning the effectiveness of a new diagnostic or therapeutic intervention.

If the new engine saves gasoline but increases the price of the car, the car buyer can determine whether the savings in gasoline is worth the extra cost. The automobile manufacturer, knowing that buyers will make this calculation, often anticipates the result by making the assessment first. Thus, innovations that do not promise to be cost-effective are weeded out at an early stage of development. Under conventional programs of insurance and reimbursement, "buyers" of health care—patients—bear only a fraction of the cost; therefore, neither patients nor health care innovators have the incentive to carry out such assessments.

The contrast with automobile manufacturing is also apparent in the scale of the economic activity. General Motors, Ford, and Toyota each control a substantial share of the market. When they invest in technology assessment, they stand to benefit directly from the results. By contrast, individual physicians lack the incentive and ability to commit the resources needed to assess new medical technologies in part because there is a significant "public good" aspect to any such assessment. Even the largest insurance companies individually account for only a small percentage of the health care market; therefore they are understandably reluctant to pay for large-scale assessments that will benefit all. Thus the new TA in medicine is funded principally by government agencies (most notably the Congressional Office of Technology Assessment and the newly formed Agency for Health Care Policy and Research, although many branches of the Public Health Service and the Department of Veterans' Affairs also fund research on TA), private foundations (including the Pew Charitable Trusts, the Hartford Foundation, The Robert Wood Johnson Foundation, and the Kaiser Foundation), and to a lesser extent by private third-party payers and managed care plans.

Although the fragmentation of the industry may make heavy reliance on government and foundation support inevitable, private support of TA could easily be increased. The electric power industry provides a model that health insurance companies would do well to consider. A small fraction of each public utility bill goes to fund the Electric Power Research Institute, a major research organization devoted to the development and assessment of power technologies. If all private health insurers devoted just one penny out of each $10 of premium income to technology assessment, $200 million per year would become available for this purpose (Office of National Cost Estimates

1990). If research on this scale leads to changes in practice, billions of dollars could be saved in annual health care expenditures.

The Usefulness and Quality of the New TA

In order to influence practice, TA must be both credible and useful. Credibility requires the application of appropriate methodology. It is necessary to apply increasingly sophisticated methods to accomplish the expanding goals of the new TA (Eddy 1980, 1989; Phelps and Mushlin 1988; Shacter, Eddy, and Hasselbald 1990). These methods make it possible to answer broad questions with incomplete data. They can also provide greater assurance that the conclusions of a study follow from its data and assumptions. As the studies become more complex, however, the proportion of their audience who feel competent to evaluate the assumptions and methods shrinks. The audience must rely on other experts, such as reviewers of journal articles and professional societies, to appraise the validity of an analysis.

There are at least two reasons to question the validity of complicated analyses. First, the investigators might have a conflict of interest that did not become known during the review process. As in other fields of biomedical research, the evaluation of medical technology depends in part upon the integrity, objectivity, care, and expertise of the researchers who conduct it to safeguard against such errors.

Second, and more important, authors and journal reviewers might fail to detect errors due to shortcomings in the data, the analysis, or the interpretation of the results. The complexity and scope of TA give ample opportunity for error, even among impartial investigators. Recognizing that this is a genuine concern, the authors of technology assessments often take steps to minimize the impact of inadvertent errors and biases. They supply the data used for the analysis, either including it in the document or furnishing it on request. For example, assessments that use quantitative methods to combine the results of several different randomized controlled trials of similar health interventions often display the data and the criteria for selecting data sources in detail (Weinstein 1983; L'Abbe, Detsky, and O'Rourke 1987; Sacks et al. 1987; Littenberg, Garber, and Sox 1990). The investigators also describe the assumptions used for the analysis and perform sensitivity analysis to show the consequences of altering uncertain assumptions. Studies that follow these steps enable knowledgeable readers to reject or confirm the conclusions in a way that is rarely feasible for laboratory research. The best assessments build upon expertise in the technology and its alternatives, along with impartiality and scientific rigor, to produce evaluations that are complete, explicit, and balanced.

The Stages and Timing of TA

Technology assessment is a dynamic process that usually proceeds in three stages of progressively widening scope. The first stage focuses on technical characteristics, such as the effectiveness of an antibiotic in laboratory experiments, the resolution of a scanner, or the short-term safety of a drug. The second stage investigates broader aspects of efficacy of a diagnostic or therapeutic technology. Traditional randomized controlled clinical trials of operations or drugs often fall into this category (such trials are carefully controlled experiments that are designed to isolate the effects of treatment from the impact of the many other factors that influence health outcomes). Studies of diagnostic technologies in this stage typically emphasize aspects of the test's accuracy in diagnosing health conditions.

The third stage of TA, which distinguishes the new TA from the old, focuses on clinical, economic, and societal consequences of the technology. A third-stage assessment analyzes how an intervention should be used and what its global consequences are. Third-stage assessments of cancer therapy, for example, measure the changes in mortality and disability that result from treatment and relate these endpoints to the cost of the proposed therapy. Some third-stage assessments are beginning to incorporate information about patients' preferences regarding the multiple impacts of health interventions, such as prostate surgery, on the quality of life (Barry et al. 1988).

While TA usually proceeds sequentially from the first stage to the third, reflecting the information requirements for the broadest forms of TA, sometimes a third-stage assessment is needed well before clinical trials have been conducted. Pharmaceutical companies, for example, need to decide whether a drug in the development stage is likely to meet a need at an acceptable cost. Developers of diagnostic procedures must also perform third-stage assessments earlier than in the past, perhaps in approximate terms. A new test to detect an untreatable condition, for example, might not affect outcomes even if it were highly accurate. The developer could perform a third-stage assessment with hypothetical data before exact figures on test performance were available, because even a preliminary analysis might reveal that the diagnostic technology would be unlikely to improve health. Early assessments can help to clarify the value of a technology and determine whether it merits further investigation. Of course, while any stage of a TA could be performed before all of the data pertinent to its evaluation become available, lack of essential data may limit its value.

Because it is designed to help guide policy, the new TA must reassess technologies more frequently than the traditional TA. Both forms of assessment need to be modified as new data about safety and efficacy become available, as the technology is used for new indications, or as the intervention itself changes (Banta and Thacker 1990). For example, traditional and new TA would both need to reevaluate mammography if it required less radiation exposure or became more accurate as a screening test for breast cancer. Reevaluation is even more important for the new TA because the assessment considers additional factors, such as cost, that make a technology more or less desirable and may change over time. Costs undoubtedly were a critical issue when the Health Care Financing Administration (HCFA) rejected extra payments to hospitals that used recombinant tissue-type plasminogen activator (TPA) to treat heart-attack patients. Advocates claimed that TPA was more effective, or safer, than the major alternative (streptokinase), but at the time of the HCFA's decision TPA cost nearly ten times as much as the least expensive alternative. Many observers felt that if TPA had been priced lower, it would have been adopted as the drug of choice for dissolving blood clots in the coronary arteries during myocardial infarction. An unanticipated change in the price of a medication (or any other technology) changes its cost-effectiveness, a consideration that is irrelevant to traditional TA. Yet for the new TA, such a change is a reason to revise the assessment.

Limitations and Promise of TA

Efforts to contain costs and monitor the quality of medical care increasingly rely on formal TA (Relman 1988; Russell 1989). By helping to define appropriate care, TA is often instrumental in developing health policy and setting reimbursement guidelines. An unequivocal assessment, whether a randomized controlled clinical trial or a comprehensive, "new" assessment, can promote the dissemination or rejection of a technology. The possibility that much modern, costly medical care is "flat of the curve medicine" (Fuchs 1972), providing minimal or no health benefits, is a key motivation for engaging in TA. When TA catalyzes the abandonment of interventions whose risks exceed their health benefits, it can lower the costs of health care without sacrificing quality.

For several reasons, though, most clinical and policy decisions concerning health practices inevitably depend on more than the results of TA. Sometimes the poor quality of the study is the reason; the TA may be so flawed by gaps in the data or shortcomings of the analytic methods that it cannot answer the questions posed. This problem is less serious for traditional TA. Traditional TA also confronts imperfect data, but because its goals are narrower, it usually needs less information and the methods for analyzing the data are more straightforward.

To readers unfamiliar with the general approach, even rigorous and careful assessments can appear untrustworthy. Moreover, readers may be skeptical because the new TA uses novel methods and data from diverse sources. Many physicians believe that only a randomized controlled clinical trial can provide definitive measures of the effectiveness of an intervention.

The new TA often includes, but is not limited to, data from randomized trials. Randomized trials usually cannot provide all of the information needed for an assessment; in fact, many technologies are applied long before results of a randomized trial become available, and it is not always feasible to measure all of the relevant endpoints in a trial. Furthermore, the trials are frequently performed in clinical settings different from the settings in which the interventions are most likely to be applied. For many interventions, ethical or logistical difficulties may preclude conducting a randomized trial. Rather than ignore questions that cannot be answered in the rigorous framework of a randomized controlled trial, the new TA seeks answers by applying less traditional methods, including analysis of nonexperimental data (Moses and Brown 1984; Sechrest, Perrin, and Bunker 1990), meta-analysis, decision analysis, and economic modeling. Although the new TA's data and techniques are appropriate, they rarely answer questions with the certainty of a laboratory experiment or randomized trial.

Scientific credibility is not the most serious obstacle to using the new TA. Even well-executed assessments may not resolve whether a technology is worth using; while they characterize the consequences of applying a technology, the assessments do not always clarify whether a technology should be adopted. When TA reveals that an innovation provides no net benefits, it may be decisive. But the ability to identify useless interventions is not unique to the new TA; traditional clinical trials can also identify "flat of the curve" medicine—care that provides negligible marginal benefit.

Furthermore, eliminating the procedures that confer no benefits is laudable, but is not the only concern of employers and third-party payers. They also seek to limit the application of costly interventions that have small, albeit positive, effects on health. From a payer's point of view, the health benefits of an intervention should be commensurate with the benefits obtained from interventions that are equally or less expensive. Although the new TA explicitly addresses cost-effectiveness, it cannot tell us how much we should be willing to pay for a given health effect. That would require explicit value judgments, which are beyond the scope of even much of the new TA.

Sometimes TA influences health practices in ways unintended by the authors. The sponsors of TA and the third-party payers often expect to use the results to develop practice guidelines or reimbursement policies. For them, the best outcome of a study is a simple yes or no answer to the question: Is this intervention worthwhile? But as most physicians know, few promising technologies are simply good or bad; their value usually depends on the clinical setting and patient preferences. The benefits of immediate surgery for enlargement of the prostate gland, for example, depend on patient attitudes toward different states of health (Barry et al. 1988). It will not be easy to develop reimbursement policies that take such factors into account. It is expensive to collect detailed information about each patient, and both physicians and patients can usually circumvent policies based on these subjective criteria. Payers may assume, with some justification, that even if they agree to pay for a treatment only if it is applied to the subset of patients for whom it is highly cost-effective, the treatment will often be given to patients in whom it is much less cost-effective. Thus, assessments that demonstrate substantial benefit for a small group of patients, with minimal or no benefit for a larger group of potential recipients, may convince payers who cannot monitor or control use of the technology either to deny coverage altogether or to impose seemingly arbitrary rules for its use, such as age limits for hemodialysis.

The hazards of oversimplified assessments are particularly great for interventions whose major effect is improvement in the quality of life rather than prolongation of life. The new TA emphasizes quality of life and its relation to disease and treatment. However, it is difficult to incorporate quality-of-life considerations into an analysis. While few investigators challenge the importance of incorporating quality considerations in TA, in practice they apply quality adjustments in an ad hoc fashion or not at all. One consequence is that assessments may not properly evaluate those interventions whose major purpose is not reduction of mortality. Applications that ignore quality effects will almost certainly undervalue some interventions, while applications that include quality adjustments on an ad hoc basis may either under- or overvalue the interventions. Thus inadequacies of technology assessment, as usually applied, may discourage health interventions that improve the quality of life.

Finally, TA by itself may not affect practice because its major contribution—information—may not be implemented. Clinical information is only one of many factors that influence medical practice. Medical practice is a result of the interaction between physician and patient. Medical education and training, the organization of practice, the legal system, and peer review undoubtedly influence physician behavior. Education, the family, the workplace, and community values can have important effects on patient behavior.

These influences are important, but few influences that are amenable to policy intervention are as important as the economic incentives that both physicians and patients face. These incentives often promote inefficient health practices, which are reflected in widespread variation in rates of operations and other medical procedures in apparently similar populations (Wennberg and Gittelsohn 1973; Chassin et al. 1987; Leape et al. 1990). It seems unlikely that differences in knowledge alone account for these variations. Although TA is helpful for setting reimbursement policies, voluntary guidelines based on TA are insufficient to impel changes in physician behavior (Lomas et al. 1989). To achieve such changes, policymakers must understand how incentives shape behavior and act accordingly.

These limitations give rise to a fundamental tension between the new TA and the legal environment of health care. The new TA can be used to set a benchmark for the standard of care relevant to medical liability. Yet the new TA, by incorporating differences in patients' preferences, implies that some variation in practice is appropriate. The very idea of a community standard, in contrast, suggests uniformity and consensus. Because the new TA incorporates preferences toward length of life and aversion to pain or disability, it might lead to the conclusion that two physiologically similar patients should get different treatments. This does not imply that all practices are equally acceptable, but the incorporation of preferences and other nonphysiologic factors poses real difficulties for defining and implementing a standard of care.

Conclusions

The new technology assessment is a tool that can be used to help decide how to limit health expenditures while maintaining or improving health. Like any tool, though, its impact depends on the way it is used. The new TA can give health professionals essential information to evaluate and improve their clinical practices. It can also offer payers a rational basis for deciding which health practices should be covered. It can also be misused or ignored; a flawed assessment could be used to rationalize denial of coverage for cost-effective care. Payers may use it to limit expenditures by restricting provider discretion, even when discretion is exercised appropriately. For all its potential and real faults, though, the new TA offers payers, providers, and the public an explicit approach to evaluate specific kinds of health care. It is itself more open and subject to evaluation than the less formal methods of the past. Ongoing efforts to reform American health care have created an important role for TA; as long as new health interventions are created or used in new ways, the new technology assessment will play an essential role.

14

National Health Insurance Revisited

Proposals for national health insurance are once again making the headlines, as they have periodically in the United States since World War I. Advocates of national health insurance have, as always, diverse goals: to expand access to health care for millions of uninsured Americans; to stem the rapid escalation in the cost of health care; and to improve the overall health status of the population and reduce socioeconomic differentials in life expectancy. Vigorous opposition to national health insurance is also not a new phenomenon. Insurance companies, physicians, and others directly involved in the health field see national health insurance as a threat to their roles and interests; in addition, many Americans with no direct involvement in health issues oppose expansion of government on general principle. The huge federal budget deficit contributes to the difficulty of enacting a major new domestic program, in health or any other area. Thus, the debate among those for and against national health insurance does not appear to be headed for resolution any time soon.

In 1976 I discussed the popularity of national health insurance around the world and offered four reasons why the United States was the last major holdout: distrust of government; heterogeneity of the population; a robust voluntary sector; and less sense of *noblesse oblige* (Fuchs 1976). In this chapter I consider whether these explanations are as relevant today as they were in the past. First, however, I discuss several issues that put the universal insurance controversy in clearer perspective. Why are so many Americans uninsured? How do conflicting views of health insurance shape attitudes toward national health insurance? What is the connection between national health insurance and the cost of care? Would national health insurance reduce socioeconomic differentials in health?

The Uninsured

With some exceptions, such as Medicare, health insurance in the United States is a private, voluntary matter. The demand for insurance, like the demand for any product or service, depends on consumers' ability and willingness to pay for it. Some of the uninsured cannot afford health insurance; others are unwilling to acquire it. In all, the uninsured can be grouped into six categories.

THE POOR

The largest group of uninsured consists of individuals and families whose low income makes it infeasible for them to acquire insurance, either on their own or as a condition of employment. About 20 percent have no connection with the work force, but nearly 80 percent either are employed or are the dependents of employed persons (Chollet 1990). The Health Insurance Association of America (HIAA) estimates that 31 percent of the working uninsured earned less than $10,000 in 1989; another estimate puts the figure at 63 percent (Health Insurance Association of America 1990). In any case, it is clear that the great majority of uninsured workers cannot afford to give up a substantial fraction of their wages to obtain health insurance.

Most uninsured workers are employed in small firms, but the frequently heard explanation, "Small employers can't afford health insurance," is as misleading as the phrase "employer-provided health insurance." Employers do not bear the cost of health insurance; workers do, in the form of lower wages or forgone nonhealth benefits. A more accurate description of the problem would be, "Many workers in small firms can't afford health insurance." Note that lawyers, accountants, computer consultants, and other highly paid professionals organized in small firms usually have health insurance, although they often face extra costs, as discussed below.

THE SICK AND DISABLED

Many men and women who are not poor are still unable to afford health insurance because they have special health problems and therefore face very high premiums or are excluded from coverage entirely (see, for example, DeJong, Batavia, and Griss 1989).

THE "DIFFICULT"

Some individuals are neither poor nor sick but have difficulty obtaining insurance at average premiums. They may be self-employed, work in small firms, or be out of the labor force entirely. To insure such individuals, insurance companies incur abnormally high sales and administrative costs. They also encounter the problem of adverse selection: if an insurance company offers a policy to individuals or small groups at an average premium, those who expect to use a great deal of medical care are likely to buy, and those who do not will refrain from buying.

THE LOW USERS

Some people do not expect to use much medical care. They may be in particularly good health; they may dislike going to physicians; or, like Christian Scientists, they may not believe in medical care. For them, health insurance is a bad buy unless they can acquire it at a below-average premium.

THE GAMBLERS

Most people buy health insurance in part because they are risk averse. They would rather pay a fixed, known premium (even above the actuarial level) than risk a huge expense in the event of serious illness. But not everyone is risk averse about health expenditures, or risk averse to the same degree. People in this category prefer to take their chances with continued good health and save the premium payment.

THE FREE RIDERS

The final category consists of individuals who remain uninsured because they believe that in the event of serious illness they will get care anyway, and others will pick up the bill. They save the cost of insurance and "ride free" on the coattails of those who pay into the health care system. There may be elements of free riding in the behavior of the low users and the gamblers as well; it is often difficult to distinguish among the three categories of individuals who are able to pay for insurance but are unwilling to do so.

From an analytical perspective, it is not difficult to achieve a national health insurance system; all it requires is subsidizing those who are unable to afford insurance and requiring purchase by those who are unwilling to acquire it voluntarily. No nation achieves universal coverage without subsidization and compulsion. Thus far, Americans have resisted both.[1]

Two Models of Health Insurance

Part of the current debate over national health insurance is rooted in two conflicting visions of how the cost of health care should be shared. We can designate one as the casualty insurance model and the other as the social insurance model. Casualty insurance, which usually refers to automobile collision, residential fire, and similar risks, is premised on the idea that premiums should (to the extent feasible) be set according to expected loss. Other things being equal, policyholders with better driving records or with smoke detectors in their homes pay lower premiums; poorer risks pay higher premiums. Social insurance, which is the basis for national health insurance, provides for extensive cross-subsidization among different risk groups; it ignores expected loss in allocating costs.

Advocates of the casualty approach argue that, as applied to health insurance, it is more efficient and more equitable than the social insurance model. They assert that use of care depends, to some extent, on personal behavior and choice. If premiums vary with expected use, individuals have an incentive to choose healthier behavior and to make more cost-conscious decisions about their use of care for any given health condition.[2] A clear example is charging cigarette smokers higher premiums than nonsmokers are charged. This may decrease the number of smokers, and even if it does not, advocates of the casualty model argue that it is fair for smokers to bear the extra cost of their unhealthy habit.

Even when there is no possibility of altering behavior, and even if use of care is unrelated to insurance coverage, the casualty model still offers an efficiency advantage in any system of voluntary health insurance. The alternative—a uniform premium for all individuals, including those with major health problems—will discourage purchase of insurance by those without such problems because the premium would be unreasonably high.

Advocates of the social insurance model rely heavily on arguments that appeal to one's sense of justice or collective responsibility. In earlier times, these feelings of mutual responsibility were often evident within families and within religious communities. In modern times, many countries have extended the concept to encompass the entire nation. The philosophical foundation for such arguments can be discerned in John Rawls's discussion of making choices behind a veil of ignorance (Rawls 1971). For example, suppose, before you were born, you did not know if you were going to be rich or poor, sick or healthy; you might (assuming some risk aversion) prefer to be born into a society that would provide health care on the same basis for, say, persons born with a genetic disease as for those born without such a problem. Advocates of the social insurance model also point to efficiency arguments. Because everyone must participate, there can be savings in sales and administrative costs that offset other efficiencies achieved through the casualty approach.

Whether one model or the other is more conducive to an efficient health care system is primarily an empirical question (interwoven with value judgments) that cannot be answered *a priori*. Which approach is more just is primarily a value question (individual versus collective responsibility), but empirical information concerning the reasons for variation in use of care is relevant. In my experience, the same audiences that overwhelmingly approve charging smokers a higher premium because they use more care strongly oppose a premium surcharge for individuals whose high use is attributable to genetic factors. If cigarette smoking should turn out to have a significant genetic component, opinions concerning the smoker surcharge would presumably change. One consequence of the genetics revolution may be to shift public sentiment toward the social insurance model.

National Health Insurance and Health Care Costs

Opponents of national health insurance frequently assert that it would result in a substantial increase in total health care costs. Both theoretical and empirical research support the view that the lower the price of care to the patient, the more care he or she will want. The logic of this argument suggests that those countries with universal coverage spend more on medical care than does the United States. In fact, the reverse is true. Adjusting for differences in real income, the United States spends much more per person on medical care than does any other country. For instance, the average person in the United States spends about 40 percent more than the average Canadian, even though the difference in real income per capita is less than 10 percent. And Canada spends more per capita than does any European country. How can this be? Countries with universal coverage find other methods to contain health care spending, methods that apparently are more effective than financial constraints on patients.

The most obvious source of savings under a national health insurance system is in reduced administrative costs. According to the Health Care Financing Administration, approximately 6 percent of U.S. health expenditures are in program administration and net cost of private health insurance. Several additional percentage points must be added to account for costs incurred by providers for billing and other administrative activities directly attributable to the U.S. system of financing care. By contrast, the Canadian system of provincial health insurance imposes minimal administrative and billing costs on providers and payers; the insurance plans themselves are inexpensive to run because everyone must join, and premiums are collected through the tax system.

But savings in administrative costs are only part of the answer. Nearly all countries with national health insurance rely heavily on what I call "upstream resource allocation." The key to this is control over capital investment in facilities and equipment, specialty mix of physicians, and the development and diffusion of high-cost new technologies. Such control usually results in less excess capacity, in both physical and human capital. In Canada, for example, relatively scarce high-tech equipment, such as magnetic resonance imaging (MRI) or computerized axial tomography (CT) scanners, is used intensively, while the proliferation of such equipment in the United States results in considerable idle time. There are more physicians per capita in Canada than in the United States, but fewer physicians there specialize in complex surgical and diagnostic procedures. As a result, the average Canadian specialist has a full work load, while his or her American counterpart does not (see Chapter 6).

The price that Canadians and Europeans pay for such controls is delay or inconvenience in receiving high-tech services, or sometimes not receiving such services at all. Whether such delays or denials have a significant effect on the health of the population is not known with certainty; the limited evidence now available suggests that they do not.

Countries with national health insurance also contain costs by using their centralized buying power to squeeze down the prices of resources, especially drugs and physician services. Drug prices in the United States usually contain significant monopoly rents, as evidenced by the willingness of the drug manufacturers to sell the identical products overseas at much lower prices.

Canadian and European physicians do not enjoy net incomes that are as high as those of U.S. physicians, even after adjustment for international differences in the general level of wages. But this does not mean that U.S. physicians are more satisfied with their lot or that U.S. medical schools find it easier to attract high-quality, well-motivated applicants. Compared with physicians in most countries with national health insurance, U.S. physicians experience more bureaucratic supervision from public and private insurance plans and greater interference with the day-to-day practice of medicine.

It is important not to overestimate the amount that can be saved by reducing physicians' incomes. U.S. physicians' net incomes account for about 10 percent of all health care spending. If these incomes were reduced by 20 percent (the approximate differential between the United States and Canada after adjusting for specialty mix, the exchange rate, and the general level of wages), the saving would be only 2 percent of health care spending. Also, this is not a saving of real resources, but only a money transfer from physicians to patients and taxpayers.

Cost containment under a national health insurance system often relies on single-source funding set prospectively (for example, the global budget given to each Canadian hospital at the beginning of each year). Samuel Johnson once said, "When a man knows he is to be hanged in a fortnight, it concentrates his mind wonderfully." Much the same seems to be true of health care. When physicians and hospital administrators know that there is a certain pool of resources at their disposal and that no more will be forthcoming, they seem to figure out ways to do the job with what they have. To be sure, this inevitably involves

212

limitation of some services, but most health professionals prefer having some control over the allocation of the scarce resources available to them.

National Health Insurance and Health

Does national health insurance improve the health of the population by increasing access to care, or does it worsen health by constraining the introduction of new technology and destroying incentives for physicians and hospitals? There is no conclusive answer to this question; in my judgment, such a system has little effect on health one way or the other.[3]

The evidence regarding life expectancy differentials, however, is more compelling. Universal coverage does not eliminate or even substantially reduce differentials across socioeconomic groups. In England, for instance, infant mortality in the lowest socioeconomic class is double the rate of the highest class, just as it was prior to the introduction of national health insurance (Townsend and Davidson 1982). The relatively homogeneous populations of Scandinavia not only enjoy universal coverage for health care but also have many other egalitarian social programs. Nevertheless, life expectancy varies considerably across occupations; the age-standardized mortality ratio for male hotel, restaurant, and food service workers is double that for teachers and technical workers (Andersen 1991). A study of age-standardized death rates in Sweden among employed men aged 45 to 64 found substantial differentials across occupations in 1966–1970 and slightly greater differentials in 1976–1980 (Calltorp 1989).

The failure of national health insurance to eliminate or reduce mortality differentials is not necessarily a decisive argument against its adoption. Bruce Vladeck (1991) argues that curing disease and improving functional outcomes are not the only benefits of medical care. He writes, "We expect the health system to take care of sick people whether or not they are going to get better, as much for our benefit as theirs." The caring services provided by health professionals have value even when they do not change health outcomes (Fuchs 1974b).

Prospects for National Health Insurance in the United States

What changes have occurred since 1976 that might modify Americans' resistance to national health insurance? Here I evaluate the four factors I advanced then to explain the absence of national health insurance in the United States in light of recent sociopolitical trends.

DISTRUST OF GOVERNMENT

The typical American's distrust of government is probably stronger now than it was in the mid-1970s. Jimmy Carter was elected as an outsider, and he did little to enhance the image of the presidency or of government in general during his four-year term; Ronald Reagan maintained an antigovernment posture throughout his two terms; and George Bush, while he may be more pragmatic and less ideological, commanded wide support with the message "Government is the problem, not the solution."

The recent debacle with the savings and loan industry also provides ample cause for concern. It did not come upon us suddenly; it was a well-diagnosed, localized cancer that government allowed to metastasize to its present level. What is particularly disturbing is that the blame cannot be laid on one political party or branch of government. Moreover, not just the federal government was derelict; state regulatory agencies and legislatures also failed to meet their responsibilities to the public.

Our government is built on checks and balances. If these checks and balances failed so badly with savings and loan institutions, many observers wonder how well they would do with health care, which is so much larger, more complex, and more vulnerable to mismanagement and dishonesty.

HETEROGENEITY OF THE POPULATION

In 1976, I argued that the heterogeneity of the U.S. population helped explain a reluctance to embrace national health insurance. Unlike the Swedes, Germans, Japanese, and many other peoples, most Americans do not share centuries of common language, culture, and traditions; thus, there is less sense of national identification and empathy. At present, this explanation probably has even more force. The celebration of multiculturalism in the United States in the past fifteen years appears to have led to a heightened sense of separateness among the country's many ethnic, religious, and racial groups. Glorification of the *pluribus* at the expense of the *unum* does not enhance the prospects for national health insurance.

Heterogeneity of values also fuels resistance to national health insurance. No nation should expect or desire uniformity of opinion, but the name-calling and physical violence that often accompany debates in the United States over values undermine the ability of the nation to undertake collective efforts for collective well-being. Americans might consider the words of British historian R. H. Tawney (1926): "The condition of effective action in a complex civilization is cooperation. And the condition of cooperation is agreement, both as to the ends to which efforts should be applied and the criteria by which its success is to be judged."

A ROBUST VOLUNTARY SECTOR

The United States has always been distinguished by its highly developed private, nonprofit institutions devoted to health, education, and social services. These institutions, often founded and supported by religious groups, perform many of the functions that government undertakes in other countries. During the past fifteen years, however, the ability of nonprofit hospitals and the Blue Cross and Blue Shield organizations to provide a form of social insurance through free care, cost shifting, and community rating of insurance premiums has been seriously compromised. The "competition revolution" has imposed the casualty approach to health insurance as a condition for survival (see Chapter 11). The growth of managed-care entities and tough bargaining by all third-party payers have sharply diminished the capacity of nonprofit institutions to act as redistributive agents. The declining importance of philanthropy relative to private and public health insurance also decreases the ability of nonprofit institutions to act as quasi-governmental agencies. In health care, the "thousand points of light" are fainter now than in the past. I conclude that the voluntary-sector explanation for the absence of national health insurance in the United States has less force now than it had in the 1970s.

LESS *NOBLESSE OBLIGE*

The two central ideological forces of American society have been a commitment to individual freedom and, at least in the abstract, to equality. Tension has always existed between these forces, with the emphasis on individual opportunity and achievement prevailing most of the time, but the egalitarian emphasis much in evidence in the 1930s and 1960s. Even the egalitarian ideology, however, has focused more on equality of social status, equality under the law, and equality of opportunity than on equality of outcomes. Because so many Americans of humble origins could and did gain wealth and high social position, the sense of *noblesse oblige* that motivates many of the well-born in other nations to vote for social programs to aid the less fortunate has never been as evident in the United States. While I find it difficult to judge accurately, I suspect that the absence of *noblesse oblige* may be slightly more relevant today than in 1976. In the 1980s, the rhetoric of most of the American right wing was laissez-faire, not Tory conservative. Moreover, the left wing's infatuation with the vocabulary of rights (divorced from obligations) often diminishes a feeling of mutual responsibility.

In summary, the distrust of government, the population heterogeneity, and the lack of *noblesse oblige* are explanations probably more relevant today than in 1976. Only one explanation—the robustness of the voluntary sector—is definitely weaker now. It is ironic that the "competition revolution," which erodes the ability of not-for-profit health care institutions to provide a modicum of social insurance, may prove to be a significant factor leading the country toward national health insurance.

Nevertheless, in my view, the prospects for national health insurance in the short run are poor. The forces actively opposed to it are strong and well organized, and have a clear sense of what they do not want. The forces actively in favor are relatively weak, disorganized, and frequently at odds regarding the reasons for wanting national health insurance or the best way to obtain it. The great majority of Americans are not actively involved in the debate one way or the other but tend to be opposed for the reasons I have indicated. Some public opinion polls seem to indicate a readiness for national health insurance, but they are not credible indicators of political behavior because the answers vary widely depending on how the questions are framed.

In the long run, national health insurance is far from dead; the need to curb cost while extending coverage will continue to push the country in that direction. The process will accelerate as nonprofit health care institutions lose their ability to provide some social insurance as an alternative to national health insurance. Moreover, the current trend of basing insurance premiums on expected utilization will strike more people as unjust because most disease will be found to have a significant genetic component. Also, as employers' hiring decisions and employees' job choices become increasingly constrained by health insurance considerations, there will be more appreciation of the efficiency advantages of making health insurance independent of the labor market.

The timing of adoption of national health insurance will depend largely on factors external to health care. Major changes in health policy, like major policy changes in any area, are political acts, undertaken for political purposes. That was true when Bismarck introduced national health insurance to the new German state over a hundred years ago. It was true when England adopted national health insurance after World War II, and it will be true in the United States as well. National health insurance will probably come to the United States in the wake of a major change in the political climate, the kind of change that often accompanies a war, a depression, or large-scale civil unrest. Short of that, we should expect modest attempts to increase coverage and contain costs, accompanied by an immodest amount of sound and fury.

Notes

5. U.S. Health Expenditures and the Gross National Product

1. The health sector's components, in order of expenditures in 1987, are hospital care, physician services, nursing home care, drugs, dentist services, program administration and net cost of private health insurance, other professional services, public health, other personal health care, noncommercial research, eyeglasses and appliances, and construction of facilities.
2. The prices of output depend entirely on the prices of inputs (including entrepreneurial profits) and the quantities of input needed to produce any given output.
3. These estimates are based on multivariate analyses of the Public Use Sample (1 in 100) of the 1950 *Census of the Population* (U.S. Bureau of the Census 1950a) and the March 1986 *Current Population Survey* (U.S. Bureau of the Census 1986b), with controls for education, age, geographic location, and sex.
4. Calculated from *Economic Report of the President* (1989) and from *Socioeconomic Characteristics of Medical Practice* (American Medical Association 1987b, 1988), table 43, p. 124.
5. Calculated from the 1950 and 1980 *Census of the Population* (U.S. Bureau of the Census 1950a, 1980a) and from *Health United States 1988*, table 80, p. 129 (National Center for Health Statistics 1989b).

6. How Canada Does It: Physicians' Services

1. Sources include the following: American Hospital Association 1986; American Medical Association 1986; Health and Welfare Canada 1987, 1988a; Iowa Development Commission 1987; Levit 1985; Or-

ganisation for Economic Co-operation and Development 1987; Statistics Canada 1985, 1987b, 1988a, 1988b, 1988c, 1989a; U.S. Bureau of the Census 1986a, 1987, 1988b, 1989a; U.S. Department of Commerce 1988; Waldo, Levit, and Lazenby 1986.

2. See NAPS document no. 04801 for twenty pages of supplementary material. Order from National Auxiliary Publications Service of the American Society for Information Sciences, 8720 Georgia Ave., Suite 501, Silver Spring, MD 20910-3602.

7. How Canada Does It: Acute Hospital Care

1. Sources include the following: American Hospital Association 1988; Donham and Maple 1989; Health and Welfare Canada 1988b; The Hospital Medical Records Institute 1987; Levit 1985; National Center for Health Statistics 1987; Office of the Registrar General of Ontario 1990; Office of Statewide Health Planning and Development 1990; The St. John's Hospital, *Quarterly Financial and Utilization Reports Submitted to Office of Statewide Health Planning and Development* (1987) and *Annual Disclosure Report Submitted to Office of Statewide Health Planning and Development* (Feb. 14, 1988); Schieber, Poullier, and Greenwald 1991; Stanford University Medical Center, *Annual Disclosure Report Submitted to Office of Statewide Health Planning and Development* (Dec. 30, 1987) and *Auditor's Report on Examinations of Financial Statements* (1987); State of California Department of Finance 1990; Statistics Canada 1988a, 1989b, 1990, 1991a, 1991b, 1991d; Sunnybrook Health Sciences Center, *Annual Return of Health Care Facilities, Part I, Submitted to Health and Welfare Canada* (June 16, 1988); Treasurer of Ontario and Minister of Economics 1990; U.S. Bureau of the Census 1988b, 1990; U.S. Department of Health and Human Services 1988; U.S. Department of Labor 1990; The Wellesley Hospital, *Annual Return of Health Care Facilities, Part I, Submitted to Health and Welfare Canada* (Aug. 31, 1988); personal communications from California Association of Hospitals and Health Systems confidential survey of wages (March 4, 1991), The Hospital Medical Records Institute (April 8, 1991), Statistics Canada data on hospital employee wages (April 30, 1991), Statistics Canada Health Care Section (Aug. 21, 1991), State of California, Department of Health Services, Health Data and Statistics Branch (Feb. 4, 1992),

State of New York, Department of Health, Bureau of Biometrics (Feb. 6, 1992), State of Texas, Department of Health Services (Feb. 7, 1992); and unpublished computer data analyses from Ontario Ministry of Health, Information Systems Division (Nov. 9, 1990, and Aug. 21, 1991).

9. America's Children

1. See, for instance, many of the papers in Blankenhorn, Bayme, and Elshtain, eds., *Rebuilding the Nest* (1990).
2. That is, the GNP-implicit deflator for government purchases. See *Economic Report of the President* (1991), p. 291.
3. Reported money income is a good but not perfect measure of command over goods and services because it does not include fringe benefits, such as health insurance, or income from the underground economy, nor does it exclude personal income taxes. Estimation of the effects of these variables on the true net income available to households is very difficult, and even more difficult if separate estimates for children and adults are required.
4. Because the data gathered by the Bureau of the Census through the *Current Population Surveys* differ slightly from those gathered in the decennial censuses, the 1988 figures were adjusted to census levels by linking changes in the *Current Population Survey* results between 1980 and 1988 to the 1980 census levels. The number of persons in the samples are: 175,123 in 1960; 197,345 in 1970; 220,916 in 1980; and 155,654 in 1988.
5. Alternative calculations in which each child is weighted as some fraction of an adult (for example, 0.75 or 0.50) show that the trends over time discussed here are not sensitive to assumptions about the "adult equivalence" of children unless the assumption is changed appreciably from one year to another. We have no basis for making such changes.
6. That is, the GNP-implicit deflator for personal consumption expenditures. See *Economic Report of the President* (1991), p. 290.
7. The rapid growth in the female labor force participation rate since 1960 is accounted for primarily by women in households with children. Participation rates among childless women have always been high and show little change. Participation rates of older

women whose children no longer live with them have shown only modest increases since 1960.

8. The purpose of this calculation is to show the contribution of women's earnings to the income available to children, not to suggest that women should not have paid jobs.

9. The statistical adjustment does not capture all the labor market and income effects of the increase in mothers taking paid jobs; to do so would require a complex model beyond the scope of this chapter.

10. The weighted average of $7,640 and $2,397 is $7,273 when the weights are 93 percent and 7 percent, but only $6,644 when the weights are 81 percent and 19 percent.

11. That is, in more than 25 percent of the households without an adult male, women's earnings were the only source of income.

11. The "Competition Revolution" of the 1980s

1. Boulding (1968) says, "The integrative system . . . involves such things as status, identity, love, hate, benevolence, malevolence, legitimacy—the whole raft of social institutions which defines roles in such a way that you do things because of what you are and because of what I am, that is, because of some kind of status or respect."

2. Mathematically, it means that the demand curve facing each seller (or supply curve facing each buyer) is completely horizontal.

3. These calculations were made from computer tapes of the *Current Population Surveys* of March 1980 and March 1986. Overall, real earnings of American workers declined between 1979 and 1985; this analysis focuses on differential rate of change by sector.

14. National Health Insurance Revisited

1. The United States has some compulsion and some subsidization in large companies. In the typical case, all workers participate, and the firm rarely adjusts the individual worker's wages or premiums to take full account of differences in expected utilization.

2. The RAND Health Insurance Experiment clearly showed that utilization is greater when patients do not bear some of the cost of care. See Manning et al. 1987.

3. The effect of national health insurance on health depends on the product of two elasticities: the responsiveness of the quantity of medical care to national health insurance, and the responsiveness of health to changes in the quantity of medical care. In developed countries, the product of these terms is apparently very small.

References

Afriat, S. N. 1977. *The Price Index*. New York: Cambridge University Press.

American Hospital Association. 1984. *Hospital Statistics*. Chicago: American Hospital Association.

—— 1986. *Hospital Statistics*. Chicago: American Hospital Association.

—— 1988. *Hospital Statistics*. Chicago: American Hospital Association.

—— 1990. *Hospital Statistics*. Chicago: American Hospital Association.

American Medical Association. 1983. *Socioeconomic Characteristics of Medical Practice*. Chicago: American Medical Association.

—— 1986. *Physician Characteristics and Distribution in the U.S.* Chicago: American Medical Association.

—— 1987a. *SMS Detailed Tables*. Chicago: AMA Center for Health Policy Research, October.

—— 1987b. *Socioeconomic Characteristics of Medical Practice*. Chicago: American Medical Association.

—— 1988. *Socioeconomic Characteristics of Medical Practice*. Chicago: American Medical Association.

Andersen, O. 1991. "Occupational Impacts on Mortality Declines in the Nordic Countries." In *Future Demographic Trends in Europe and North America*, ed. W. Lutz. New York: Academic Press.

Andreopoulos, S., ed. 1975. *National Health Insurance: Can We Learn From Canada?* New York: Wiley.

Applebee, A. N., J. A Langer, and I. V. S. Mullis. 1989. *Crossroads in American Education*. Princeton, NJ: Educational Testing Service.

References

226

Arrow, Kenneth J. 1963. "Uncertainty and the Welfare Economics of Medical Care." *American Economic Review* 53:941–973.

Auster, Richard, Irving Leveson, and Deborah Sarachek. 1969. "The Production of Health, an Exploratory Study." *Journal of Human Resources* 4:411–436.

Bandura, Albert. 1991. "Self-Efficacy Mechanism in Physiological Activation and Health-Promoting Behavior." In *Neural Biology of Learning, Emotion, and Affect,* ed. John Madden IV. New York: Raven Press.

Bane, M. J., and D. T. Ellwood. 1989. "One Fifth of the Nation's Children: Why Are They Poor?" *Science* 245:1047–1053.

Banta, H. D., and S. B. Thacker. 1990. "The Case for Reassessment of Health Care Technology: Once Is Not Enough." *Journal of the American Medical Association* 264:235–240.

Barer, M. L., and R. G. Evans. 1986. "Riding North on a South-Bound Horse? Expenditures, Prices, Utilization and Incomes in the Canadian Health Care System." In *Medicare at Maturing: Achievements, Lessons, and Challenges,* ed. R. G. Evans and G. L. Stoddart. Proceedings of the Health Policy Conference on Canada's National Health Care System. Calgary, AB: University of Calgary Press.

Barry, Michael J., et al. 1988. "Watchful Waiting vs. Immediate Transurethral Resection for Symptomatic Prostatism: The Importance of Patients' Preferences." *Journal of the American Medical Association* 259:3010–3017.

Berger, Mark C., and J. Paul Leigh. 1989. "Schooling, Self-Selection, and Health." *Journal of Human Resources* 24:435–455.

Bergstrom, Theodore C. 1974. "Preference and Choice in Matters of Life and Death." Unpublished ms.

Blankenhorn, D., S. Bayme, and J. B. Elshtain, eds. 1990. *Rebuilding the Nest.* Milwaukee: Family Service America.

Bombardier, C., et al. 1977. "Socioeconomic Factors Affecting the Utilization of Surgical Operations." *The New England Journal of Medicine* 297:699–705.

Boulding, Kenneth. 1968. *Beyond Economics.* Ann Arbor: University of Michigan Press.

Brook, R. H., et al. 1983. "Does Free Care Improve Adults' Health? Results from a Randomized Controlled Trial." *The New England Journal of Medicine* 309:1426–1434.

Bruce, Neil, and Michael Waldman. 1991. "Transfers in Kind: Why They Can Be Efficient and Nonpaternalistic." *American Economic Review* 81:1345–1351.

Budetti, P., et al. 1981. "The Costs and Effectiveness of Neonatal Intensive Care." In *The Implications of Cost-Effectiveness Analysis of Medical Technology.* Case Study no. 10. Washington, DC: Office of Technology.

Califano, Joseph. 1986. *America's Health Care Revolution.* New York: Random House.

Calltorp, J. 1989. "The 'Swedish Model' under Pressure—How to Maintain Equity and Develop Quality?" *Quality Assurance in Health Care* 1 (1): 13–22.

Capdevielle, P. 1988. "International Differences in Employers' Compensation Costs." *Monthly Labor Review* 111 (5): 44–46.

Carr-Hill, Roy. 1987. "The Inequalities in Health Debate: A Critical Review of the Issues." *Journal of Social Policy* 16:509–542.

Centers for Disease Control. 1983a. *Abortion Surveillance, 1979–1980.* Atlanta: Centers for Disease Control.

———— 1983b. *Surgical Sterilization Surveillance, 1979–1980.* Atlanta: Centers for Disease Control.

Chassin, Mark R., et al. 1987. "Does Inappropriate Use Explain Geographic Variations in the Use of Health Care Services? A Study of Three Procedures." *Journal of the American Medical Association* 258:2533–2537.

Chollet, D. 1990. "Update: Americans Without Health Insurance." *EBRI Issue Brief.* Washington, DC: Employee Benefit Research Institute, July.

Coate, Stephen, Stephen Johnson, and Richard Zeckhauser. 1992. "Robin-Hooding Rents: Exploiting the Pecuniary Effects of In-Kind Programs." Mimeo. Cambridge, MA: Harvard University, March.

Coyte, P. C., D. N. Dewees, and M. J. Trebilcock. 1991. "Medical Malpractice—The Canadian Experience." *The New England Journal of Medicine* 324:89–93.

Culyer, A. J. 1989. "Cost-Containment in Europe." Discussion Paper 62, Centre for Health Economics. York, England: University of York.

Culyer, A. J., J. Wiseman, and A. Walker. 1977. *An Annotated Bibliography of Health Economics.* London: Martin Robertson; New York: St. Martin's Press.

Danzon, P. M. 1985. *Medical Malpractice: Theory, Evidence, and Public Policy.* Cambridge, MA: Harvard University Press.

Davis, M. M., and C. R. Rorem. 1932. *The Crisis in Hospital Finance.* Chicago: University of Chicago Press.

DeJong, G., A. I. Batavia, and R. Griss. 1989. "America's Neglected

228

Health Minority: Working-Age Persons with Disabilities." *The Milbank Quarterly* 67 (Supplement 2, Part 2): 311–351.

Detsky, A. S., et al. 1986. "Global Budgeting and the Teaching Hospital in Ontario." *Medical Care* 24:89–94.

Detsky, A. S., S. R. Stacey, and C. Bombardier. 1983. "The Effectiveness of a Regulatory Strategy in Containing Hospital Costs: The Ontario Experience, 1967–1981." *The New England Journal of Medicine* 309:151–159.

Doherty, K. 1989. "Is the Canadian System as Good as It Looks for Employers?" *Business Health* 7 (7): 31–34.

Donham, C. S., and B. T. Maple. 1989. "Health Care Indicators." *Health Care Financing Review* 11 (3): 113–132.

Dubos, René. 1959. *The Mirage of Health.* New York: Harper and Bros.

Economic Report of the President. 1989. Washington, DC: Government Printing Office.

———— 1991. Washington, DC: Government Printing Office.

———— 1992. Washington, DC: Government Printing Office.

Eddy, David M. 1980. *Screening for Cancer: Theory, Analysis, and Design.* Englewood Cliffs, NJ: Prentice Hall.

———— 1989. "The Confidence Profile Method: A Bayesian Method for Assessing Health Technologies." *Operations Research* 37 (2): 210–228.

Enthoven, Alain C. 1978. "Consumer-Choice Health Plan." *The New England Journal of Medicine* 298:650–658, 709–720.

———— 1986. "Managed Competition in Health Care and the Unfinished Agenda." *Health Care Financing Review Annual Supplement:* 105–119.

———— 1988. "Managed Competition: An Agenda for Action." *Health Affairs* 7:25–47.

Evans, R. G. 1974. "Supplier-Induced Demand: Some Empirical Evidence and Implications." In *The Economics of Health and Medical Care: Proceedings of a Conference Held by the International Economic Association at Tokyo, April 1973,* ed. Mark Perlman. London: Macmillan; New York: Halsted Press.

Evans, R. G., et al. 1989. "Controlling Health Expenditures—The Canadian Reality." *The New England Journal of Medicine* 320:571–577.

Evans, R. G, and G. L. Stoddart, eds. 1986. *Medicare at Maturity: Achievements, Lessons, and Challenges.* Proceedings of the Health Policy Conference on Canada's National Health Care System. Calgary, AB: University of Calgary Press.

Farrell, P., and V. R. Fuchs. 1982. "Schooling and Health: The Cigarette Connection." *Journal of Health Economics* 1:217–230.

Feder, Judith, Jack Hadley, and Stephen Zuckerman. 1987. "How Did Medicare's Prospective Payment System Affect Hospitals?" *The New England Journal of Medicine* 317:867–873.

Fein, R. 1958. *Economics of Mental Illness.* New York: Basic Books.

Feldschuh, J., and R. Feldschuh. 1982. "Frozen Semen and Artificial Insemination." In *Current Therapy of Infertility, 1982–1983,* ed. C.-R. Garcia, L. Mastroianni, and R. Amelar. Trenton, NJ: B. C. Decker.

Feldstein, M. S. 1967. *Economic Analysis for Health Service Efficiency.* Amsterdam: North-Holland.

Feldstein, P. 1983. *Health Care Economics.* 2nd ed. New York: John Wiley and Sons.

Fowler, Floyd J., et al. 1988. "Symptom Status and Quality of Life Following Prostatectomy." *Journal of the American Medical Association* 259:3018–3022.

Fox, A. J. 1984. *Social Class and Occupational Mobility Shortly before Men Become Fathers.* OPCS series LS, no. 2. London: HMSO.

Friedman, B. 1978. "On the Rationing of Health Services and Resource Availability." *Journal of Human Resources* 13 (Supplement): 57–75.

Friedman, M., and S. Kuznets. 1945. *Income from Independent Professional Practice.* General series no. 45. New York: National Bureau of Economic Research.

Fuchs, Victor R. 1965a. "Some Economic Aspects of Mortality in the United States." Mimeo. New York: National Bureau of Economic Research.

——— 1965b. "Toward a Theory of Poverty." In *The Concept of Poverty,* 77–91. Task Force on Economic Growth and Opportunity, First Report. Washington, DC: Chamber of Commerce of the United States.

———, ed. 1969. *Production and Productivity in the Service Industries.* New York: National Bureau of Economic Research.

——— 1972. "Health Care and the United States Economic System: An Essay in Abnormal Physiology." *Milbank Memorial Fund Quarterly* 50 (April): 211–237.

——— 1974a. "Some Economic Aspects of Mortality in Developed Countries." In *The Economics of Health and Medical Care: Proceedings of a Conference Held by the International Economic Association at Tokyo, April 1973,* ed. Mark Perlman. London: Macmillan; New York: Halsted Press.

230

—— 1974b. *Who Shall Live? Health, Economics, and Social Choice.* New York: Basic Books.

—— 1976. "From Bismarck to Woodstock: The 'Irrational' Pursuit of National Health Insurance." *Journal of Law and Economics* 19 (August): 347–359.

—— 1978. "The Supply of Surgeons and the Demand for Operations." *Journal of Human Resources* 13 (Supplement): 35–56.

—— 1982. "Time Preference and Health: An Exploratory Study." In *Economic Aspects of Health,* ed. Victor R. Fuchs. Chicago: University of Chicago Press.

—— 1984. " 'Though Much is Taken': Reflections on Aging, Health, and Medical Care." *Milbank Memorial Fund Quarterly* 62 (Spring): 143–166.

—— 1986a. *The Health Economy.* Cambridge, MA: Harvard University Press.

—— 1986b. "Paying the Piper, Calling the Tune: Implications of Changes in Reimbursement." *Frontiers of Health Services Management* 2:4–27.

—— 1986c. "Sex Differences in Economic Well-Being." *Science* 232:459–464.

—— 1988. *Women's Quest for Economic Equality.* Cambridge, MA: Harvard University Press.

—— 1992. "The Best Health Care System in the World?" *Journal of the American Medical Association* 268:916–917.

Fulda, T. K., and P. F. Dickens. 1979. "Controlling the Cost of Drugs: The Canadian Experience." *Health Care Financing Review* 1 (2): 55–64.

Galbraith, John K. 1956. *American Capitalism.* Boston: Houghton Mifflin.

Ginzberg, E. 1954. "What Every Economist Should Know about Health and Medicine." *American Economic Review* 44:104–119.

—— 1969. *Men, Money, and Medicine.* New York: Columbia University Press.

Glass, R., and R. Ericsson. 1982. *Getting Pregnant in the 1980s.* Berkeley: University of California Press.

Gortmaker, Steven L., et al. 1987. "Increasing Pediatric Obesity in the United States." *American Journal of Diseases of Children* 141 (May): 535–540.

Grabowski, H. G. 1986. "Health Care Cost Containment and Pharmaceutical Innovation." In *Pharmaceuticals for the Elderly: New Research and New Concerns.* Washington, DC: Pharmaceutical Manufacturers Association.

Grabowski, H. G., J. M. Vernon, and L. G. Thomas. 1978. "Estimating the Effects of Regulation on Innovation: An International Comparative Analysis of the Pharmaceutical Industry." *Journal of Law and Economics* 21 (April): 133–163.

Grossman, Michael. 1972. *The Demand for Health: A Theoretical and Empirical Investigation.* NBER occasional paper no. 19. New York: National Bureau of Economic Research.

——— 1975. "The Correlation between Health and Schooling." In *Household Production and Consumption,* ed. Nestor Terleckyj. New York: National Bureau of Economic Research.

Grossman, Michael, and Lee Benham. 1974. "Health, Hours and Wages." In *The Economics of Health and Medical Care: Proceedings of a Conference Held by the International Economic Association at Tokyo, April 1973,* ed. Mark Perlman. London: Macmillan; New York: Halsted Press.

Haber, S. G., et al. 1993. "Hospital Expenditures in the United States and Canada: Do Hospital Worker Wages Explain the Differences?" *Journal of Health Economics* 11 (4):453–465.

Hamilton, P. M., et al. 1984. "Radiation Procedures Performed on U.S. Women during Pregnancy: Findings from Two 1980 Surveys." *Public Health Reports* 99:146–151.

Hamilton, Walton H. 1932. *Medical Care for the American People: The Final Report of the Committee on the Cost of Medical Care, Adopted October 31, 1932.* Chicago: University of Chicago Press.

Health and Welfare Canada. 1987. *National Health Expenditures in Canada, 1975–1985.* Ottawa, ON: Health and Welfare Canada.

——— 1988a. *Active Civilian Physicians by Type of Physician, Canada, by Province, December 31, 1987.* Ottawa, ON: Health and Welfare Canada.

——— 1988b. *Canada Diseases Weekly Report* 14:15.

——— 1988c. *Physicians' Income by Specialty Study, 1985.* Ottawa, ON: Health and Welfare Canada.

——— 1988d. *Salaries and Wages in Canadian Hospitals, 1962 to 1985.* Ottawa, ON: Health and Welfare Canada.

Health Care Financing Administration. 1985. *Average Allowed Charges for Selected Procedure Codes by Type of Service, 1985: Part B, Medicare Annual Data Procedure File.* Baltimore: Health Care Financing Administration.

——— 1987. "National Health Expenditures, 1986–2000." *Health Care Financing Review* 8 (4): 1–36.

Health Insurance Association of America. 1982. *The Cost of Having a Baby.* Washington, DC: Health Insurance Association of America.

———— 1985. *Source Book of Health Insurance Data, 1984–1985.* Washington, DC: Health Insurance Association of America.

———— 1990. *Providing Employee Health Benefits: How Firms Differ.* Washington, DC: Health Insurance Association of America.

Helyar, C. 1991. *Notebook on Data for Quality Measurement.* Don Mills, ON: The Hospital Medical Records Institute.

Henshaw, S. K. 1982. "Freestanding Abortion Clinics: Services, Structure, Fees." *Family Planning Perspectives* 14:248–256.

Henshaw, S. K., J. D. Forrest, and E. Blaine. 1984. "Abortion Services in the United States, 1981 and 1982." *Family Planning Perspectives* 16:119–127.

Himmelstein, D. U., and S. Woolhandler. 1986. "Cost without Benefit: Administrative Waste in U.S. Health Care." *The New England Journal of Medicine* 314:441–445.

———— 1991. "The Deteriorating Efficiency of the U.S. Health Care System." *The New England Journal of Medicine* 324:1253–1257.

The Hospital Medical Records Institute. 1987. *Length of Stay Database by CMG.* Don Mills, ON: The Hospital Medical Records Institute.

Hughes, R. G., S. S. Hunt, and H. S. Luft. 1987. "Effects of Surgeon Volume and Hospital Volume on Quality of Care in Hospitals." *Medical Care* 25:489–503.

Iglehart, J. K. 1986. "Canada's Health Care System." *The New England Journal of Medicine* 315:202–208, 778–784, 1623–1628.

———— 1990. "Canada's Health Care System Faces Its Problems." *The New England Journal of Medicine* 322:562–568.

Inman, R. P., ed. 1985. *Managing the Service Economy.* New York: Cambridge University Press.

Institute of Medicine. 1985. *Assessing Medical Technologies.* Washington, DC: National Academy Press.

Iowa Development Commission. 1987. *Statistical Profile of Iowa.* Des Moines: Iowa Development Commission.

Jones-Lee, M. 1974. "The Value of Changes in the Probability of Death or Injury." *Journal of Political Economy* 82:835–849.

Kaplan, Abraham. 1964. *The Conduct of Inquiry.* Scranton, PA: Chandler Publishing.

Katz, S. J., H. F. Mizgala, and H. G. Welch. 1991. "British Columbia Sends Patients to Seattle for Coronary Artery Surgery." *Journal of the American Medical Association* 266:1108–1111.

Keeler, E. B., et al. 1977. "Deductibles and Demand: A Theory of the Consumer Facing a Variable Price Schedule under Uncertainty." *Econometrica* 45 (April): 641–655.

Kenkel, Donald S. 1991. "Health Behavior, Health Knowledge, and Schooling." *Journal of Political Economy* 99:287–304.

Kerem, Bat-Sheva, et al. 1989. "Identification of the Cystic Fibrosis Gene: Genetic Analysis." *Science* 245:1073–1080.

Kessel, Reuben A. 1958. "Price Discrimination in Medicine." *Journal of Law and Economics* 1 (October): 20–53.

Keynes, John Maynard. 1923. "Introduction." In D. H. Robertson, *The Control of Industry*. New York: Harcourt, Brace.

Kirchner, M. 1982. "Fee Increases: Restraint Takes Over." *Medical Economics* 59:218–249.

Klarman, H. E. 1965. *The Economics of Health*. New York: Columbia University Press.

Kleinman, J., et al. 1983. "Variation in Use of Obstetrical Technology." In *Health United States 1983*. Washington, DC: National Center for Health Statistics.

L'Abbe, Kristan A., Allan S. Detsky, and Keith O'Rourke. 1987. "Meta-Analysis in Clinical Research." *Annals of Internal Medicine* 107 (August): 224–233.

Lave, J. R., and L. B. Lave. 1970. "Hospital Cost Functions: Estimating Cost Functions for Multi-Product Firms." *American Economic Review* 60:379–395.

Leape, Lucian L., et al. 1990. "Does Inappropriate Use Explain Small-Area Variations in the Use of Health Care Services?" *Journal of the American Medical Association* 263:669–672.

Lees, D. S. 1961. *Health Through Choice*. Hobart Paper no. 14. London: Institute of Economic Affairs.

Lemna, Wanda K., et al. 1990. "Mutation Analysis for Heterozygote Detection and Prenatal Diagnosis of Cystic Fibrosis." *The New England Journal of Medicine* 322:291–296.

Letsch, Suzanne W., Katharine R. Levit, and Daniel R. Waldo. 1988. "National Health Expenditures, 1987." *Health Care Financing Review* 10 (2): 109–122.

Levit, K. 1985. "Personal Health Expenditures by State, 1976–1982." *Health Care Financing Review* 6 (4): 1–49.

Levit, K., et al. 1991. "National Health Expenditures, 1990." *Health Care Financing Review* 13 (1): 29–54.

Lipset, S. M. 1990. *Continental Divide*. London: Routledge.

234

Littenberg, Benjamin, Alan M. Garber, and Harold C. Sox. 1990. "Screening for Hypertension." *Annals of Internal Medicine* 112 (1 February): 192–202.

Lomas, Jonathon, et al. 1989. "Do Practice Guidelines Guide Practice? The Effect of a Consensus Statement on the Practice of Physicians." *The New England Journal of Medicine* 321:1306–1311.

London, Kathryn. 1989. "Children of Divorce." *Vital and Health Statistics,* Series 21, no. 46. Washington, DC: Government Printing Office.

Louv, R. 1990. *Childhood's Future.* Boston: Houghton Mifflin.

Lubitz, J., and R. Prihoda. 1984. "The Use and Costs of Medicare Services in the Last Two Years of Life." *Health Care Financing Review* 5 (3): 117–131.

Luft, H. S. 1981. *Health Maintenance Organizations: Dimensions of Performance.* New York: John Wiley and Sons.

Luft, H. S., John C. Hershey, and Joan M. Gianaris. 1974. "Factors Affecting the Use of Physicians' Services in a Rural Community." Mimeo. Stanford, CA: Stanford University School of Medicine, December.

Major, Ralph H. 1954. *A History of Medicine.* Springfield, IL: C. C. Thomas.

Malenbaum, Wilfred. 1970. "Health and Productivity in Poor Areas." In *Empirical Studies in Health Economics,* ed. Herbert E. Klarman. Baltimore: The Johns Hopkins University Press.

Manning, Willard G., et al. 1987. "Health Insurance and the Demand for Medical Care: Evidence from a Randomized Experiment." *American Economic Review* 77:251–277.

Marshall, Alfred. [1890]. 1936. *Principles of Economics.* 8th ed. London: Macmillan.

McCormick, M. 1985. "The Contribution of Low Birth Weight to Infant Mortality and Childhood Morbidity." *The New England Journal of Medicine* 312:82–90.

McCormick, M., S. Shapiro, and B. Starfield. 1980. "Rehospitalization in the First Year of Life for High-Risk Survivors." *Pediatrics* 66:991–999.

McNeil, Barbara J., Ralph Weichselbaum, and Stephen G. Pauker. 1978. "Fallacy of the Five-Year Survival in Lung Cancer." *The New England Journal of Medicine* 299:1397–1401.

McPherson, K., et al. 1981. "Regional Variations in the Use of Common Surgical Procedures: Within and between England and Wales,

Canada and the United States of America." *Social Science and Medicine* 15:273–288.

McRae, J. J., and F. Tapon. 1985. "Some Empirical Evidence on Post-Patent Barriers to Entry in the Canadian Pharmaceutical Industry." *Journal of Health Economics* 4:43–61.

Medical Group Management Association. 1986. *The Cost and Production Survey Report: 1986 Report.* Denver: Medical Group Management Association.

Melnick, Glenn A., and Jack Zwanziger. 1987. "Hospital Behavior under Competition and Cost Containment Policies: The California Experience, 1980–1985." Mimeo. Santa Monica, CA: The RAND Corporation.

Menning, B. E. 1982. "Psychosocial Issues in Donor Insemination." In *Current Therapy of Infertility, 1982–1983,* ed. C.-R. Garcia, L. Mastroianni, and R. Amelar. Trenton, NJ: B. C. Decker.

Mishan, E. J. 1971. "Evaluation of Life and Limb: A Theoretical Approach." *Journal of Political Economy* 79:687–705.

Moloney, T. W., and B. Paul. 1989. "A New Financial Framework: Lessons from Canada." *Health Affairs* 8:148–159.

Morris, J. N. 1964. *Uses of Epidemiology.* 2nd ed. Baltimore: Williams & Wilkins.

Moses, Lincoln E., and Byron Wm. Brown, Jr. 1984. "Experiences with Evaluating the Safety and Efficacy of Medical Technologies." *Annual Review of Public Health* 5:267–292.

Mosher, W. 1984. "Fecundity and Infertility in the United States, 1965–1982." Paper presented at the annual meeting of the Population Association of America, Minneapolis, May 3–5.

Moss, A. J., and M. A. Moien. 1987. "Recent Declines in Hospitalization: United States, 1982–1986." *AdvanceData* 140. Hyattsville, MD: National Center for Health Statistics.

Mullner, Ross, Peter Kralovec, and David McNeil. 1987. "45 Percent More Community Hospitals Closed in '86." *Hospitals* 61 (5 May): 32–34.

Mushkin, S. J., ed. 1964. *The Economics of Health and Medical Care.* Ann Arbor: University of Michigan Press.

National Center for Health Statistics. 1960. *Vital Statistics of the United States,* vol. II, part A. Washington, DC: Government Printing Office.

——— 1970. *Vital Statistics of the United States,* vol. II, part A. Washington, DC: Government Printing Office.

—— 1980. *Vital Statistics of the United States,* vol. II, part A. Washington, DC: Government Printing Office.

—— 1982. "Data from the National Survey of Family Growth." *Vital and Health Statistics,* series 23. Washington, DC: U.S. Department of Health, Education, and Welfare.

—— 1983. "Patterns of Ambulatory Care in Pediatrics: The National Ambulatory Medical Care Survey, United States, January 1980–December 1981." *Vital and Health Statistics,* series 13, no. 75. Washington, DC: National Center for Health Statistics.

—— 1984a. "Patterns of Ambulatory Care in Obstetrics and Gynecology: The National Ambulatory Medical Care Survey, United States, January 1980–December 1981." *Vital and Health Statistics,* series 13, no. 76. Washington, DC: National Center for Health Statistics.

—— 1984b. "Use of Contraception in the United States, 1982." *AdvanceData* 102. Washington, DC: National Center for Health Statistics.

—— 1984c. "Use of Services for Family Planning and Infertility: United States, 1982." *AdvanceData* 103. Washington, DC: National Center for Health Statistics.

—— 1984d. "Utilization of Short-Stay Hospitals, United States, 1982, Annual Summary." In *Vital and Health Statistics,* series 13, no. 78. Washington, DC: National Center for Health Statistics.

—— 1985a. "Diagnosis-Related Groups Using Data from the National Hospital Discharge Survey: United States, 1982." *AdvanceData* 105. Washington, DC: National Center for Health Statistics.

—— 1985b. "Fecundity and Infertility in the United States, 1965–1982." *AdvanceData* 104. Washington, DC: National Center for Health Statistics.

—— 1987. *National Hospital Discharge Data Survey.* Washington, DC: U.S. Department of Health and Human Services, Public Health Service.

—— 1988. *Vital Statistics of the United States,* vol. II, part A. Washington, DC: Government Printing Office.

—— 1989a. *Health United States 1987.* Washington, DC: Government Printing Office.

—— 1989b. *Health United States 1988.* Washington, DC: Government Printing Office.

—— 1990. "Advance Report of Final Natality Statistics, 1988."

Monthly Vital Statistics Report 39 (Supplement). Washington, DC: Government Printing Office.

National Commission on Children. 1991. *Beyond Rhetoric: A New American Agenda for Children and Families.* Final Report. Washington, DC: Government Printing Office.

National Institutes of Health. 1985. "Health Implications of Obesity." Consensus Development Conference Statement 5 (February). Washington, DC: U.S. Department of Health and Human Services.

Naylor, C. D. 1991. "A Different View of Queues in Ontario." *Health Affairs* 10:110–128.

Nestor, B., and Gold R. Benson. 1982. "Public Funding of Contraceptive, Sterilization and Abortion Services, 1982." *Family Planning Perspectives* 16:128–133.

Newhouse, J. P., et al. 1981. "Some Interim Results from a Controlled Trial of Cost Sharing in Health Insurance." *The New England Journal of Medicine* 305:1501–1507.

———— 1982. "Does the Geographical Distribution of Physicians Reflect Market Failure?" *Bell Journal of Economics* 13 (Autumn): 493–505.

Newhouse, J. P., G. Anderson, and L. L. Roos. 1988. "Hospital Spending in the United States and Canada: A Comparison." *Health Affairs* 7:6–16.

Office of National Cost Estimates. 1990. "National Health Expenditures, 1988." *Health Care Financing Review* 11 (4): 1–41.

Office of the Registrar General of Ontario. 1990. *Vital Statistics for 1987.* Ottawa, ON.

Office of Statewide Health Planning and Development. 1990. *Aggregate Hospital Discharge Data Summary, January 1, 1987–December 31, 1987.* Sacramento, CA.

———— 1991. *Annual Report of Hospitals, 1990: Licensed Services and Utilization Profiles.* Sacramento, CA.

Office of Technology Assessment, U.S. Congress. 1980. *The Implications of Cost-Effectiveness Analysis of Medical Technology.* Washington, DC: Government Printing Office.

Organisation for Economic Co-operation and Development. 1987. *National Accounts.* Vol. 1, *Main Aggregates, 1960–1985.* Paris: Organisation for Economic Co-operation and Development.

Palmer, John L., Timothy Smeeding, and Christopher Jencks. 1988. "The Uses and Limits of Income Comparisons." In *The Vulnerable,* ed. John L. Palmer, Timothy Smeeding, and Barbara Boyle Torrey. Washington, DC: Urban Institute Press.

Pauly, M. V. 1968. "The Economics of Moral Hazard: Comment." *American Economic Review* 58:531–536.

—— 1971. *Medical Care at Public Expense: A Study in Applied Welfare Economics.* New York: Praeger.

Peltzman, S. 1973. "An Evaluation of Consumer Protection Legislation: The 1962 Drug Amendments." *Journal of Political Economy* 81:1049–1091.

Perlman, M., ed. 1974. *The Economics of Health and Medical Care.* London: Macmillan.

Phelps, Charles. 1973. *The Demand for Health Insurance: A Theoretical and Empirical Investigation.* No. R-1054-OEO. Santa Monica, CA: The RAND Corporation.

Phelps, Charles E., and Alvin I. Mushlin. 1988. "Focusing Technology Assessment Using Medical Decision Theory." *Medical Decision Making* 8 (October–December): 279–289.

Phibbs, C. S., R. L. Williams, and R. H. Phibbs. 1981. "Newborn Risk Factors and Costs of Neonatal Intensive Care." *Pediatrics* 68:313–321.

Placek, P. J., et al. 1984. "Electronic Fetal Monitoring in Relation to Cesarean Section Delivery, for Live Births and Stillbirths in the U.S., 1980." *Public Health Reports* 99:173–183.

Pomerance, J. J., et al. 1978. "Cost of Living for Infants Weighing 1,000 Grams or Less at Birth." *Pediatrics* 61:908–910.

Rawls, J. 1971. *A Theory of Justice.* Cambridge, MA: Harvard University Press.

Relman, Arnold S. 1988. "Assessment and Accountability: The Third Revolution in Medical Care." *The New England Journal of Medicine* 319:1220–1222.

Rice, D. P. 1966. "Estimating the Cost of Illness." Public Health Service Publication 947-6. Washington, DC: U.S. Department of Health, Education, and Welfare.

Ries, Peter. 1987. "Health Care Coverage by Age, Sex, Race, and Family Income: United States, 1986." *AdvanceData* 139. Hyattsville, MD: National Center for Health Statistics.

The Robert Wood Johnson Foundation. 1987. *Access to Health Care in the United States: Results of a 1986 Survey.* Special Report no. 2. Princeton, NJ: The Robert Wood Johnson Foundation.

Roberts, Ffrangcon. 1952. *The Cost of Health.* London: Turnstyle Press.

Robinson, James C., and Harold S. Luft. 1987. "Competition and the

Cost of Hospital Care, 1972 to 1982." *Journal of the American Medical Association* 257:3241–3245.

Roos, L. L., et al. 1990. "Postsurgical Mortality in Manitoba and New England." *Journal of the American Medical Association* 263:2453–2458.

Roper, William L., et al. 1988. "Effectiveness in Health Care: An Initiative to Evaluate and Improve Medical Practice." *The New England Journal of Medicine* 319:1197–1202.

Rosenzweig, M. R., and T. P. Schultz. 1982. "The Behavior of Mothers as Inputs to Child Health: The Determinants of Birth Weight, Gestation, and Rate of Fetal Growth." In *Economic Aspects of Health,* ed. Victor R. Fuchs. Chicago: University of Chicago Press.

Rosett, R. N., ed. 1976. *The Role of Health Insurance in the Health Services Sector.* New York: National Bureau of Economic Research.

Russell, Louise B. 1979. *Technology in Hospitals.* Washington, DC: Brookings.

——— 1989. "Some of the Tough Decisions Required by a National Health Plan." *Science* 246:892–896.

Sacks, Henry S., et al. 1987. "Meta-Analyses of Randomized Controlled Trials." *The New England Journal of Medicine* 316:450–455.

Sandier, S. 1989. "Health Services Utilization and Physician Income Trends." *Health Care Financing Review Annual Supplement,* 33–48.

Schacter, R. D., David M. Eddy, and V. Hasselbald. 1990. "An Influence Diagram Approach to Medical Technology Assessment." In *Influence Diagrams, Belief Nets and Decision Analysis,* ed. Robert M. Oliver and J. Q. Smith. London: J. Wiley.

Schelling, T. C. 1968. "The Life You Save May Be Your Own." In *Problems in Public Expenditure Analysis,* ed. S. B. Chase. Washington, DC: Brookings.

Scherer, F. M. 1985. "Post-Patent Barriers to Entry in the Pharmaceutical Industry." *Journal of Health Economics* 4:83–87.

Schieber, G. J., and J.-P. Poullier. 1988. "DataWatch: International Health Spending and Utilization Trends." *Health Affairs* 7:105–112.

Schieber, G. J., J.-P. Poullier, and L. M. Greenwald. 1991. "Health Care Systems in Twenty-four Countries." *Health Affairs* 10:22–28.

Scitovsky, A. A. 1967. "Changes in the Costs of Treatment of Selected Illnesses, 1951–65." *American Economic Review* 57:1182–1195.

Sechrest, L., E. Perrin, and J. Bunker, eds. 1990. *Research Methodology: Strengthening Causal Interpretations of Nonexperimental Data.* DHHS pub. no. (PHS) 90-3454. Washington, DC: Government Printing Office.

Simmons, Larry K. 1987. "Hospital Profits During the Second Year of PPS." Testimony before the Subcommittee on Health of the Ways and Means Committee, U.S. House of Representatives, 26 February 1987.

Sloan, F., and R. Feldman. 1978. "Competition Among Physicians." In *Competition in the Health Care Sector: Past, Present, and Future,* ed. W. Greenberg. Washington, DC: Federal Trade Commission.

Social Security Bulletin. 1987 (September). Washington, DC: Social Security Board.

Somers, H. M., and A. R. Somers. 1961. *Doctors, Patients, and Health Insurance.* Washington, DC: Brookings.

Sonnefeld, S. T., et al. 1991. "Projections of National Health Expenditures through the Year 2000." *Health Care Financing Review* 13 (1): 1–27.

State of California Department of Finance. 1990. *California Statistical Abstract, 1990.* Sacramento, CA.

Statistics Canada. 1985. *Canada Year Book 1985.* Ottawa, ON: Statistics Canada.

——— 1987a. *Annual Return of Hospitals—Hospital Indicators, 1984–1985.* Catalogue 83-233. Ottawa, ON: Statistics Canada.

——— 1987b. *Hospital Annual Statistics, 1984–85.* Catalogue 82-232 Annual. Ottawa, ON: Statistics Canada.

——— 1988a. *The Canada Year Book 1988.* Ottawa, ON: Statistics Canada.

——— 1988b. *Life Tables, Canada and Provinces, 1985–1987.* Catalogue S41-044. Ottawa, ON: Statistics Canada.

——— 1988c. *Postcensal Annual Estimates of Population by Marital Status, Age, Sex, and Components of Growth for Canada, Provinces, and Territories, June 1, 1985.* Vol. 3, 3rd Issue. Catalogue 91-210 Annual. Ottawa, ON: Statistics Canada.

——— 1989a. *Canadian Economic Observer, Historical Statistical Supplement, 1988/1989.* Catalogue 11-210. Ottawa, ON: Statistics Canada.

——— 1989b. *Hospital Statistics Preliminary Annual Report, 1987.* Ottawa, ON: Canadian Government Publishing Center.

——— 1990. *List of Canadian Hospitals, 1989.* Ottawa, ON: Canadian Government Publishing Center.

——— 1991a. *The Canada Year Book, 1990 Edition.* Ottawa, ON: Statistics Canada.

—— 1991b. *Hospital Annual Statistics, 1987–88: Outpatient Services.* Ottawa, ON: Canadian Government Publishing Center.

—— 1991c. *Hospital Statistics Preliminary Annual Report, 1989.* Ottawa, ON: Statistics Canada.

—— 1991d. *Vital Statistics.* Vol. 3. Ottawa, ON: Statistics Canada.

Steinwald, B., and L. A. Dummit. 1989. "Hospital Case-Mix Change: Sicker Patients or DRG Creep?" *Health Affairs* 8:35–47.

Stern, J. 1983. "Social Mobility and the Interpretation of Social Class Mortality Differentials." *Journal of Social Policy* 12:27–49.

Stettler, H. Louis, III. 1970. "The New England Throat Distemper and Family Size." In *Empirical Studies in Health Economics,* ed. Herbert E. Klarman. Baltimore: The Johns Hopkins University Press.

Sweden Now. 1986. "A Land Where Father (Sometimes) Is Left Holding the Baby." *Sweden Now* 6:27.

Tawney, R. H. 1926. *Religion and the Rise of Capitalism.* New York: Harcourt, Brace.

Thaler, Richard, and Sherwin Rosen. 1975. "The Value of Saving a Life: Evidence from the Labor Market." In *Household Production and Consumption,* ed. Nestor Terleckyj. New York: National Bureau of Economic Research.

Torres, A., and J. D. Forrest. 1983. "The Costs of Contraception." *Family Planning Perspectives* 15:70–72.

Townsend, P., and N. Davidson, eds. 1982. *Inequalities in Health: The Black Report.* Harmondsworth, England: Penguin Books.

Treasurer of Ontario and Minister of Economics. 1990. *1990 Ontario Budget.* Toronto, ON: Queens Printer for Ontario.

Tversky, Amos, and Daniel Kahnemann. 1986. "Rational Choice and the Framing of Decisions." *Journal of Business* 59 (4), part 2: S251–S278.

U.S. Bureau of the Census. 1950a. *Census of the Population, 1950.* Washington, DC: Government Printing Office.

—— 1950b. *Census of Population and Housing, 1950.* Computer file. Ann Arbor, MI: Inter-university Consortium for Political and Social Research.

—— 1960. *Census of Population and Housing, 1960.* Computer file. Ann Arbor, MI: Inter-university Consortium for Political and Social Research.

—— 1970. *Census of Population and Housing, 1970.* Computer file. Ann Arbor, MI: Inter-university Consortium for Political and Social Research.

———— 1973. *Statistical Abstract of the United States, 1973.* Washington, DC: Government Printing Office.

———— 1975. *Historical Statistics of the United States, Colonial Times to 1970.* Vol. 2, series B221–235. Washington, DC: Government Printing Office.

———— 1980a. *Census of the Population, 1980.* Washington, DC: Government Printing Office.

———— 1980b. *Census of Population and Housing, 1980.* Computer file. Ann Arbor, MI: Inter-university Consortium for Political and Social Research.

———— 1980c. *Current Population Survey, Annual Demographic File, March 1980.* Computer file. Ann Arbor, MI: Inter-university Consortium for Political and Social Research.

———— 1980d. *Statistical Abstract of the United States, 1980.* Washington, DC: Government Printing Office.

———— 1983. *Statistical Abstract of the United States, 1982–83.* Washington, DC: Government Printing Office.

———— 1984. *Current Population Reports.* Series P-25, no. 952. Washington, DC: Government Printing Office.

———— 1985. *Current Population Survey, Annual Demographic File, March 1985.* Computer file. Ann Arbor, MI: Inter-university Consortium for Political and Social Research.

———— 1986a. *City and County Data Book.* Washington, DC: Government Printing Office.

———— 1986b. *Current Population Survey, Annual Demographic File, March 1986.* Computer file. Ann Arbor, MI: Inter-university Consortium for Political and Social Research.

———— 1987. *Statistical Abstract of the United States, 1987.* Washington, DC: Government Printing Office.

———— 1988a. *Current Population Survey, Annual Demographic File, March 1988.* Computer file. Ann Arbor, MI: Inter-university Consortium for Political and Social Research.

———— 1988b. *Statistical Abstract of the United States, 1988.* Washington, DC: Government Printing Office.

———— 1989a. "Money Income and Poverty Status in the U.S., 1989." *Current Population Reports, Consumer Income,* series P-60, no. 168. Washington, DC: Government Printing Office.

———— 1989b. *Statistical Abstract of the United States, 1989.* Washington, DC: Government Printing Office.

—— 1990. *Statistical Abstract of the United States, 1990*. Washington, DC: Government Printing Office.

—— 1991. *Statistical Abstract of the United States, 1991*. Washington, DC: Government Printing Office.

U.S. Department of Commerce. 1988. Bureau of Economic Analysis. *Survey of Current Business, May 1988*. No. 337-790. Washington, DC: Government Printing Office.

U.S. Department of Health and Human Services. 1988. *Morbidity and Mortality Weekly Report* 36 (50, 51): 827.

—— 1989. "Children of Divorce." *Vital and Health Statistics*, series 21, no. 46: 14.

U.S. Department of Labor. 1990. "Industry Wage Survey: Hospitals, March 1989." *Bureau of Labor Statistics Bulletin*, no. 2364 (August).

Valdez, R. B., et al. 1985. "Consequences of Cost-Sharing for Children's Health." *Pediatrics* 75:952–961.

Vayda, E., W. R. Mindell, and I. M. Rutkow. 1982. "A Decade of Surgery in Canada, England and Wales, and the United States." *Archives of Surgery* 117:846–853.

Viscusi, K. W. 1978. "Labour Market Valuations of Life and Limb: Empirical Evidence and Policy Implications." *Public Policy* 26 (Summer): 359–386.

Vladeck, Bruce C. 1991. "Unhealthy Rations." *The American Prospect*, no. 6 (Summer): 101–103.

Wadsworth, M. E. J. 1986. "Serious Illness in Childhood and Its Association with Later Life Achievement." In *Class and Health: Research and Longitudinal Data*, ed. Richard G. Wilkinson. London and New York: Tavistock Publications.

Waldo, Daniel, Katharine R. Levit, and Helen Lazenby. 1986. "National Health Expenditures, 1985." *Health Care Financing Review* 8 (1): 1–21.

Waldo, Daniel, et al. 1989. "Health Expenditures by Age Group, 1977–1987." *Health Care Financing Review* 10 (4): 111–120.

Weinstein, M. C. 1983. "Cost-Effective Priorities for Cancer Prevention." *Science* 221:17–23.

Weisbrod, B. A. 1961. *Economics of Public Health*. Philadelphia: University of Pennsylvania Press.

Wennberg, J. E. 1984. "Dealing with Medical Practice Variations: A Proposal for Action." *Health Affairs* 3:6–32.

Wennberg, J. E., and A. Gittelsohn. 1973. "Small Area Variations in

Health Care Delivery: A Population-Based Health Information System Can Guide Planning and Regulatory Decision-Making." *Science* 182:1102–1108.

White, Kerr L. 1973. "Life and Death in Medicine." *Scientific American* 229 (September): 16, 22–33, 198.

Wilkinson, Richard G. 1986. "Socioeconomic Differences in Mortality: Interpreting the Data on Their Size and Trends." In *Class and Health: Research and Longitudinal Data,* ed. Richard G. Wilkinson. London and New York: Tavistock Publications.

Yett, D. E. 1975. *An Economic Analysis of the Nurse Shortage.* Lexington, MA: D. C. Heath.

Zeckhauser, R., and C. Zook. 1981. "Failures to Control Health Costs: Departures from First Principles." In *A New Approach to the Economics of Health Care,* ed. Mancur Olson. Washington, DC: American Enterprise Institute for Public Policy Research.

Zill, N., and C. A. Schoenborn. 1990. "Developmental, Learning, and Emotional Problems: Health of Our Nation's Children, United States, 1988." *AdvanceData* 190. Washington, DC: National Center for Health Statistics.

Sources

The chapters in this book were adapted from the following:

"Concepts of Health—An Economist's Perspective," *The Journal of Medicine and Philosophy* 1, 3 (September 1976):229–237, by permission of Kluwer Academic Publishers. Copyright © 1976 by The Society for Health and Human Values. All rights reserved.

"Health Economics," in *The New Palgrave: A Dictionary of Economics,* Vol. 2, ed. John Eatwell, Murray Milgate, and Peter Newman (London: Macmillan, 1987), pp. 614–619.

Victor R. Fuchs and Richard Zeckhauser, "Valuing Health—A 'Priceless' Commodity," *American Economic Review, Papers and Proceedings 7,* 2 (May 1987):263–268.

"Poverty and Health: Asking the Right Questions," in *Medical Care and the Health of the Poor,* ed. David E. Rogers and Eli Ginzberg (Boulder, CO: Westview Press, 1993), by permission of Westview Press, Boulder, Colorado.

"The Health Sector's Share of the Gross National Product," *Science* 247 (February 2, 1990):534–538. Copyright 1990 American Association for the Advancement of Science.

Victor R. Fuchs and James S. Hahn, "How Does Canada Do It? A Comparison of Expenditures for Physicians' Services in the United States and Canada," *The New England Journal of Medicine* 323, 13 (September 27, 1990):884–890.

Donald A. Redelmeier and Victor R. Fuchs, "Hospital Expenditures in the United States and Canada," *The New England Journal of Medicine* 328, 11 (March 18, 1993):772–778.

Victor R. Fuchs and Leslie Perreault, "Expenditures for Reproduction-Related Health Care," *Journal of the American Medical Association* 255, 1 (January 3, 1986):76–81. Copyright 1986, American Medical Association.

Index

Index

Index